The
Formation
of a
Planter
Elite

The Formation of a Planter Elite

Jonathan Bryan and the Southern Colonial Frontier

by Alan Gallay

The University of Georgia Press

Athens and London

© 1989 by the University of Georgia Press
Athens, Georgia 30602
All rights reserved
Designed by Rich Hendel
Set in 10/13 Sabon
The paper in this book meets the guidelines for permanence and
durability of the Committee on Production Guidelines for Book
Longevity of the Council on Library Resources.

Printed in the United States of America

93 92 91 90 89   5 4 3 2 1

Library of Congress Cataloging in Publication Data

Gallay, Alan.
    The formation of a planter elite: Jonathan Bryan and the southern
colonial frontier / Alan Gallay.
        p. cm.
    Bibliography: p.
    Includes index.
    ISBN 0-8203-1143-X (alk. paper)
    1. Bryan, Jonathan, 1708–1788. 2. Plantation owners—Georgia—
Biography. 3. Frontier and pioneer life—Georgia. 4. Frontier and
pioneer life—Southern States. 5. Georgia—History—Colonial period,
ca. 1600–1775. 6. Southern States—History—Colonial period, ca.
1600–1775. 7. Georgia—History—Revolution, 1775–1783. 8.
Southern States—History—Revolution, 1775–1783.   I. Title.
F289.B888G35 1989
975'.02—dc19   88-38688
                                                          CIP

British Library Cataloging in Publication Data available

For Carolina

CONTENTS

MAPS

ix

ACKNOWLEDGMENTS

I gratefully acknowledge permission to reprint portions of this manuscript. Part of chapter 2 previously appeared in different form in "The Origins of Slaveholders' Paternalism: George Whitefield, the Bryan Family, and the Great Awakening in the South," *Journal of Southern History* 53 (August 1987), 369–94; and in "The Great Sell-out: George Whitefield on Slavery," in *Looking South: Chapters in the Story of an American Region,* edited by Joseph F. Tripp and Winfred B. Moore (Westport, Conn.: Greenwood Press, in press). Part of chapter 4 previously appeared in "Jonathan Bryan's Plantation Empire: Land, Politics, and the Formation of a Ruling Class in Colonial Georgia," *William and Mary Quarterly,* 3d series, 45 (April 1988): 253–79. Part of chapter 6 has been published in "The Search for an Alternate Source of Trade: The Creek Indians and Jonathan Bryan," *Georgia Historical Quarterly,* in press.

Many kind people helped this manuscript to fruition. My good friend David Teasley sat through innumerable lunches discussing Jonathan Bryan and his world. R. Emmett Curran, Ronald Johnson, and Marcus Rediker also contributed much in the early stages for which I am most grateful. The last named, through his own pursuit of history, influenced me to ask a lot of the right questions about the past. John Boles, Donald Critchlow, Hardy Jackson, and Michael McGiffert read portions of the manuscript and provided both encouragement and valuable suggestions. Douglas Egerton, fellow time-traveler through the southern past, shared both his friendship and knowledge. Sylvia Frey, Winthrop Jordan, Charles Wilson, and Peter Wood read and provided helpful comments on the entire manuscript.

I am also indebted to family, friends, and colleagues who have supported me and my work. They make a difference. In particular, I would like to thank my siblings, Robin, Joel, and Sandy; my parents, Harold and Leona Gallay; my in-laws, Leon and Rachel Coleman; and Linda Egerton, Phil Gordon, Bob Haws, Tom Lastrapes, Michael Murray, Brett Roach, and Barbara Shuttleworth.

My wife, Carolina, has read and edited this manuscript more times than I care to admit. Her groans and witty pen have improved my prose. Her love has improved the man.

None of these people can be held responsible for errors of fact or opinion—these are my own.

A NOTE ON THE TEXT

Eighteenth-century Americans chose a variety of ways to spell words. I have retained their spelling and punctuation within quotations. I have also chosen to spell Charleston in the colonial manner, by not dropping the *w* as in modern usage. For Indian words in which there is no agreed-upon spelling, I have selected the form most often used in the original documents.

INTRODUCTION

On the southern frontier people of different races, religions, and ethnic groups lived in close proximity and greatly influenced each other's lives. They exchanged ideas and technology, traded goods, fought with one another, moved from place to place, and intermarried. The intimacy that accompanied trade, alliance, warfare, adoption, immigration and miscegenation led to adaptations in all the region's cultures. The appropriation of knowledge from one culture by another was often the best way to compete with aggressive neighbors. It was no accident that the aborginal nations of the southern frontier were alike in their social, political, and economic organization. Several millennia of interaction had taught the Indians to select from and adapt to each other's mode of living to improve the chances of survival and prosperity. In much the same way, the peoples of Europe had developed a cosmology and forms of social, economic, and political organization that reflected their mutual historical experience. It should come as no surprise that as soon as the diverse peoples of the Old and New Worlds came into contact, the process of adoption and adaptation took on greater meaning. The Europeans had to learn to survive in an environment of which they were woefully ignorant, one in which Old World concepts had little meaning; the aborigines were faced with new peoples whose aggressiveness and technology could not be ignored; removal from their homeland and bondage forced blacks into a melting pot of African cultures within a hostile European society. Thus, *all* the peoples of the southern frontier had to learn from each other and adapt themselves and their institutions to an environment undergoing vast demographic, social, economic, and political changes.

Adaptation was the means of preserving and enriching a group's way of life: seldom did people desire or expect to change the basic values of their society. Thus, aborigines adopted European firearms to use in their ancient wars with each other and to expedite hunting, as well as to withstand the territorial encroachments of whites. European weaponry became a tool for fulfilling an old agenda, though the use of European technology led to unforeseen changes in the structure and texture of Indian life: dependence on European goods forever bound aborigines to European society. The Europeans were not immune to far-reaching changes that resulted from the adaptation of new technologies: they used the Indian flat-bottomed boats, piraguas, to move goods to market and extend their influence and power through the region; they fed themselves on Indian and African crops; they exported staples produced by Indian and African methods of cultivation and labor.

The effects of adaptation and competition upon European society in the New World have been studied since Frederick Jackson Turner described the formative influence of the frontier on American institutions and character in his 1893 essay "The Significance of the Frontier in American History." Turner and his followers found a frontier demarcated between the advancing forces of a white Christian civilization and a wilderness inhabited by "savages" doomed to extinction. Recent students of the frontier have questioned the chauvinistic assumptions by which Indians were termed savage and whites civilized. Furthermore, the frontier has been perceived as a place on which interaction between peoples was of greater importance than segregation. Francis Jennings, for instance, has emphasized those characteristics shared by Indians and Euramericans, while James Axtell has examined the interchange that took place in the "contest of cultures." Peter H. Wood has explored the appropriation of knowledge, and William Cronon has studied the effect of the frontier upon the biological environment.[1]

This new generation of historians has been particularly concerned with the evolution of the frontier. For instance, Cronon analyzed how the introduction of the market economy altered the floral and animal life of New England; Wood elucidated how Afro-American life and labor changed in South Carolina from 1670 to 1739. For Turner, however, the frontier was a process where the basic interactions between white society and savage wilderness were repeated in the westward movement across the North American continent. The present work shares with the new generation of historians a deep concern for examining the evolutionary aspects of the frontier, especially relations between social groups, but I maintain great respect for the Turnerian emphasis on the frontier as process, one repeated in kind, over time, and in different areas.

The frontier experience, I believe, was the most important factor in the creation of the South. The frontier gave meaning to the basic facts of southern history: after two and a half centuries of intimate contact, cultural exchange, competition, and warfare with aborigines, Frenchmen, and Spaniards, the British plantation system prevailed in the Southeast. This system, based upon the exploitation of thousands of enslaved Africans, was shaped by the exigencies of frontier life. The selection of crops, laborers, the peculiarities of local government and religion, and the implementation of legal, land, and police systems were all predicated upon adaptation to frontier conditions. In other words, Euramericans, operating within a Western tradition of thought and experience, adapted their language, food, clothing, medicine, technology, economy, agriculture, social organization, government, and cosmology to a New World environment, one in which they were forced to contend with and learn from many strange peoples who were guided by different rules and goals, and who possessed an understanding of the universe that perplexed, irritated, and challenged the newcomers.

The frontier was seminal in the creation of an American character—there are numerous parallels between the frontier of the Southeast and other geographic regions in North America. Arguably, the similarities are more important than the differences, but my interest lies in exposing some of the ways in which the frontier experience shaped the South's development.

It is necessary to focus upon what is southern on the colonial frontier because many scholars persist in believing that the South was born in 1789, 1820, or at another date selected to coincide with some political event that gives meaning to southern nationalism. Before southerners knew they were southern, however, a region had been born. Slavery, the plantation system, the centrality of race, the importance of family, the legacy of violence, and the prominence of evangelical religion—characteristics that define a southern way of life—all were in various stages of development in the colonial era. Rhys Isaac, Allan Kulikoff, Edmund S. Morgan, and Peter H. Wood have led the way in recapturing the legacy of the southern colonial past in the region and the nation's history. All of them emphasize class and race relations, and the emergence of the plantation system. They all owe a great debt to Verner W. Crane, whose 1929 work *The Southern Frontier* recognized the centrality of intercultural relations and economic activities.[2] The study of these factors must continue if we are to move forward in our understanding of the region; we should reexamine the colonial experience, especially the competition between Indian, African, and European systems of thought, social organization, technology, and culture.[3] The eventual dominance of the British must be explained in terms of over two centuries of competition and adaptation.

In this book I will analyze the manner in which the British planter elite responded to frontier conditions: the mechanics by which they built their estates, assumed political power, and formed relationships with diverse groups of people. Although my focus is upon the elite, I have tried to view them not only from their vantage point but through the eyes of those whom they terrorized, brutalized, cajoled, co-opted, appeased, befriended, belittled, and defended. I assume that all parties in a relationship possessed their own particular interests and goals and that, although members of the elite frequently had the upper hand, the weaker party had enough power to modify elites' expectations and behavior.

This work is a case study, an examination of the life of Jonathan Bryan, whose fortune and government offices gave him membership among the southern colonial elite. An entrepreneur who was born and lived the first half of his life on South Carolina's southern frontier, Bryan became familiar with the Georgia frontier before it became a British colony and then participated in the establishment of British authority. When the Trustees of Georgia, the proprietors of that colony from 1732 to 1754, transferred their control of Georiga to the Crown and paved the way for the development of a plantation society, Bryan played a pivotal role in the formation of the new slaveholding order.

As with all case studies, it is hazardous to project the life experiences of the individual to the larger groups of which they were members. In his ambitions and his social, political, and economic successes, Bryan was not typical of the majority of planters. But he was representative of the slaveholding elite—the small group of men who ruled Georgia in the quarter-century before the American Revolution. The Georgia elite was composed of the governor and council. In common with Bryan, these men possessed not only great wealth and political power but a wide knowledge concerning the economic and political affairs of their colony and the Atlantic world. They were men of talent who understood the importance of patronage, political preferment, and public works projects and who were familiar with the native soils, the marketing of crops, and the intricacies of English law. Their knowledge and their political offices allowed them to use black labor to transform the colony's best land into rice plantations which were of much greater value than those belonging to other slaveholders. In a calculated manner the members of the Georgia Council controlled the disbursement of public land to the benefit of themselves, family, and friends; they directed public works projects to be built to their own personal advantage; they created patron-client relationships that left other whites dependent upon them for land and jobs. Through Bryan's life I hope to elucidate the frontier process: the means by which British Americans interacted with Indians, appropriated knowledge and territory, and then used government to secure their gains and extend their wealth and influence.

Bryan's life largely has been ignored. Yet his role in the Great Awakening, the evangelization and education of slaves, and the founding of Georgia and his leadership in the American Revolution demand that his story be recounted. Bryan's life touched the lives of a wide variety of peoples over a period of eighty years, in South Carolina, Georgia, and Florida. A man of immense energy, his ambitions led him to traverse the southern frontier in pursuit of wealth, power, and personal fulfillment. He was equally comfortable dining at the governor's table, trading with German-speaking immigrants, and negotiating a treaty with Creek Indians.

A man of piety and charity, Bryan earned a reputation for compassion and tolerance. Yet, he also displayed an intense accumulative spirit: at times, his desire for land became insatiable. The tension between the quest for personal profit and Bryan's responsibilities to his family, neighbors, and slaves was similar to that experienced by other southern elites. The members of the ruling class had grasped economic and political power for the purpose of forwarding their own interests, only to learn that their dependents and the community-at-large expected them to wield power for other purposes. In the First Great Awakening, Evangelical preachers arrived on the southern frontier and demanded that the slaveholding elite face up to its responsibilities. Most elites were aghast at their demands, but a few, like Bryan, recognized the expediency of reform, became Evangelicals, and shaped the new religion into one that justified their positions and allowed them to perceive themselves as moral Christian patriarchs. Thus was born the paternalistic ideology of the great southern planters. Rather than drawing from the remnants of a medieval chivalric tradition, the paternalism of the southern master class was the product of the transformation from frontier to plantation society. And it is in this transformation—from frontiersman to pillar of a slaveholding community—that Jonathan Bryan's life best illustrates the formation of a planter elite.

The
Formation
of a
Planter
Elite

1

THE SOUTHERN FRONTIER

Between the Mississippi River and the Atlantic Ocean lay one of the largest expanses of fertile land in the world. Bounded on the south by the Gulf of Mexico and the north by the rolling hills of Tennessee and North Carolina, the Southeast possessed a mild climate and an abundance of plant and animal life.[1] This bountiful region supported a culturally rich collection of aboriginal peoples. The southeastern Indians of the "Mississippi Tradition" resided in large towns, erected substantial buildings and palisaded forts, formed complex political organizations, and produced dynamic works of art. Their sophisticated cosmology of the universe led them to build the most impressive pre-Columbian religious monuments north of Mexico. Thus, when Europeans first stepped on southeastern shores in the early sixteenth century they found no wilderness but an inhabited area populated by a civilization of native peoples who farmed, hunted, warred with one another, and exchanged goods over an extensive regional network. Their cosmology, system of justice, technology, and habits differed greatly from those of the newcomers, but like them they were a long-established people with great concern for tradition, family, health, survival, and the afterworld.[2] Some Europeans found it convenient to characterize them as wanderers and savages. It provided a rationale for dispossession: a peripatetic and violent people could hardly have a better claim to the land than a Christian civilization.[3]

The population of native southeasterners declined drastically as a result of the introduction of European diseases. Estimates of the number of pre-Columbian Indians in the region are currently undergoing radical revision as new methods of demographic assessment are being employed by anthropologists and archaeologists. Henry Dobyns recently suggested that in Florida alone the precontact population may have approached one million.[4] Whatever population figures further research will disclose, disease and warfare clearly wiped out many southeastern nations and reduced others to a fraction of their former size. Nevertheless, several aboriginal nations remained strong and others rose in prominence by filling the vacuums of power created by the demise of their neighbors. Life was altered permanently by the European presence. New technologies created dependencies on weaponry, tools, textiles, and alcohol. Those Indians who survived the biological onslaught of European diseases adapted to the arrival of their aggressive neighbors and used military power and diplomacy to withstand domination.

The European arrival forever connected the aborigines to outside peoples and affairs. Decisions and events thousands of miles away shaped the course of the region's history. Economic and military competition in Europe reverberated across the Atlantic. European ships maintained the region's connections with other parts of the world by bringing goods and people and carrying away the same, including many Indians as slaves. The southeast had never been a closed region—the Iroquois, for instance, traveled more than a thousand miles from the North to conduct trade, raids, and diplomacy—but despite the influx of new peoples and outside influences, the Southeast remained a distinct region, its inhabitants' lives intermeshed as a result of their mutual dependency, geopolitics, trade, and the extraordinary mobility of the aborigines.

Viewing the Southeast as a collection of discrete areas demarcated by the political boundaries of the European powers distorts the nature and character of the region in several ways. The Europeans had little idea of the geographic boundaries of their respective domains and little respect for the claims of each other and the aboriginal inhabitants. Force and effective occupation rather than discovery and prior settlement determined ownership.[5] Boundaries between Indian groups were as fluid as those which divided the Europeans, but the latter's encroachments forced the aborigines to contest overlapping claims and insist upon treaty-defined borders with the British. Thus, the compartmentalization of the Southeast into a series of political entities distorts more than just the fluid boundaries of colonial America: it subordinates, if not hides, the basic factors which defined and shaped life on the southern frontier—namely, the economic, political, and military connections between the region's inhabitants. Events in any portion of the Southeast could have a dramatic effect upon any and all of the region's inhabitants. For instance, South Carolina's quest for slaves had a lasting (and devastating) impact upon the aboriginal population of Florida; Choctaw-Chickasaw relations along the Mississippi River affected Creek power in their relations with the British in Georgia.

Trade involved all peoples of the region and made for strange bed-
fellows. Southeasterners frequently suppressed racial, religious, and
ethnic animosities to exchange goods. The Spanish and English sought
each other's destruction and removal from the Southeast but conducted
a mutually profitable trade in goods and slaves.[6] European traders
broke the laws of their respective nations to conduct illegal trade with
the Indians, and they resided in Indian towns although aware that a
sudden change in political or economic circumstances could result in
death at the hands of their hosts. The traders possessed a deservedly
infamous reputation as a group who frequently created dissensions
within and between nations. Their ability to affect the destiny of the
region was immense. As an example, British traders incited the Yamassees to war in 1715 and fostered large cessions of land from the Cherokees and Creeks in the 1770s; British and French traders played a
major role in leading the Choctaws into civil war in the 1740s.[7] Control of the Indian trade was a key factor in both the economic and
political standing of the European powers in the Southeast, while access to European goods shaped the diplomacy of the Indians.

Exchange between Indians and Europeans was not always conducted over great distances. Large Indian populations lived among and
in close proximity to the Spanish in Florida and the French in Louisiana. Indians provisioned Europeans with farm goods and animal
products and provided labor on a daily basis. A similar relationship
existed between the Yamassees and the Carolinians until war divided
these erstwhile allies and convinced many southeastern Indians that
the English were best dealt with from afar.

Travel in preindustrial societies was both difficult and hazardous.
Thus, European settlements in North America invariably were located
along the seacoasts and select inland waterways. Besides slaves and
soldiers, who were forced to migrate, only the adventurous, the hearty,
or the desperate dared make the three-month voyage across the ocean.
The Europeans' ability to cross three thousand miles of sea was not
matched by a similar ability to traverse the continent. Migration inland, therefore, proceeded slowly, confined mostly to those driven by
economic circumstances to leave the safer confines of eastern society. In
contrast, the southeastern Indians traveled great distances overland,
their mobility facilitated by ancient trading routes that crisscrossed the
Southeast. They toted heavy loads quickly over long distances, a feat
which many European observers believed impossible to replicate.[8]
From cypress and cedar trees the Indians carved the piraguas used on

the Southeast's many creeks and rivers. In addition, they created porta-
ble small canoes out of leather and other materials, on which they
traveled smaller creeks. Mobility enhanced their power. British officials, for example, held virtually no hope of conquering the Creek Indians, not only because of their large number of warriors, but because an
invasion of their territory was deemed impractical, if not impossible: a
European army could not pursue the Creeks over their own terrain.[9]

The Spanish of the Southeast placed little pressure on the Indians for
their land, unlike elsewhere in New Spain. Since Florida attracted few
settlers from Spain and its possessions, the colony remained essentially
a military outpost. For a century after the brutal murder in 1565 of the
French colonists at Fort Caroline and the subsequent establishment of
St. Augustine, Europeans challenged the Spanish only on the periphery
of the region: the British settled in Virginia to the north, while the
French explored the Mississippi region from Canada. Once the English
and French began colonizing the Southeast in the 1670s, Spanish
power rapidly declined. The extensive network of mission villages
which the Spanish built among the aborigines in Florida and Guale
(Georgia) in the sixteenth and seventeenth centuries was largely destroyed by the the British and their allies before the second decade of
the eighteenth century. This forced the Spanish to locate their Christian
Indians close to the Castillo de San Marcos at St. Augustine, so that the
aborigines could seek the protection of the fort in times of invasion. As
John Jay Tepaske noted, the Spanish gave their Indian allies walled
protection against their enemies but were unwilling to leave their castle
to help them. The main concern of the Spanish was survival: lack of
funds and new settlers prevented them from extending their domain in
the eighteenth century.[10]

The French adapted Indian technologies for their own use far more
quickly than their European competitors. Less interested in Indian
land and more interested in trade and containing British power along
the eastern seaboard, the French penetrated the inland continent and
established forts and spheres of influence from Louisiana to Canada in
the first half of the eighteenth century. French success was due to the
minimal pressure they applied upon the Indians for land and their willingness to treat some aborigines with more respect than that usually
accorded by the British.[11] Many of the Indians who lived and traded
with the French in Louisiana enjoyed a far more hospitable environment than that allotted Indians in any portion of British America.

The British presence in the Southeast differed from that of the French and Spanish in several respects. A steady influx of settlers induced the British to seek frequent cessions of land from the Indians, which led to numerous wars that resulted in the destruction or near destruction of entire nations. Relations with the aborigines generally improved in the 1730s but the British remained an ever-present threat to most southeastern Indians in the colonial period because of their growing numbers, military power, and economic strength. Although the British ability to offer superior trade goods at lower prices than the French and Spanish gave them a distinct advantage in competition for Indian friendship and alliance, many of the southeastern Indian nations exploited the competition among European powers. The Creeks, for instance, assumed a posture of neutrality by which they conducted trade and accepted gifts from the Spanish, French, and English. Until the end of the French and Indian War in 1763, the southeastern Indians held the balance of power in the Southeast.

French and Spanish settlements were composed mainly of soldiers and their families. The British, however, included a conglomeration of peoples from many parts of Europe and Africa. The initial group of British settlers in the Southeast was led by a contingent of West Indies planters (particularly from Barbados) who brought with them dependent laborers to establish plantations to produce commodities for export. Arriving from land-scarce islands, these immigrants were peculiarly voracious in their appetite for cultivable land. Once they uncovered a valuable commodity for export, rice, they devoted their efforts to accumulating land and laborers to produce the crop. By the early eighteenth century, rice surpassed Indian deerskins and cattle as South Carolina's major export, and though the Indian trade remained important for the economy, a large number of settlers became willing to risk both the trade and peaceful relations with the aborigines in order to obtain Indian land and Indian slaves.

Rice cultivation created a large class of wealthy planters in the Southeast, while also promoting the growth of a large class of nonindigenous servile laborers. Carolinians enslaved Indians to work their plantations but increasingly imported and relied upon black slaves, many of whom were familiar with the crop in Africa. By the first decade of the eighteenth century, the majority of South Carolina's inhabitants were blacks, and they participated in virtually every aspect of the colony's economy.[12] Despite their lack of political independence, blacks played a significant role in the interchange between south-eastern peoples as soldiers, purveyors of goods, laborers, pilots, and so on. They also represented an ever-present menace to the political integrity of British settlements, forcing the latter into both warfare and new alliances. Nevertheless, the successful exploitation of African labor allowed the British to grow stronger than their European counterparts, which led to the eventual dominant position of the Anglo-Saxon people and the spread of their plantation system through the region.[13]

The Southeast was an area of great fluidity, where boundaries were ill-defined and often disputed, where trade goods were exchanged between friends and enemies over great distances, where the threat of war constantly hung over the entire region, and where people of different races, religions, and ethnic groups came into daily contact with one another. By the late seventeenth century, the peoples of the Southeast had become mutually dependent upon one another for trade and diplomatic alliance. Although southeastern Euramericans looked across the ocean for political guidance, military help, and commercial exchange, relationships with other southeastern peoples shaped the quality of life for all the region's inhabitants. By exploring these relationships in the life of Jonathan Bryan, we come to a better understanding of the manner in which British elites dominated the region and extended their power over people and places. For Bryan realized, as well as anyone who inhabited the southern frontier, that the quality of relations between people of diverse races, religions, ethnicities, and classes shaped the quality of life for all.

PORT ROYAL: THE BRYANS AND THEIR NEIGHBORS

Perhaps no one should have been surprised when Port Royal, South Carolina, erupted into war in 1715. A century and a half of misfortune had accompanied every European attempt to settle the area. The French tried first in 1562, when they built Charlesfort (near modern-day Beaufort, South Carolina), only to have the expedition succumb to starvation, disease, and cannibalism. The Spanish then settled the region but also without success. Until the British colonized the area a century later, the only Europeans to visit Port Royal were shipwrecked sailors and an occasional missionary or reconaissance party from St. Augustine.

Port Royal is an unofficial name for the region bounded by the Savannah River to the south, the Combahee River to the north, the Atlantic Ocean to the east, and the mainland to the west: it comprises a series of islands separated from one another by Port Royal Sound, St. Helena Sound, and numerous freshwater rivers and streams. The superb harbor of Port Royal Island promised future development of the area's rich resources. When in 1669 the English sent three ships to Port Royal to establish the new colony of Carolina, it appeared to be the perfect place from which to challenge Spanish designs in the Southeast.[14] Upon arrival, however, the colonists followed the advice of friendly Indians and made their home on the Ashley River, near the modern-day city of Charleston, farther removed from the Spanish. Perhaps the colonists realized that Port Royal's location permitted easy invasion by sea. A more dangerous area did not exist on the British North American mainland. No one expected the Spanish to acquiesce in British settlement, and small pox, malaria, and yellow fever threatened all, especially the unseasoned settler. These factors did not deter a group of Presbyterian Scots from settling Port Royal in 1684. The attraction of religious freedom and fertile land overcame their misgivings. Their optimism was ill-founded: the Spanish destroyed the settlement two years later, and the area lay abandoned for another decade. Dissenters from the Church of England, mostly Presbyterians and Baptists, continued to colonize the region, but most of them settled to the north of Port Royal in Colleton County.

Why Jonathan Bryan's father, Joseph, decided to immigrate to Port Royal is a mystery. The family hailed from Hereford County, England, and were members of the Anglican church. Therefore, they were not attracted to the southern frontier by the offer of religious asylum. The first appearance of the family in the colony's legal records was on a warrant Joseph received for "Two hundred acres of Land in Colleton County now in his possession Date the Tenth Day of ffebry: 1697." He received another grant of land in Granville County in 1705, but agriculture appears to have been only a secondary pursuit: Joseph Bryan's main source of income accrued from engagement in trade with the Yamassee Indians.[15]

Joseph Bryan and Janet Cochran's fourth child, Jonathan, was born on September 12, 1708, at Port Royal. His mother died when he was two weeks old. Jonathan, however, did not suffer lack of attention from family members. He and his two brothers, Joseph and Hugh, and his

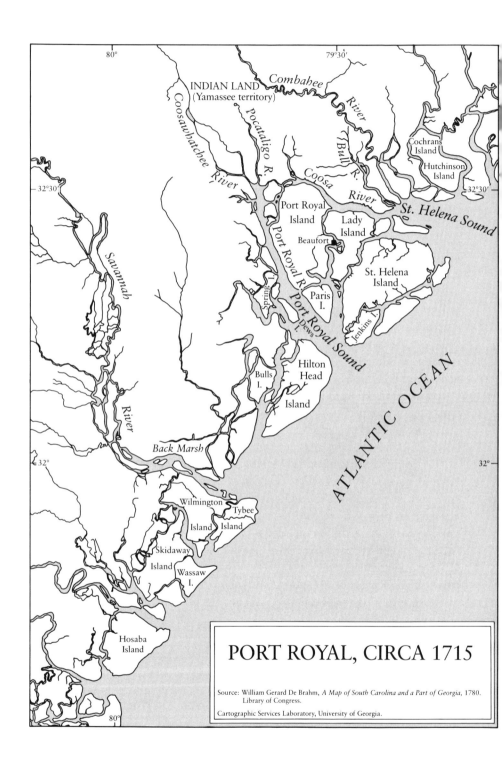

80°

79°30'

INDIAN LAND
(Yamassee territory)

Combahee

River

Coosawhatchee River

Pocataligo R.

Bull R.

Coosa River

Cochrans Island

Hutchinson Island

32°30'

32°30'

St. Helena Sound

Port Royal Island

Lady Island

Beaufort

St. Helena Island

Port Royal R.

Savannah

Spring I.

Paris I.

Jenkins I.

Port Royal Sound

Dews I.

River

Hilton Head

Bulls I.

Island

ATLANTIC OCEAN

Back Marsh

32°

32°

Wilmington

Tybee

Island   Island

Skidaway

Island   Wassaw I.

Hosaba Island

PORT ROYAL, CIRCA 1715

Source: William Gerard De Brahm, *A Map of South Carolina and a Part of Georgia*, 1780.
Library of Congress.

Cartographic Services Laboratory, University of Georgia.

80°

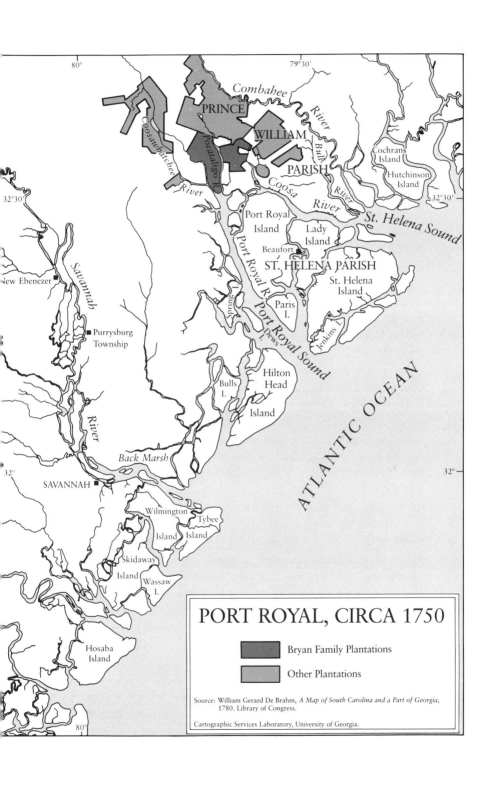

80°

79°30'

Combahee

PRINCE

River

Coosawhatchee

WILLIAM

Bull

Pocataligo R.

PARISH

Cochrans
Island

River

Hutchinson
Island

River

32°30'

Coosa

River

St. *Helena* Sound

32°30'

Port Royal
Island

Lady
Island

Beaufort

ST. HELENA PARISH

Savannah

New Ebenezer

St. Helena
Island

Spring I.

Paris
I.

Jenkins I.

Port Royal R.

Port Royal Sound

Purrysburg
Township

Dews I.

Hilton
Head

Bulls
I.

Island

River

Back Marsh

ATLANTIC OCEAN

32°

32°

SAVANNAH

Wilmington

Tybee

Island

Island

Skidaway

Island

Wassaw
I.

PORT ROYAL, CIRCA 1750

Bryan Family Plantations

Other Plantations

Source: William Gerard De Brahm, *A Map of South Carolina and a Part of Georgia*,
1780. Library of Congress.

Cartographic Services Laboratory, University of Georgia.

Hosaba
Island

80°

sister, Hannah, remained close throughout their lives. Their economic affairs and those of their children and grandchildren were thoroughly intertwined. They bought and sold property together and administered and probated each other's estates. Moreover, Bryan grew up in a small, tightly knit community, where families were tied together by marriage, economic interests, and shared experiences. As a result of marriage and remarriage, Jonathan's mother-in-law also became his sister-in-law, and a brother-in-law was married to his niece. The importance of family in the Bryan clan was emphasized in the repetition of first names among family members. Jonathan named a child after each of his siblings and they followed suit. His father, brother, son, and nephew all were named Joseph; a brother, son, and nephew were named Hugh; a sister and daughter were named Hannah. The repetition of names was reproduced in succeeding generations. As a member of a strong extended family, Jonathan could count on support and assistance throughout his life.

The Carolina Bryan grew up in was scarred by severe religious disputes, which impeded the colony's development. The policies of Dissenter proprietors clashed with the interests of Anglican settlers. To counteract Anglican power, the proprietors initiated a campaign to attract new settlers from Europe. They portrayed Carolina as a religious haven for oppressed Protestants. Scotch and English Presbyterians, English Baptists, Quakers, and other sectarians, and a large number of French Huguenots flocked to the colony. They were followed in the early eighteenth century by Irish, Swiss, and German Protestants. The intention of the proprietors was to create a Dissenter stronghold in the southern parishes. As members of the Anglican church, the Bryans would have been expected to unite politically with their religious brethren in the northern parishes. But many southern Anglicans united politically with their Dissenter neighbors. Even as the colony was rent by internal discord, the southern parishes stood united. What appeared as religio-ethnic factionalism, according to Clarence L. Ver Steeg, was actually a north versus south dispute, in which the spoils of office and taxation revenues were at stake. The needs of the southerners for defense and internal improvements were vital, and although northerners were cognizant of the south's needs, they were not inclined to part with government revenue for the sake of their southern neighbors. To prevent southern control of the government, it became expedient for northerners to disenfranchise Dissenters and thus weaken the whole political fabric of the southern parishes.[16] Despite temporary disenfranchisement in 1704, the northerners' ploy failed to split southerners along religious lines. In Colleton and Granville counties relations between Anglicans and Dissenters remained on amiable terms. Presbyterians, for instance, allowed the minority Anglicans use of their meeting houses for divine services.[17] The spirit of religious tolerance became a cornerstone of Jonathan Bryan's political career.

In the early eighteenth century, the low country was made up mostly of the northern parishes of Carolina. An area of rice plantations serviced by large numbers of black laborers and extending from the Edisto River to the Pee Dee River, the low country provided the social and economic models which Bryan's family and their Euramerican neighbors wished to emulate. The area's rice planters quickly became one of the richest group of men on the British North American mainland. Their wealth helped turn Charlestown into a major port city with stately houses and a gaiety of life that had few peers. To Charlestown came the ships which plied the Atlantic trade and tied the colony's planters to European and Caribbean markets. To Charlestown also came the growing numbers of unfree black laborers, the major source of the planters' wealth. Port Royal's inhabitants desired their own window on the Atlantic, which would allow them to possess a great port city like Charlestown. Jonathan Bryan inherited this dream. In the 1730s and 1740s he and his brothers worked diligently to make Port Royal a great market center. In later years he helped build the port at Savannah, and he intended to establish new port cities on the Altamaha and Apalachicola rivers. Life at Port Royal instructed Bryan in the difficulties of transporting goods to world markets, and his mastery of this problem played no small role in his becoming one of the Southeast's richest men.

The initial concern for a port arose among the Euramericans of Port Royal as a direct response to the decline of the Indian trade at the beginning of the eighteenth century. The traders hoped to increase profits by cutting out the Charlestown middlemen. Failing that, the traders vented their frustrations on their Indian partners, the Yamassees, who resided in ten towns on the mainland, west of Port Royal. An aggressive, warlike people, the Yamassees were extremely valuable to South Carolina as economic and military allies. By relocating their towns on Carolina's southern border they provided a buffer against an overland Spanish attack. Additionally, they frequently invaded Florida and were largely responsible for pushing Spain out of the Apalachee region and confining its effective occupation of the Southeast to St. Augustine.

On many of these forays the Yamassees' chief purpose was to obtain Indian slaves for the Carolina traders. Their slaving expeditions were so successful—they decimated numerous towns of Florida Indians— that they were running out of victims by the onset of the eighteenth century. The Port Royal traders responded to the reduction of Indian slaves by harassing the Yamassees. An alarmed Carolina government could not afford to lose its most valuable ally and took steps to protect the Indians. In 1702 the South Carolina Commons House of Assembly sought methods "to remove the Abuses done to the Yamassee Indians by them that live among them." The house singled out Joshua Brinan as a trader who had "Committed Several Abuses to our neighbor and friendly Indians ye Ja:ma:sees and wth all Conteintiously Disobeyed the order of this Gover^mt." This Joshua Brinan was later referred to by the house as Joseph Brinan, and, since the Indians made later complaints against Indian trader Joseph Bryan, we may assume that Brinan and Jonathan's father were one and the same. The house found that "Brinan" had stolen a canoe, killed "Po:ca:Saba's hoggs," burned down an Indian house of powder and corn, destroyed the goods of a certain Phillip, and stolen from "Tho:ma:Sa . . . six Hoogs Chest and Goods." Despite these transgressions he continued unapprehended from spring until September. Brinan posted a bond and received permission to return to the Yamassees to "gett in his Debts." He was forbidden from trading with the Indians and reminded not to "Misbehave himself during ye time he remanes amongst the s^d Yamassees."[18]

Bryan not only continued to trade with the Yamassees, he and his fellow traders began to pressure the Indians for their land. In 1705 Joseph Bryan received acreage in Granville County, most of which was inhabited by the Yamassees.[19] Two years later, after a decade of steady white encroachment, the house passed an act to protect the Yamassees by defining the boundaries of their land. The mainland of Granville County was reserved for usage by the Yamassees, between the Combahee, Port Royal, and Savannah rivers. Only the Sea Islands were reserved for white settlement.[20] But Euramericans continued to occupy Yamassee land and disturb them in their persons and property. This prompted action by the commissioners of the Indian trade, whose primary function, it appears, was to prevent abuses and protect the Indians from the traders' land hunger. The commission was sympathic to Indian grievances, the most baleful of which were the selling of free Indians into slavery and the settlement of whites on their land. The Yamassees complained that they were "damnified by the Stock of the white Men," to which the president of the commission replied, "that those Persons who are settled within their Limitts shoold effectualy be prosecuted." Among the six trespassers whom the Indians named was Joseph Bryan.[21]

This episode is instructive in several respects. The surnames of guilty white men reads like a who's who of St. Helena Parish twenty years later.[22] The list included such names as Bryan, Palmer, Bull, and Bellinger.[23] The traders' activities provoked the Yamassees to war in 1715. Several historians have cited Yamassee frustration with trade and fear of enslavement as the major sources of conflict.[24] Overlooked has been the traders' desire for the Indians' land, described by the governor of Carolina as "ye best part of this province."[25] The Port Royal traders coveted the Yamassees' land—they wished to become rice planters instead of traders—but their own government protected the Indians in their possession. By provoking the Yamassees to war the traders forced the hand of the government against the Indians. When the Indians struck in 1715 the local militia struck back, knowing that the South Carolina government had to support them. When it was all over there was no need to protect the Yamassees' land. Those Indians left alive fled to Florida, where they allied with the Spanish and with a vengeance conducted raids on South Carolina until peace was made in 1728.[26]

The war was a disaster for South Carolina. It quickly spread into a general Indian war, for many aborigines were disgruntled over trade relations with the British.[27] Massacres perpetrated by both sides left Port Royal and its environs desolate of both peoples for years to come. Irreparable damage was done to the colony's defense system. When the war ended no Indian nation could be persuaded to inhabit the buffer zone between South Carolina and its enemies, the Spanish and French. This left the colony's southern border open to invasion. Instead of economic development, defense became the chief concern of settlers along South Carolina's southern frontier. Moreover, the traders lost their economic lifeline. What remained of the Indian trade was redirected to Charlestown, and those whites who desired to stay at Port Royal were forced to take employment in the colony's new defense network: manning scout boats, building and maintaining forts, and providing food and supplies for the soldiers. Unfortunately for Port Royal's Eur-americans, a colony-wide quitrent problem led to the closing of the land office in 1719. Until the colony reached agreement with the Crown as to the payment of quitrents, no land patents could be issued. Thus the traders could not claim the so-called Indian Land, the Yamassee domain which would enable them to become rice planters. The promise of Indian land had turned to the desolation of war.

Port Royal's Euramerican community survived the financially strapped times because of money infused in the region for defense, and because few outsiders were willing to move to the unsecured frontier to compete for the area's resources. Port Royal's economy stagnated until the 1730s. The Sea Islands were ill-suited to the production of rice, for only salt water was available to flood the fields.[28] Indigo could have been grown on the islands but was not discovered as a cash crop until the 1740s. Many whites moved away in search of economic opportunities and security from the ravages of disease and marauding bands of Indians. Yet, several families willing to risk the hazards remained at Port Royal. The Bryans, Bulls, Barnwells, Mottes, Cochrans, Bellingers, Hexts, and Palmers were tied by the economic promise of the future to a land that was not yet their own. They awaited the day when the land office would open and they could seize the rich Indian land they had fought for in the Yamassee War.[29]

AN APPRENTICESHIP IN LAND, WEALTH, AND POLITICS

In the 1720s the Bryans held more than 1,500 acres of land in South Carolina. Joseph Bryan possessed more than 500 acres in Granville County and between 900 and 1,100 acres in Colleton County, although most of it was undeveloped. The date of Joseph Bryan's death cannot be determined, but it appears that he died some time before 1731.[30] His eldest son, Joseph, who probably inherited his father's holdings, sold portions of the land in the 1730s.[31] His local prominence was reflected by election to the South Carolina Commons House of Assembly in 1728. Hannah Bryan, Jonathan's sister, married into their mother's family, the Cochrans, which further enmeshed the Bryans into the Port Royal community and extended their ties through the colony. Hugh Bryan displayed the greatest promise of all the Bryans. He quickly rose through the militia ranks to lieutenant, captain, and then major. His ambitions led him to undertake a variety of enterprises, which included establishing plantations and provisioning the militia. In 1726 Hugh purchased 250 acres from Timothy Hendrick, and between 1727 and 1731 he made two more purchases totaling 711 acres from Landgrave John Bailey.[32] The later acquisitions were risky. Landgraves held large tracts of land under patent from the colony's former proprietors. The legal ownership of Landgrave land was undetermined by South Carolina's royal government.[33] Hugh's purchase might have been voided, yet his speculation paid off: the Commons House sanctioned the legality of the Landgraves' claims, and Hugh found himself in possession of several excellent tracts. His success must have bolstered his confidence, for he soon undertook an even wider variety of economic enterprises, from the buying and selling of land to fulfillment of government contracts.

Jonathan Bryan held no land in the 1720s. In 1729, at the age of twenty-one, he was part of a reconnaissance expedition which explored the no-man's region south of the Savannah River to the St. Johns River in Florida. It is likely that Jonathan continued his employment in the colony's defense for several more years, for in 1733 we find him commanding a scout boat that patrolled the frontier.[34] These experiences enlarged Jonathan's horizons. He came in close contact with the Creek Indians, from whom it appears he learned the skill of carving piraguas from cedar and cypress trees.[35] His knowledge of the southern terrain aided him immeasurably when he established plantations on numerous Georgia rivers in the 1750s and 1760s. His familiarity with the southeastern Indians furthered his political career: it led him to a place by James Oglethorpe's side in negotiations with the Creeks for the new colony of Georgia and to conducting diplomatic relations with the Indians for both the royal and revolutionary governments of Georgia; earning the Indians' trust he persuaded many Creeks to lease him more than four million acres of Florida land in the 1770s. It appears that Bryan learned from the mistakes his father and the other traders made in their treatment of Indians.

While Bryan received his frontier education, a series of events dramatically altered the fortunes of his family and their neighbors. In 1731 an act of Parliament permitted the direct shipment of rice to ports south of Cape Finistere, Spain. This allowed Carolinians to sell their rice without first shipping the staple to London, thus considerably lowering transportation costs. The legislation had an immediate effect in South Carolina, where the amount of land devoted to rice cultivation doubled in less than ten years.[36]

The second event to alter life on the southern frontier was settlement of the colony's quitrent problem. This resulted in the reopening of South Carolina's land office in late November 1731. Port Royal settlers wasted no time in making their claims to the rich land vacated by the Yamassees more than a decade before.[37] Three weeks after the land office opened, Hugh and Joseph Bryan, Jr., submitted a plat for 3,140 acres, which they were granted a year later.[38] The speed with which the Bryans put forth their claim resulted from Hugh's talents as a surveyor.[39] In March and April of 1732, less than four months after the opening of the land office, at least thirty-six patents encompassing more than 40,000 acres of land surveyed by Hugh were submitted by Carolinians.[40] Possessing a much-desired skill brought Hugh into close contact with the richest and most powerful men of the province, which improved his social position in the community and earned him political patronage.[41] The fees from surveying also helped Hugh capitalize many of the economic enterprises that he undertook in the coming decade. His biggest capital expenditures, like those of neighboring planters, were made for the purchase of slaves.

Slave labor enabled the Bryans and their neighbors to transform the Indian land from a frontier to a commercial economy in just a few years. The Bryans owned at least a few slaves at the time of the Yamassee War. In 1721 there were about twenty slaves in the region; by the end of the 1730s there were several thousand.[42] The number of slaves which the Bryans possessed in the 1730s is not recorded, though in the early 1750s Hugh held between seventy-five and one hundred, and Jonathan at least sixty-six.[43] The Bryans rarely questioned the morality of holding slaves, but they were very concerned with the treatment of bondspeople and the spiritual state of black souls. Jonathan and Hugh's attempts to reform the institution of slavery brought upon them the wrath of government and many Carolinians in the 1740s. Nevertheless, despite their attempts at reform, at no time did they become willing to free their laborers. They fully recognized that they owed their wealth to slave labor.[44]

Most of the planters of the Indian Land devoted their labor force to the production of rice, but the Bryan brothers followed Hugh's lead and produced a variety of agricultural goods. In addition to rice, they raised cattle and provisioned the local troops that guarded the frontier. They also became involved in speculating, shipping, lumber, the production of shingles, and other enterprises related to defense and internal improvements. Utilizing patronage, Hugh adeptly procured a multitude of government contracts.[45] He received a seven-year monopoly to run a ferry from Port Royal Island to his property on the mainland. The placement of a fort adjacent to the ferry increased his opportunities for provisioning the local troops.[46] In addition, Hugh contracted with the government to provide scout boats and men to patrol the southern frontier, and when occasion warranted, he hired men to pursue escaped convicts and runaway slaves. With these contracts Hugh became one of Port Royal's richest men and received election to the assembly from 1733 to 1736.[47]

Life at Port Royal shaped Jonathan Bryan in numerous ways. The necessity of white settlers overcoming religious differences in order to forward political interests promoted his later tendency for tolerance and charity toward different religious groups. He also learned from his family's experience in the Yamassee War—during which his brother Hugh spent a year as a prisoner of the Yamassees—both the destructiveness of war with the Indians and the importance of negotiation. Perhaps Hugh's imprisonment and release and the time Jonathan spent as a scout taught him to view the Indians differently from the way his father had. Whereas the latter employed violence and thievery with the Yamassees, Jonathan used diplomacy, generosity, and amicability in his relations with Indians. Perhaps we should not be surprised. A major reason for Jonathan's later political and economic success lay in his ability to establish profitable working relationships with a wide variety of people. In a region inhabited by myriad races, religions, and ethnic groups, many of whom were mutually dependent, the most successful individuals crossed the cultural boundaries that divided people and employed the available human resources to best advantage. Bryan's father and his fellow Indian traders opted to abuse Indians in order to obtain what they wanted: land, wealth, and power. Likewise, many of Jonathan Bryan's contemporaries believed that abusing black slaves by working them seven days a week, rather than "coddling" them with a day off, provided the surest way to profit on a plantation. Jonathan Bryan did things differently. He found that satisfaction of his self-interests could often be best attained by looking after the interests of others, whether they were slaves, Indians, or poor whites.

Bryan's career provides an alternative model for relationships between cultural groups in the Southeast—a path to wealth and power rarely associated with southern planters. Furthermore, Bryan's economic activity, though hardly indicative of that of all white southerners, may be more representative of elite South Carolinians than is usually recognized. Plantation slavery, it has been argued, inhibited the economic development of the South because whites with capital invested in "larger plantations rather than into innovative ventures that might have diversified the southern economy."[48] Hugh Bryan, however, taught Jonathan the importance of diversification and of entrepreneurship. Together they helped build the economic infrastructure of the Port Royal area by surveying, establishing ferryboat routes, building forts and roads, filling government contracts, and, later, by improving port facilities, cultivating new markets, supplying immigrants, and producing a variety of goods for export abroad. The Bryans' frontier experience taught them how to build, maintain, and expand an estate on a dangerous frontier in an uncertain world market.

THE EXPANDING FRONTIER: PURRYSBURG AND GEORGIA

Increasing wealth and political power did not diminish the threats to the security of the white settlers. With the growth of the slave population, the Euramericans on the southern frontier found themselves hardpressed to circumscribe slave mobility. They required assistance to prevent slave escapes to Florida and collusion between runaways and the Spanish.[49] Moreover, the French threat loomed larger in the 1730s. French expansion in the interior continent and diplomatic success among the Indians led South Carolina government officials to send frequent pleas to London for help. At any moment they expected the French and their Indian allies to overrun the colony from the south and west. In addition, paranoid South Carolina officials sent home frequent reports that a Spanish flotilla from Havana was expected to sail into Port Royal or Charlestown harbor, that St. Augustine's governor was about to lead Spanish regulars and runaway slaves in an overland invasion from the south, or that all their foes were about to attack in concert.[50] Threatened by enemies from within and without, plans were developed to establish new buffer settlements. The colony's hope for security lay in attracting poor British and foreign

Protestants to inhabit the "debatable land" between the European powers and in convincing members of the British government that South Carolina and the southern frontier had indeed become an important part of the British Empire and therefore worthy of significant financial outlays for defense.[51]

Plans for South Carolina's defense originated from within the province. In 1729 Governor Robert Johnson revived John Barnwell's township scheme and received official approval of it in London and South Carolina. The plan called for the establishment of ten townships at crucial points along the southern and western borders of the colony. These would guard the frontier as a complement to the forts. In areas between the townships, scouts would patrol on land and by canoe.[52]

The township plan never came close to full realization. Only one of the projected townships, Purrysburg, met with a degree of success.[53] Located on cliffs overhanging the Savannah River, Purrysburg lay thirty miles south of the Indian Land, now part of St. Helena Parish. Purrysburg's strategic location limited access to the parish via the Savannah River.[54] Enemies intending to invade the parish overland from the south had first to travel inland along the Savannah River to the vicinity of Purrysburg, because the numerous swamps and waterways along the coast prevented easy passage. With the establishment of Purrysburg the overland invasion route from Florida was guarded.

The people of St. Helena welcomed with open arms the French- and German-speaking Swiss who settled Purrysburg because the newcomers strengthened their defensive network without occupying any of the parish's rich alluvial land.[55] The Bryans, especially, became active in Purrysburg's affairs and remained so for the remainder of their lives. Hugh surveyed much of the town's land and produced a map of the area in 1735.[56] Jonathan and Hugh both purchased tracts in Purrysburg, and the former may have built a warehouse there on waterfront property.[57] In the 1750s and 1760s, when Jonathan established a string of plantations along the Savannah River, he located several of them in and around Purrysburg township. Few great planters settled in Purrysburg because of the paucity of valuable land, but Bryan's intimate knowledge of the area helped him locate prime tracts with excellent port facilities.

The failure of the township scheme to attract large numbers of foreign Protestants did not deter others from formulating colonization plans for the periphery of South Carolina. The most important of these, and the most successful, began under the auspices of a group of philanthropists, the Associates of Thomas Bray, many of whom had been members of Parliament and the Society for the Propagation of the Gospel in Foreign Parts (SPG). These men joined together as the Trustees of Georgia and received a grant from King George II in 1732 to settle the region below the Savannah River. For the king they would expand the realm; for themselves they had the business of a great philanthropic enterprise; and for the poor and indebted of England they expected to bestow a new lease on life.

The Spanish viewed Georgia with trepidation and anger. They claimed the region themselves. In private, Englishmen recognized Spain's rightful claim, but Spanish inability to occupy the region effectively provided a temptation too strong for Britain to resist. The audacity of the British in settling land long recognized as Spain's emphasized to St. Helena's inhabitants the commitment of the royal government to both South Carolina and Georgia. When the first 113 colonists arrived at Port Royal in 1733, the people of St. Helena Parish, particularly the Bryans, extended a significant amount of assistance.

Hugh McCall wrote in 1811 that Jonathan Bryan and William Bull led James Oglethorpe, Georgia's first leader, to the spot chosen to settle the new colony. Harvey H. Jackson could find no proof to substantiate McCall's claim but added, "No doubt McCall had heard Bryan's name so often that the man had taken on heroic proportions, for of those Carolinians who supported, and exploited the fledgling province Jonathan Bryan was surely the most famous. Therefore, to put such a man with the founder at the founding was only natural—if he was not there, he should have been."[58] It is very possible that Jonathan or one of his brothers did in fact lead Oglethorpe to Yamacraw bluff either by recommendation or in person, for the Bryans' familiarity with the Savannah River probably exceeded that of anyone else at Port Royal. Jonathan's experience as a scout and Hugh's as a surveyor, cartographer, and employer of local Indians, as well as the family's local prominence and their involvement with Purrysburg (also located on the Savannah River), gave great creditability to their opinions for the establishment of the new colony. Whichever actual role they played in selecting the site of first settlement, the family was rewarded for their efforts by having Savannah's first street named Bryan.

The Bryans helped the new colony in a variety of ways. Joseph Bryan allowed Oglethorpe the free use of his slaves to clear land and erect buildings.[59] Hugh Bryan became a major supplier of cattle for the colony, barreling beef and transporting herds to Ebenezer, Savannah, and Frederica.[60] Whenever supplies were short—which they often were—the colony's leaders knew they could call on the Bryans to provide foodstuffs. Jonathan Bryan also provided slaves to work for the colony, assisted Oglethorpe in his negotiations with the Indians, served as a guide, and provided advice on the layout of the country. Oglethorpe asked the Trustees to give Jonathan Bryan five hundred acres of land, for he is "a very brave young man, who himself with four of his Negroes worked for us gratis some months."[61] Bryan became a part of Oglethorpe's inner circle.[62] Familiar with the local Indians, he stood at Oglethorpe's left side during the treaty negotiations with the Yamacraws. While it is often pointed out that Oglethorpe's talents induced the neighboring Indians to make peace with the British, the role of local Carolinians in the treaty-making process has been overlooked. Men like Jonathan Bryan, on intimate terms with Georgia's Indian neighbors as scouts, traders, and employers, advised Oglethorpe concerning the natives they knew so well. The presence of Jonathan at Oglethorpe's side added legitimacy to the Englishman's word in his negotiations with the Indians.[63]

Jonathan Bryan and his brothers remained actively involved in Georgia throughout the Trustee period. They traded with Georgia colonists, provisioned her garrisons, and became major sponsors of the Bethesda Orphan House, the colony's largest private institution in the 1740s. Despite their personal attachment to the colony, they, like most Carolinians, had little motivation to move to Georgia. The Trustees hoped to create a society of yeoman farmers and artisans in Georgia by limiting land ownership and prohibiting slavery. These measures effectively deterred the Bryans and other slaveholders from migrating. It might not have mattered. In the 1730s South Carolina enjoyed great prosperity; few planters would have wanted to leave.

The Bryans benefited from the booming economic conditions of the 1730s as much as anyone in their parish. All three brothers became wealthy planters and were selected to public office. Not only did they complete the difficult tasks of establishing rice plantations—they had to purchase laborers, construct dikes, build slave quarters, and find factors for their crops—but they continued to pursue a variety of entrepreneurial activities. Hugh Bryan personally handled the selling of rice and cattle in the Georgia market, and both Hugh and Jonathan remained active in public works projects and in provisioning troops. In 1735, Jonathan proposed building a road in Georgia for Oglethorpe. He shrewdly stipulated that the eighteen laborers he was to be provided with first be used to extend a road from his own plantation to St. Helena Parish to the Savannah River.[64] The road Bryan envisioned would have made his plantation a major terminus between Charlestown and Georgia. Oglethorpe rejected Bryan's offer, but it was indicative of the latter's recognition of the importance of placing one's operations in the most expeditious location and of his willingness to enlist government support for his personal designs.

While the Bryans and their neighbors took advantage of favorable economic circumstances, the Georgians experienced little of the same. The Trustees searched for a cash crop that could be produced by the yeomen on their farms and promoted silk production and vineries, but these enterprises failed. Many settlers left the colony, but despite these setbacks, the Trustees were disinclined to alter their plan for Georgia. This led a group of colonists to organize themselves to defeat Trustee policies.[65] The latter, labeled in history as the "malcontents," eyed prosperity in South Carolina and published numerous tracts proclaiming the necessity of slave labor and the removal of restrictions on land ownership. The Trustees resisted the intense pressure provided by the malcontents and earned a reprieve when Parliament began making yearly grants to the colony, which not only improved Georgia's defense but put money into the economy. Carolinians probably did not care whether or not Georgia allowed slavery: few were interested in migrating to this backward and relatively unprotected frontier. Carolinians preferred to view Georgia as their own colony, which they could exploit, rather than as a potential base of operations.[66] For St. Helena residents, and especially the Bryans, the colony provided a market for their crops and a buffer for their recently settled lands.

Yet men like Jonathan and Hugh Bryan forged bonds with the colony that went beyond self-interest. The Bryans' free donation of labor and their steady supply of goods at reasonable rates bespoke a sincere commitment to Georgia's impoverished immigrants. Johann Martin Boltzius, leader of the poor Salzburger community in Georgia, frequently spoke of the help Jonathan Bryan provided for his people. He described him as "a Christian man and a good friend of our congregation." Three Germans who visited South Carolina found warm hospitality at Jonathan's plantation: they reported that "they received so much love and kindness that they cannot praise it enough; and they saw and heard many edifying things in his house, where God's word dwells abundantly, which is sometimes very rare in this country."[67] The Bryans also became the leading benefactors of Georgia's Bethesda Orphan House during its first ten years of operations. In addition, Hugh was responsible for collecting and distributing poor relief in St. Helena Parish. He became one of the first South Carolina slaveholders to attempt to convert his slaves.[68] Throughout their adult lives, the Bryan brothers devoted extraordinary energy to the pursuit of both profit and improving the lot of others.

THE DESIRE FOR CONQUEST

The inability of Georgia to prosper did not lessen its importance to the denizens of St. Helena Parish nor to the officers of empire in London. The yearly parliamentary grants displayed Britain's commitment to defend and expand her position in the Southeast. Spain could do little to stem English expansion in the region, but it had several assets to help keep Britain out of Florida. The superb Castillo de San Marcos, with walls strongly constructed of coquina shells cemented together with limestone, gave St. Augustine an imposing fortress to withstand British attacks. Moreover, Spain's Caribbean fleet, based in Havana and responsible for defending Florida, provided an ever-present threat against South Carolina and Georgia; on several occasions the Havana fleet helped save St. Augustine from British invaders. Florida's value to Spain lay in its location along the sea-lanes between the Caribbean and Spain's possessions in Mexico and South America. Spain also envisioned Florida as the first line of defense against British encroachments into New Spain. Otherwise, Spain lacked the ability to exploit Florida's natural resources, and the nation's soldiers and bureaucrats viewed the colony as one of the least desirable assignments in its vast empire. Prime Minister Robert Walpole sought to soften British belligerency toward Spain by negotiating a border for the Southeast at the Convention of El Prado. Continued British smuggling with Spain's South American empire and expansion in Georgia wounded Spanish pride, however, and led to an aggressive policy of resistance.[69]

The governor of St. Augustine responded to British expansion by promoting the escape of slaves from South Carolina. The policy was an old one, but in 1738 the manner and vigor with which St. Augustine prompted these escapes terrified South Carolina whites. Officials in St. Augustine issued a widely publicized proclamation that offered freedom to all slaves who fled the British. The acting governor of South Carolina, William Bull, parlayed with the Spanish to amend the situation, but to no avail. St. Helena's whites grew alarmed when fifty of their slaves responded to the Spanish call and slipped away to St. Augustine. Then, the worst nightmare of South Carolina whites came true: in September 1739 between sixty and one hundred blacks revolted in the Stono Rebellion. More than twenty whites and many more blacks died in the rebellion and its aftermath. White Carolinians blamed St. Augustine for the revolt.

Word of war with Spain "reached Charlestown the very weekend that the uprising began."[70] Shortly thereafter, Oglethorpe arrived in South Carolina from England with instructions to strengthen South Carolina's and Georgia's defenses and to "annoy" the Spanish. He appeared before the South Carolina Commons House and offered to lead a combined force of Georgians, Indians, Carolinians, and English army regulars to subdue the Spanish.[71] The usually miserly assembly appropriated the stately sum of £120,000 for the leveling of St. Augustine.

Young Carolinians like Jonathan Bryan enlisted in the expedition. Bryan raised a company of "gentlemen volunteers," which he commanded as lieutenant. The conquest promised to reward its participants with unmatched honor and glory. Captain Richard Wright spoke for the Carolina volunteers when he stated that they joined the expedition "from a sincere Motive of serving their Country and of sharing somewhat in the Reputation of taking St. Augustine."[72] Although the colony was only seventy years old, it already had its legendary military heroes; John Barnwell, James Moore, John Palmer, and James Cochran, all had earned fame in wars against Spain and its allies. Related to both the Barnwell and Cochran families, Jonathan Bryan hoped—in this final showdown with Spain—to join his name to theirs in the annals of Carolina history.[73] Oglethorpe promised that this conquest would remove the Spanish once and for all time from the Southeast. Of course, fame did not provide the sole motive for the "gentlemen volunteers." In lieu of pay, they made an agreement with Oglethorpe to receive booty in the form of captured slaves and horses. Governor Don Manuel de Montiano of Florida suspected, however, that the Carolinians' true motive for invasion was in their desire for Indian land. Montiano believed that Spanish defeat would deprive the Apalachee

Indians of protection. The British would then exterminate the Apalachee and take their land. The volunteers probably did not give much thought to the Apalachee, and though they looked forward to collecting booty, it was doubtful that they would risk their lives for it. Certainly Jonathan Bryan and his fellow planters had easier ways of attaining wealth.

At thirty years of age Bryan must have been the envy of his peers. His youth belied the extent of his accomplishments: he had explored the interior, accumulated 1,200 acres of prime rice land on which he built a profitable plantation, received appointment as church warden for his parish, and counted among his close associates James Oglethorpe, one of the most esteemed men in the British Empire. Now the opportunity of a lifetime beckoned him to display his prowess as a leader of men in pursuit of the traditional enemy, the kind of enterprise of which legends were made.

The expedition got under way in early May 1740 when Oglethorpe arrived on the Spanish side of the St. Johns River with approximately one thousand men. Spanish forces in northern Florida numbered close to six hundred.[74] In the following weeks British troops filtered into northern Florida, bivouacked, and awaited Oglethorpe's instructions. Oglethorpe consulted with Commodore Pearse of the Royal Navy to coordinate the invasion. They agreed to drive the people of St. Augustine into the Castillo de San Marcos, occupy the town, and then bombard the "densly packed" fort into submission from close quarters.[75]

On May 21 and 22 Oglethorpe reconnoitered the narrow peninsula which faces St. Augustine from the northeast. He recklessly pushed his men and horses, leaving the party weakened with exhaustion and abandoning the horses along the way. While Oglethorpe returned to camp on the twenty-second, Jonathan Bryan arrived at the St. Johns River with twelve Carolina volunteers and an unknown number of Indian allies. The force Bryan led was small but composed of socially prominent men who were experienced in southern topography and warfare. Larry Ivers described them as "well-born gentlemen, several of whom had extensive Indian fighting experience [and] were accustomed to voicing their opinions and making decisions by virtue of their social and financial positions."[76] The gentlemen volunteers expected and demanded an elevated position among Oglethorpe's troops as befitted men of their experience and station. They badgered the general to undertake offensive operations, but throughout the expedition he remained hesitant and refused their advice.

At Fort Diego the Carolina volunteers and their allies were slighted by the general. Forced to "shift for themselves," Bryan and his men found it difficult to understand why they had to pay the Spaniard Don Diego for his cattle when he should have been chained as a prisoner of war and had his property confiscated. Oglethorpe raised the ire of the volunteers when he berated their Cherokee allies for killing Diego's cattle. A perplexed Cherokee headman told Jonathan, "It was a strange Thing that they were permitted to kill the Spaniards but not their Beef."[77]

On May 27 Oglethorpe conducted a "leisurely reconaissance" with a "large Detachment of his own Men." Bryan joined the general with six of the volunteers, some of their slaves, and a "party of Indians." After marching all night they came in sight of five scattered houses, about five or six miles from St. Augustine. The general halted the troops one-quarter mile from the makeshift village and ordered the Carolina volunteers to attack the settlement. The volunteers followed the general's orders in full sight of the troops. They captured two blacks "some others escaping for Want of more Assistance." The general approached the Carolinians "with the whole Party" and stated, "Well, I see the Carolina Men have Courage but no Conduct." Bryan replied, "Sir, the Conduct is yours."

Hostility between the general and the volunteers did not abate. The latter continued to question Oglethorpe's courage.[78] The Carolinians tried to goad Oglethorpe into attacking St. Augustine. A disgusted Colonel John Palmer, renowned hero of the Yamassee War, offered several times to burn the town with a "Party of Carolina Men and Indians." The Carolinians were cocksure that the Spanish were no match for themselves and their Indian allies. Oglethorpe refused and decided to occupy abandoned Fort Mosa, two miles from St. Augustine. Unsure of himself and a course of action, he determined not to attack. Bryan reconnoitered the city and came away with three horses. He reported to the general that "the Town was in a great Tumult and Confusion, the Inhabitants screeching and crying." When Oglethorpe stated he would withdraw British forces, Bryan implored him to attack, for now "was the Time to do it . . . if he retreated they would make Preparations against his Return." Oglethorpe refused, believing that if he stormed the town he would lose three hundred men.[79]

At Fort Mosa the Carolinians were further alienated by Oglethorpe when he refused them admittance to a house in the fort during a driving rain. Bryan reported that the general ordered "several of those volunteers and Carolina Officers [to] go out again into the Weather," though, "the said House was big enough to have contained all the Arms of the Forces, as well as a great part of the People." The "Carolina Arms particularly were rendered unfit for Action" by the rain. If "the Spaniards at that Juncture made any Attack," the men would have been unable to defend themselves.[80]

The next day Oglethorpe abandoned Fort Mosa and retreated to Fort Diego. The house at Fort Mosa was burned though Bryan urged the general to preserve the building as a hospital (for which it was soon needed). On the retreat, Bryan saw several "of the General's Men give out and drop under the march" and heard him give a general order to shoot stragglers. The order was not executed, Bryan believed, because of the officers' compassion, for the men had left Fort "Diego with only three Days Provisions and were both very hungry and greatly fatigued with marching."

After the return of the troops to Fort Diego, all of the Carolina volunteers except Bryan's brother-in-law Colonel Nathanial Barnwell, who was aide-de-camp to Oglethorpe, and William Steads abandoned the expedition. Disappointed in not having attacked St. Augustine, alienated by their shoddy treatment by Oglethorpe, and irked by the confiscation of their baggage horses, Bryan's men returned home. Oglethorpe had reneged on their agreement for dividing plunder and withheld the respect they expected as "gentlemen volunteers." Bryan escorted the volunteers to the St. Johns River, where they met with a company of volunteers just arrived from South Carolina. He returned southward with the new recruits.[81] Richard Wright, captain of the South Carolina Volunteers, welcomed the recruits and later commended Bryan, "who assisted the General as long as he stayed on the [Spanish] main."[82]

THE FAILURE OF ARMS

Oglethorpe banished the Carolina volunteers to Point Quartell and Anastasia island, opposite St. Augustine, to build batteries, though "the Volunteers in general discovered a great Desire of having an Opportunity to come to Action." The laurels to be won erecting batteries could scarcely compare with that to be gained from hand-to-hand combat. The men and their slaves applied themselves diligently to the task of building batteries but to little purpose, for the location selected by Colonel Cook was useless for invoking damage.

Furthermore, they had an insufficient number of cannon and shell to reduce the fort, and only two soldiers possessed artillery experience. Life continued as usual in St. Augustine throughout the sporadic bombardments of the Carolinians. Bells rang in the castle to warn the inhabitants whenever British canon hurled its load across the Matanzas River. Nevertheless, Bryan had good fortune in being stationed at Point Quartell.

On June 14 disaster struck the British. A force of three hundred Spanish and their allies attacked poorly defended Fort Mosa and inflicted a devastating assault on the invaders. Of the 137-man "flying party," 63 were killed and many others captured and wounded.[83] Colonel Alexander Vanderdussen, a Carolina officer and Oglethorpe's most talented tactician, believed the fort could still be subdued through siege warfare, but the shaken general refused to take any further offensive action except for the continued ineffectual bombardment from Point Quartell. When Spanish ships appeared and reinforced the fort, Oglethorpe accepted defeat and initiated retreat. Poorly managed, the retreat further lessened the army's self-esteem. Nothing, it appeared, had been accomplished by the invasion except for the loss of men and supplies. The invasion of St. Augustine had come to an ignominious end.

As a Spanish counterinvasion seemed imminent, perhaps in league with South Carolina slaves, terror spread over Georgia and the southern parishes of South Carolina. Many Georgians abandoned the colony for safer havens, the magistrates impotent to deter the exodus. Numerous St. Helena slaveholders left their homes as well. Distraught Carolinians uncovered numerous alleged slave conspiracies. Some feared, and the Spanish certainly contemplated, the sending of a flotilla into Port Royal Sound. This would subdue the low country while effectively cutting off Georgia from South Carolina. The colony needed help, but none was forthcoming. The South Carolina Commons House determined that Whitehall, not the colony, should foot the bill. Its tax sources depleted, its pride wounded, and its troops much maligned, the assembly decided to conduct a full-scale investigation to impress upon the officers of empire in London that Oglethorpe, and not the colony's lack of effort, was responsible for the failed invasion and the colony's perilous position. The scramble to lay blame detracted from the task at hand: the preparation of defense against the expected Spanish counterattack.

After a decade of peace and prosperity, St. Helena Parish seemed ready to revert to its frontier stage. In addition to the Spanish and slave threat, drought and a smallpox epidemic ravaged the colony, and the market for rice fell. Prices declined 70 percent from 1741 to 1746.[84] Hugh Bryan, falling on hard times, had to unload five thousand acres of land. The inhabitants of St. Helena lay perilously close to losing all they possessed.

Security of life at Port Royal appeared no better than at the close of the Yamassee War. Georgia no longer provided a buffer. Vulnerable to Spaniard, Indian, and slave alike, the white inhabitants of the southern frontier required outside assistance to brook the disastrous times. The South Carolina Commons House declared itself unable to help.[85] Nor could assistance be expected from across the Atlantic, for Britain was occupied in its war with Spain.[86]

The disaster of the invasion left Bryan with many nagging suspicions. He always believed that if Oglethorpe had taken the offensive and conducted a siege, then St. Augustine would have fallen.[87] Bryan expressed his disappointment with the general in the account he provided the South Carolina Commons House of Assembly on the failure of the invasion.[88] He depicted the general in his deposition as dilatory, arbitrary, cowardly, incapable of taking advice, and insouciant, if not purposefully negligent to the welfare of the Carolinians and their allies. Bryan's bitterness was compounded by the fact that formerly he had been a member of Oglethorpe's inner circle and probably had looked up to the general. Oglethorpe personified the paternalistic political leader who had achieved fame and fortune while zealously serving others—a blending of characteristics to which Bryan aspired.[89] Bryan's loyalty to the general was made evident by his return to Florida, after the other "gentlemen volunteers" had departed. Captain Wright elucidated the extent of that loyalty: Bryan "assisted the General *as long* as he stayed on the [Spanish] main."[90]

Under pressure of arms, the general not only performed poorly but displayed little of the qualities of leadership that Bryan and others had come to expect of him. Oglethorpe's promises of glory and conquest had turned into a nightmare similar to the one Bryan had known as a child during the Yamassee War. The sword that Bryan, his family, and their neighbors lived by again left them battered by the enemy and on the verge of further disaster. At precisely this moment the Great Awakening took South Carolina and Georgia by storm.

2

IMPASSIONED DISCIPLES

The Great Awakening, George Whitefield,

and the Reform of Slavery

In the 1740s the Bryans became close associates of George Whitefield, the best-known figure to step on British North American territory in the colonial period. No one could have guessed that this twenty-five-year-old son of an obscure tavern keeper was about to move to the forefront of a popular religious movement which would soon sweep through the American colonies and Great Britain. Jonathan Edwards, John and Charles Wesley, and Gilbert Tennant were among the most illustrious names associated with this great transatlantic movement, but none compared in popularity with Whitefield. The greatest orator of his day, Whitefield crisscrossed the American colonies spreading the message of the "new birth" in Christ to audiences that frequently numbered in the thousands.[1] Ben Franklin calculated that Whitefield's booming voice could be heard by 30,000 people at a single sermon; during one three-month tour in the summer of 1750, Whitefield spoke ninety times to crowds estimated to have totaled 240,000 people. Samuel Johnson thought Whitefield "would be followed by crowds were he to wear a night-cap in the pulpit, or were he to preach from a tree." David Hume, after hearing Whitefield preach, cried out, "Stop, Gabriel, stop, ere you enter the sacred portals, and yet carry with you the news of one sinner converted to God!"[2]

The rise of Evangelical Christianity spurred a revival of religion in the English-speaking world that had not been seen since the days of the Puritan revolution. It brought a storm of interest to religion in colonial society and became the premier issue discussed in taverns, newspapers, and pamphlets. The rise of Evangelical religion in the 1740s forced people to reassess the nature of churches, religion, and their own personal relationship with the divine. Its influence extended into the secular as well. Throughout the British Empire people reexamined their social relationships, institutions, and ideas. Evangelicals attacked the religious and secular values of their opponents, who then had to define and defend their way of life. Moved by the euphoria of attracting hundreds of thousands of people to the new religion, Evangelicals undertook a crusade to change society and lead the people to Christ. Whitefield persuaded Jonathan and Hugh Bryan to lead the way in reforming the institution of slavery in South Carolina, to herald the dawning of a new age in Christianity, one in which both whites and blacks would be called to Christ. The Evangelicals' evolution in status from outsider to the mainstream of southern culture was initiated by Whitefield and his major followers in South Carolina, the Bryans, who by altering their approach to the reform of slavery prepared the way for the spread of evangelism in the nineteenth century.

RELIGION IN SOUTH CAROLINA

Whitefield entered a society that appeared removed from religious fervor, when in actuality religious conflict seethed beneath the surface. The political disputes of the colony's first fifty years spilled over into the religious realm, so that at various times the Anglicans attempted (and temporarily succeeded) in disenfranchising Dissenters, and Dissenters attempted to disenfranchise French Huguenots. The Anglicans succeeded in attaining state establishment of their church in 1706, and religious divisions did not begin to abate until the 1730s.[3]

The bishop of London and the Society for the Propagation of the Gospel in Foreign Parts held responsibility for the spiritual life of South Carolina's colonists. The former was effectively the bishop of all Anglican churches in overseas colonies, while the latter was a missionary society whose primary function was to convert Indians and slaves.[4] By the Yamassee War the SPG had given up its attempts to convert Indians: the missionaries refused the task and the aboriginal population proved unreceptive.[5] Conversion of slaves was not undertaken with enthusiasm until the 1740s and enjoyed only limited success.[6] The bishop of London's principal goal was establishment of the Anglican church, while the SPG worked to meet the ministerial needs of the white population.

The Anglican establishment was extremely weak in the southern parishes, and if not for the tireless efforts of the Bryans' minister, Lewis

Jones, it might well have disappeared. Jones's devotion to the Anglican community was displayed in a letter he wrote to Bishop Gibson in London regarding his transfer to wealthier Goose Creek Parish in 1730. Jones requested he be allowed to remain at St. Helena until a replacement could be found, one who was preferably "sober, diligent, and prudent": "I am apprehensive that if this Parish were left vacant, or fill'd with an unworthy Missionary, the people that have been brought over and settled in the Church since my arrival would return to their old Profession, there being a Presbyterian Meeting close by the Church." Jones further argued that the Goose Creek Parish could be readily filled by neighboring clergy once every three weeks, while his church was eighty miles from the nearest Anglican establishment and had to compete with several Presbyterian chapels. If he were transferred the parish would be left without a single Anglican minister. The SPG determined that Jones should remain at St. Helena Parish, a decision which pleased both the shepherd and his flock.[7]

The expansion of St. Helena Parish in the 1730s found the movement of population away from the Anglican church located at Beaufort on Port Royal Island. The Bryans and their neighbors had to travel ten miles if they wished to attend services. For a community in the process of establishing plantations the trip was inconvenient. In 1736 St. Helena's Anglicans proposed to the South Carolina Commons House that a chapel be built in their neighborhood. The Commons House responded by appointing Jonathan and Hugh Bryan, along with Stephen Bull, Joseph Izard, and John Mulrain as "commissioners and authorized [them] to receive benefactors and donations of land, not exceeding 500 acres . . . [and] "the rectors were required to perform Divine Service . . . once in six weeks," in a chapel to be built on the "South side of Combahee River, near Huspahs' neck."[8] Colonel William Bull donated the land for the church, which was surrounded on two sides by plantations belonging to Hugh, Jonathan, and Joseph Bryan.[9] Jones reported a larger congregation in this and his other "remote" chapel than in the main parish church at Beaufort.[10]

Religion played an important role in the lives of the Bryans. Though distant from religious institutions they made sure that their children received baptism in the established church. After building the chapel in their neighborhood, Jonathan performed duties as church warden, while Hugh served as vestryman. These offices required their attendance to parish matters in Beaufort, where the Bryan brothers built houses close to the Anglican church. Despite their apparent devotion to the religious life of the community, the Bryans' religious activities in the 1730s contrasted sharply with the evangelical fervor they displayed in the 1740s. Certainly the Bryans would have argued that a complete change had occurred in their lives. For George Whitefield informed them in 1740 that they were not true Christians. Only the mystical experience of grace could allow them to know Christ.

Hugh Bryan and his wife, Catherine Barnwell, were the two earliest converts among the Bryans to evangelicalism. They both considered themselves pious Christians before they met Whitefield. Catherine "endeavoured to follow David's rule, seven times a day to retire and pray, and to praise God, and I kept strict fasts." Hugh, "having often experienced the condescending goodness of God, . . . concluded my state safe, and counted myself amongst the true Israel of God." Both of them soon began to doubt they were true Christians. In 1739 Catherine fell sick: "Had any one told me before that illness, that we were to be born again of God . . . making so intire a change in us, as to make us new creatures . . . I should have thought it very strange, and what could not be true." During her illness she received grace and recovered. But the concept of conversion as a "common" experience was alien to the Bryans. Hugh viewed the return of Catherine's health "as a miraculous dispensation," and "began to pray publickly in my family." He "resolved on a more strict life and more devoted to his service." But he had yet to learn that God's "miraculous dispensation[s]" were "manifestations of his spirit [that] was common to his children at their new-birth in Jesus Christ."[11]

Catherine read "Mr. Whitefield's works on the New-Birth or Justification," and began to comprehend her experience. She explained the moment of grace as a "ray of light and joy into my soul . . . as if an angel had been sent to tell me of it." Hugh was left in the dark. He tried to understand conversion but could not, for comprehension was impossible without the mystical transformation. He learned, as he confided to his diary, "that I must repent of my sins, and cast my self by a lively faith on the mercies of God in Christ, to be justified, sanctified, and saved thro' him; but yet I continued ignorant of the state of my heart, and of the change which was to be wrought in my new-birth." Upon learning that Whitefield was in Georgia, Hugh took his wife and niece to hear the evangelist preach in June 1740.[12]

Hugh listened to Whitefield expound "on the new birth, and asserted that whosoever was born of the spirit . . . would be sensible of a great change." That evening, "I went out into the *Common* to meditate, and to pray. . . . My sins which I had formerly overlook'd, now star'd me in the face." The next two days he spent in meditation, "determined, with God's permission to seek him . . . in the holy sacrament of the Lord's supper." One day, while preparing to receive the sacrament, "my heart being enlarged with a ray of light that darted into my soul," Hugh experienced salvation.[13]

Hugh and Catherine's conversion experiences undoubtedly influenced Jonathan to seek out Whitefield in the summer of 1740, shortly after his return from Florida. Bryan and his brother-in-law Stephen Bull persuaded Lewis Jones, who had befriended Whitefield, to introduce them to the evangelist in Georgia. Whitefield was ill, but Jones told him that Bryan and Bull had come a long way, "expecting to hear" him. Whitefield agreed to preach. His oratory had its promised effect: "Before I prayed long, Mr. B[ull] dropped down, as though shot with a gun." The sight of Stephen Bull convulsing set off a chain reaction of similar outbursts throughout the entire congregation.[14]

The next day Whitefield, "was sent for at noon to see Mr. Jonathan Bryan." Their meeting is well worth quoting from Whitefield's *Journals:*

> At my coming, I found him under great concern and strong convictions of sin. He reflected much of his misspent life, and blessed God for bringing him now to Savannah, and hoped that he might be found in Christ before he returned home. His wife sat weeping by. Mr. B[ull] lay on a bed groaning in bitterness of soul, under a sense of guilt, and crying out for an interest in Jesus. I asked, "What caused him to fall down yesterday?" After half an hour's conversation in the nature of the new birth and the necessity of closing in with Christ, I kneeled down, prayed with them, and took my leave, hoping the Lord would pluck them as brands from the burning. Amen and amen.

The Bryans and Bull remained another two weeks with Whitefield at the Bethesda Orphan House before returning home.[15]

One week later Jonathan Bryan met Whitefield in Charlestown, the former having arrived "much established." Hugh remained home ill, but his wife accompanied Jonathan to hear Whitefield preach to "Baptists, Church folks, and Presbyterians, all joined together, and received according to the church of England." Before Whitefield departed for

Rhode Island he persuaded Bryan to evince the changes which evangelism had brought into his life by opening a school for slaves.[16]

THE AWAKENING

At first, the Evangelicals were welcomed to preach wherever
they went. Ministers were elated when Evangelicals drew crowds into
their churches. But the enthusiastic outpourings of emotions at revival
meetings appeared dangerous to many social conservatives. Both Anglican and Puritan churches placed great emphasis on the "reason-
ableness" of Christianity. Puritan sermons were logical discourses delivered in a subdued and scholarly manner. Not only did these sermons
fail to inspire many congregants, but fewer and fewer Puritans were
achieving the regenerate experience and expressing interest in the religion of their fathers. Similarly, Anglican ministers had great difficulty
inspiring spiritual interest in their flock. Because the Anglican church
was a state church, which hoped to include all Englishmen within its
doors, most of its leaders and preachers placed little emphasis on theology. This gave the church great political, theological, and structural
malleability. This flexibility worked so well that the Methodists, for
instance, remained within the church for over fifty years, though most
contemporaries viewed the relationship as antithetical. Anglican ministers preached proper behavior not theology. Anglican sermons emphasized duty to God, king, and family; discussion of the afterlife was
barely an afterthought.[17]

Evangelicals, on the other hand, believed not only that salvation was
the central experience of a Christian's life but that regeneration must
occur instantaneously. Evangelicals disagreed as to how salvation
might be brought on but generally downplayed their theological differences to emphasize the necessity of the new birth in Christ. They
crossed denominational boundaries and united in denying the efficacy
of "good works" for achieving salvation, and they denounced ministers
who preached that salvation was attainable without a mystical instantaneous transformation of the soul. In public letters, pamphlets,
and newspapers Whitefield's message of new birth was countered by
those who argued that grace could be achieved only gradually, an argument that reflected the conservative preference for slow, moderate social change.

In late 1740 Whitefield aroused a powerful opposition in the colony by reviling an unregenerate clergy.[18] Whitefield believed that those who had not experienced salvation—that is, a mystical transformation of the soul—should not preach the word of God. What could an unregenerate minister possibly know about Christ? What could he teach the unregenerate? Evangelicals had determined that neither education, ordination, birth, wealth, pious living, nor social status entitled a man to preach the gospel. The lowliest beggar might know Christ better than the bishop of London.

The attacks of Whitefield and his fellow Evangelicals upon an unregenerate ministry closed many chapel doors to their preaching. Evangelical ministers were forced to take religion out-of-doors, giving birth to the open-air revival meeting. Itinerant ministers, many without education and license, preached the gospel of new birth through the colonies and Great Britain. Threads of social radicalism appeared as some Evangelicals included a leveling philosophy in their preachings. But whether or not Evangelicals intended to be levelers, their religious movement possessed certain characteristics which challenged social institutions and traditional channels of knowledge. The rejection of established churches for extralegal groups, of written knowledge for revealed truths, of educated, licensed, and ordained ministers for itinerant exhorters helped politicize thousands of people. Evangelical preaching provided a forum for common people to express themselves publicly and instilled in many of them a consciousness that all men were equal before God. Deference was dealt a mighty blow, as people witnessed the active, sometimes vociferous repudiation of community leaders and values.

Political authorities might subdue Evangelicals and, as we will see in South Carolina, force them to alter their criticisms of the dominant society, but they could not completely erase from people's minds the challenges posed by Evangelicals to institutions and ideas. This legacy can more easily be seen in the northern urban centers, and as Rhys Isaac has recently shown, in the Virginia countryside.[19] But in South Carolina, Evangelicals posed an even greater threat to the dominant element of that society, a threat that could not easily be dismissed. For in that colony Whitefield attacked slavery and condemned slaveholding society. He selected South Carolina for special attention because he believed the people of that colony to be particularly distant from Christ. In 1740 Whitefield began a campaign by which he hoped to save southerners, and in particular South Carolinians, from themselves and turn them to Evangelical Christianity. Whitefield was doomed to failure. The Evangelical reforms he offered were too radical for many South Carolina political leaders, who fought back with the powers of the state. This forced Whitefield and his followers to change their tactics. After posing a grave threat to the social order of South Carolina in the 1740s, Evangelicals regrouped themselves and formulated a strategy by which they hoped to convert their neighbors to their religion. But first they had to convince southerners that they intended no revolution, no overthrow of slaveholding society.

In 1740 Whitefield found four basic problems in southern society which were epitomized by South Carolina: an unregenerate clergy, excessive materialism, the people's distance from Christianity, and the institution of slavery. He considered the four to be interrelated. Nothing could be done for South Carolina, according to the evangelist, until the people overcame their "general dreadness as to divine things." Why, Whitefield pondered, were so many unwilling to seek Christ? First, there were too few men preaching the word of God and, second, too many who preached knew nothing of Christianity. Whitefield believed many southern ministers to be charlatans, who by living in comfort condoned the profligate life of the elite, which in turn inculcated in the common people a disrespect for the spirit of Christianity. Whitefield constantly railed against the materialistic excesses of the ministry and South Carolina's polite society. He wondered "whether the court-end of London could exceed [Charlestown] in affected finery," and he condemned the people's midnight balls and other amusements. His thoughts were echoed by fellow Evangelical Johann Martin Boltzius, who asserted, "Anyone who has lived in London may have seen and heard some abominations; but [in South Carolina] they have reached the highest peak."[20]

Whitefield did not have far to look to find the root cause of South Carolina's degeneracy. The materialistic excesses which allowed the clergy to lead a comfortable existence, and which deterred the people from Christ, were blamed upon slavery. Slavery had led slaveholders to become greedy. Whitefield asked them:

Is it not the highest ingratitude, as well as cruelty, not to let your poor slaves enjoy some fruits of their labour? When passing along, . . . I have viewed your plantations cleared and cultivated, many spacious houses built, and the owners of them faring sumptuously every day, my blood has frequently almost run cold within me to consider how many of your slaves had neither convenient food to eat, nor proper raiment to put on, notwithstanding [that] most of the comforts you enjoy, were solely owing to their inde-fatigable labours. The scripture says, "Thou shalt not muzzle the oxen that treadeth out the corn."[21]

Whitefield asserted that if South Carolina did not reform itself the whole society might be destroyed by God. Only recently the colony had been visited with a drought, repeated epidemics, and the Stono Rebellion. Did anyone require further proof that God had expressed his displeasure with its inhabitants? Whitefield thought not. In June 1740 he published "An Open Letter to the Inhabitants of Maryland, Virginia, North and South Carolina concerning the treatment of their Negroes." In this letter, Whitefield blamed the ills of southern society upon the slaveholders' inhumane treatment of their bondsmen. With great compassion, Whitefield pleaded on the slaves' behalf. He believed that southerners treated their dogs better than their slaves and prayed for the untold "numbers [who] have been given up to the inhuman usage of cruel task masters." The life of a slave, Whitefield believed, was so miserable, that "perhaps it might be better for the poor crea-tures themselves to be hurried out of life. . . . And indeed," he con-tinued, "considering what usage they commonly meet with, I have wondered, that we have not [had] more instances of self-murder among the negroes."[22]

Whitefield also expressed surprise that the slaves "have not more frequently risen up against their owners," but he added, "should such a thing be permitted by providence, all good men must acknowledge that the judgement would be just." Whitefield reminded the slaves who God "does not reject the prayer of the poor and destitute, nor disregard the cry of the meanest negroes." He warned slaveholders that the "blood which has been spilt, for these many years in your respec-tive provinces, will ascend up to heaven against you." Slaveholders must reform their society or face the consequences.[23]

What could southerners or, specifically, South Carolinians do to pre-vent God from inflicting further punishment upon the colony? To be-gin, blacks must be provided Christianity. For "Enslaving or misusing their bodies, comparatively speaking, would be an inconsiderable evil was proper care taken of their souls." The worst sin a slaveholder committed was neither enslavement nor brutality but the denial of Christianity to those under their care. White southerners, according to Whitefield, denied their bondsmen Christianity because they believed that conversion would make blacks proud and rebellious. Whitefield thought this ridiculous and reminded the slaveholders that nowhere in the gospel were people urged to "forget their relative duties." To the contrary, servants "are required to be subject in all lawful things to their masters." Ingeniously he argued, "if the teaching [of] slaves christianity has such a bad influence upon their lives, why are you generally desirous of having your children taught?" Do you think, "they are [in] any way better by nature, than the poor negroes?" Both are born in sin and "are naturally capable of the same improvement."[24]

The colonial government's assessment of South Carolina's problems differed markedly from that offered by Whitefield. The rebellion of blacks was not a result of God's wrath, as the Evangelicals believed, but the direct result of the perfidious behavior of the Spanish at St. Augustine, who had publicly offered freedom to the slaves of the English and thus inspired them to overthrow their taskmasters. The South Carolina government's solution lay in destruction of the Spanish, but the invasion had ended in abject failure. Whitefield's claims of impending disaster appeared to have come true, and in the unsettled atmosphere of the Anglo-Spanish War, the Awakening reached a fever pitch. In Charlestown and in the South Carolina countryside Evangelicals zealously took the offensive. People flocked to the Evangelical preachers in increasing numbers. A few months after the failed invasion, Hugh Bryan confirmed the rejuvenation of religion in St. Helena Parish church: "Mr. [Lewis] J[one]'s hall is throng'd every evening with the inhabitants who join with him in prayer and praises."[25]

THE CALL FOR REFORM

The historian Jon Butler has argued that Whitefield did "little to organize and coordinate integrated colonial revivals" and that he "failed to exercise significant authority over the ministers he inspired."[26] Compared with John Wesley, a master organizer of religious societies in England, Whitefield's record was indeed lacking, for he showed little inclination to recruit Evangelicals into religious institutions.[27] Nevertheless, he exercised significant influence over his followers, in part through correspondence. His published letters for the years from 1734 to 1769 number nearly 1,500, and this number understates the whole, since many letters remain unpublished, scattered throughout various archives.[28] In these letters Whitefield disseminated information and advice among a substantial network of followers. His correspondence linked various Evangelicals and assured his importance in evangelical affairs throughout England and the American colonies.[29] He received reports from his followers on the state of religion in their area, on fellow Evangelicals, and on events and programs of mutual interest. In return Whitefield provided information, moral support, and encouragement to those who faced rejection and persecution or who had experienced a weakening of the soul.

The network Whitefield established provided a means for mutual support among Evangelicals. In letters transmitted along the Savannah River, Hugh Bryan and James Habersham shared intimate thoughts on Whitefield's ministry, evangelism, and the state of their souls.[30] The network also worked to heal differences between Evangelicals. When William Gerard De Brahm and Johann Martin Boltzius feuded in Georgia, George Whitefield sent a letter from England to Jonathan Bryan in South Carolina, urging his assistance in ending the dispute.[31] The Bryan family formed one of the most important links in Whitefield's evangelical network. Their wealth and social status added political clout to the movement. Jon Butler, in a brief reference to the Bryans' devotion to Evangelical reform, was correct in assuming that "Whitefield seems largely to have reinforced existing urges."[32] Butler failed, however, to apprehend the extent to which Whitefield inspired the Bryans to an activism that eventually challenged the laws of the province of South Carolina.

Whitefield corresponded with the Bryans for more than ten years. As his agents in South Carolina and Georgia they performed myriad duties, such as overseeing the survival and expansion of the Bethesda Orphan House near Savannah, one of the few religious institutions Whitefield established.[33] The orphanage exerted great influence throughout Georgia: in the early 1740s, for example, it was the colony's largest civil employer. It provided jobs, education, and religious services for Georgians as it helped to spread the Evangelical religion throughout the colony. Bethesda's leaders forwarded Evangelical interests with zeal and intolerance. They organized ritual burnings of books considered heretical and were a constant source of irritation to

Savannah magistrates, claiming special privileges, exemptions, and complete authority over all of the colony's orphans. Two orphan house officials were jailed in 1742 for libelous attacks upon Savannah's unregenerate ministers.[34] In Georgia and in South Carolina Evangelicals enthusiastically worked for the reform of society by denouncing what they perceived were social evils, whether spoken, written, or performed.

The spirit of intolerance and reform was tempered by acts of charity. The Bryan brothers provided assistance for needy Georgia Evangelicals. They sold rice and cattle at below market value to the poor German Salzburgers of Ebenezer and then New Ebenezer. As wealthy benefactors of the orphan house, they provided livestock, rice, and supplies at little or no cost. In times of emergency their extensive resources helped ward off disaster. When the Spanish invaded Georgia in 1742 the Bryan plantations served as temporary refuges for the eighty-nine inhabitants of Bethesda.[35] In the mid-1740s the Bryans purchased a plantation for Whitefield in South Carolina to provide a permanent income for the orphanage.[36] When Georgia legalized slavery in the 1750s, Jonathan Bryan supervised the selection of land and the stocking of slaves for Whitefield's orphanage in Georgia. He also gave advice and assistance in the construction of buildings.[37] Hugh Bryan oversaw Whitefield's legal matters and handled the purchase and sale of the minister's land. Beyond the personal satisfaction the Bryans attained from helping Whitefield and the orphans, they achieved some renown. Whitefield praised and publicized the Bryans and their work in his widely read *Journals* and in numerous letters to others.[38] Georgians and Carolinians knew the Bryans as the leading followers and faithful friends of George Whitefield.

The Bryans' prestige fueled their zeal to pursue Evangelical reforms. The most important reform undertaken by Evangelicals concerned the institution of slavery. Led by George Whitefield, Evangelicals proposed that bondspeople be allowed to convert to Christianity and to receive education as well as more humane treatment. The conversion of slaves had long been a goal of the SPG, which provided the financial support for many of South Carolina's ministers and missionaries. But few missionaries had success convincing planters of the wisdom of slave conversion. Most planters feared their bondspeople would move from religious training to religious rights and perhaps on to civil or political rights. The few slaves who were permitted religious instruction were required to make a formal statement in which they denied any expectation that baptism would lead to freedom.[39] Other problems stood in the way of reform. Slaves were frequently employed seven days a week. Even when a planter did not work his slaves on Sunday, bondspeople often had to tend crops for their own personal consumption. Slaves in eighteenth-century South Carolina often had little time for Christianity or education.[40] When George Whitefield criticized slaveholding southerners' treatment of their bondspeople, he roused a powerful opposition that perceived his ideas as a threat to slaveholding society.

How the Bryans treated their slaves before they met Whitefield is unknown, though we do know that they were interested in slave conversion as early as 1735.[41] Whitefield provided the Bryans with a new direction for their charitable endeavors as well as with a sense of urgency and a rationale that they *must* work for the betterment of society now that they were saved. The Bryans learned that they had "obligations not to neglect the gift of God." As Hugh Bryan informed several others, including brother Jonathan, "let us who have been made partakers of the heavenly gift . . . be zealous for the honour of our master Christ, and for the welfare of our friends . . . to win over those about us." The task was arduous, but as Bryan commented, Evangelicals were to be reassured by the example of the savior: "[Jesus] was made perfect thro' sufferings, and bore not only the curse of God due for our sins, but also the contradiction of sinners." Only through suffering could the redeemed expect to enjoy the gift of grace. Bryan posed the query: "thro' much tribulation we must enter into the kingdom of heaven, . . . why then should we expect to follow him on beds of down?"[42]

With Whitefield as friend, guide, and model, the Bryans decided to take the initiative in promoting Evangelical reforms in South Carolina. Hugh Bryan composed a letter for publication in the *South Carolina Gazette* in which he blamed the miseries of the colony upon the sins of the populace and an unregenerate clergy.[43] His model was George Whitefield's letter of the previous April that had criticized the treatment of slaves and depicted the ills of the province as the results of the iniquities of the people.[44]

Few Carolinians were in the mood to receive Bryan's letter. Hugh sent it to Jonathan to forward to the printer and noted: "Our God has suffered long with us, and I fear lest the late fire may be followed with more severe strokes of his displeasure. Certainly we stand in need of having our hearts humbled by scourgings."[45] Jonathan withheld the letter from publication. Criticism of the clergy had ended, at least temporarily, in October. Would it be expedient to rekindle the dispute? He waited to confer with Whitefield in January when they met in Georgia and traveled together to Hugh Bryan's plantation in South Carolina.[46] One week later the letter was published in a special two-page postscript to the *Gazette*. Bryan wrote:

> I was last Night shock'd with the melancholy News of the South East Part of Charlestown being burnt down on Tuesday. How deplorable is the condition of many there, that are in a few Hours reduc'd to want of Bread! Surely God's just Judgments are upon us—Is there Evil befallen to a City, and the Lord hath not done it? . . . He hath at divers Times been scourging of us, by Drought; by Diseases on Man and Beast; by repeated Insurrections of our Slaves, and lately by Battling shamefully our Enterprize against our Enemy.[47]

Hugh Bryan blamed the unregenerate clergy for leading the people astray. An unfortunate reference to the British monarch's lack of Christianity led to his arrest for libeling the king, and when Whitefield admitted to having edited Bryan's letter, he was arrested for libeling the clergy.[48] Nothing came of these arrests, and evangelicals continued to rail for the reform of society. Many of their opponents would have agreed with the sarcastic sentiment of the Bostonian who claimed after the coldest weather of the century, "We have passed thro' a Winter the most tedious and severe in the Memory of Man: But neither that nor the Desolation of Charlestown, are half so bad as sectarian enthusiastick Madness."[49]

Historians of this episode have focused on the charges against Whitefield while ignoring the fate of the Bryans. Several historians have noted that the Bryans had subsequent troubles with the authorities, but none has suspected that these later challenges, inspired by Whitefield, were related to and were part of an ongoing commitment to fulfill Christian obligations.[50] Whitefield continued, however, to use his pen to reinforce the Bryans' resolve against the authorities and in favor of evangelical reform. On board the *Minerva* bound for England, he composed letters to Hugh and Jonathan Bryan. To Hugh he wrote of the arraignment, "I am persuaded our Lord will plead on your behalf. . . . The greater progress you make in the divine life, the more you will discover of the enmity . . . of the serpent. It bruised our master's heel; it will also bruise ours. Here is our comfort, . . . 'we shall bruise his head.' "[51] Whitefield's militancy was tempered with reassurance in his letter to Jonathan, whom he urged to stand firm in the face of opposition. Whitefield reminded Jonathan of his biblical namesake, soliciting him to "Follow him in his faith, and dare not to scale the wall of the Philistines. Be not afraid," he continued, "though already bound over as a libeller; shortly you shall shine in the kingdom of your Father; I say, your Father; for God is your God, and will be your guide and guard unto death. Does not this astonish you? . . . Are you not ready to cry out, 'Why me, Lord?' " Whitefield thanked Jonathan for his patronage of the orphanage and begged his continuing assistance. After a discussion of the rewards that awaited him in another life, he reminded Jonathan of his Christian duty: "Go on steadily in the use of, but do not trust in ordinances. You know what I mean."[52] A better statement of Whitefield's subornation could scarcely be made. The Christian was a law-abiding citizen except when the law contradicted his mission.[53]

THE BRYANS AND THE REFORM OF SLAVERY

The Bryans continued their reform of educating and evangelizing the slaves in their parish. Again, as Whitefield predicted, they encountered opposition. In February 1742, eighteen months after Jonathan Bryan had "resolved to begin a negro school," and one year after Hugh's published letter, the South Carolina Commons House of Assembly formed a committee to investigate the frequent assembly of blacks in St. Helena Parish. The following day the committee reported, "great Numbers of Negroes and other Slaves have several Times assembled together, to the Terror of some, and to the Disturbance of many; . . . the Fact is so public and notorious, and the Meetings of the Slaves so frequent and numerous" that no evidence need be provided nor an enquiry be made as to "what Account or Pretence these Slaves so often assemble." It was well known "they are encouraged and countenanced by several white Persons residing in those Parts." The committee continued that "however commendable" it may be to instruct slaves in the "Principles of Religion or Morality, in their own Plantations," anyone who encourages slaves "from different Plantations" to congregate together should be punished for endangering the "Safety of this Province."[54] The Commons House agreed to the committee's report and called upon the acting governor, Lieutenant Governor William Bull, Sr., to execute the laws against the assembly of slaves. The lieutenant governor responded favorably to the house and requested that he be provided with the names of the offenders. Not a few might have snickered at his request; one of Bull's plantations was surrounded on three sides by Bryan plantations, where for a year and a half the Bryans' slaves and those of neighboring plantations had received religious instruction.[55]

What exactly went on at the Bryan plantation is unknown: certainly, the Evangelicals' opponents believed that it had little to do with the dissemination of religion. Lewis Jones, who had been so intimidated by the bishop of London's commissary for South Carolina, Alexander Garden, that he finally split from the Evangelicals, was bitter at the sudden Evangelical success among slaves and wrote to his superiors at the SPG to explain it. Jones himself had made no progress in his twenty-year effort to persuade planters of St. Helena Parish to Christianize their bondspeople. Jones assured the SPG that Evangelical slave converts were "taught rather Enthusiasm, than religion," that they pretended "to see visions, and receive Revelations from heaven and to be converted by an Instantaneous Impulse of the Spirit." These false Christians, he concluded, "are among Mr. Whitefield's followers."[56]

The emotional enthusiasm of the Evangelical religion, worrisome enough to elites when it affected whites, was absolutely terrifying when it stirred blacks. What might slaves do when whipped into righteous religious frenzy? Rumors spread that Hugh Bryan was not actually evangelizing St. Helena Parish slaves but, rather, inciting them to insurrection. Hugh under his own volition appeared before the South Carolina Commons House of Assembly in March 1742 and admitted to having prophesied that slaves would destroy South Carolina down to the PonPon Bridge (which, conveniently for the Bryans, excluded St. Helena Parish). He gave to the assembly twenty pages of his journal, which contained a record of his predictions.[57]

A series of events conspired to ridicule Bryan's religious posturings while also bringing fear to his contemporaries. Bryan admitted to having undergone a mystical experience that led him to attempt parting a river with a stick. He publicly apologized for his affectations but not for his belief that South Carolina needed to be reformed. Thus reassured, the assembly was satisfied that Hugh had no intention of arming the slaves and that he was penitent for his delusions.[58]

On March 17, 1742, more than two weeks after Hugh Bryan submitted his apology to the Commons House of Assembly, the Grand Jury made a presentment based upon the "sundry enthusiastick Prophecies of the Destruction of Charles-Town, and Deliverance of the Negroes from their Servitude" found in Bryan's journal. Under Bryan's influence "great Bodies of Negroes have assembled together, on Pretence of religious Worship, contrary to Law, and destructive to the Peace and Safety of the Inhabitants of this Province." Hugh and Jonathan Bryan, William Gilbert, Robert Ogle, and all others responsible for "propagating the aforesaid Notions, or assembling of Negroes, and preaching to them at private Houses without Authority for so doing," should be punished by the court with "effectual and speedy Measures."[59] The nature and extent of the punishment inflicted upon the Bryans and their fellow Evangelicals is unknown, but it must have been severe, for shortly afterward Jonathan Bryan related to Johann Martin Boltzius that "everything had gone against them, yet the Lord helped him through gloriously, even though it did cause them great expense and effort."[60]

If Evangelicals expected to alter their society and protect South Carolina from God's wrath, they would have to change their approach to slave reform. The Bryans and their fellow South Carolina Evangelicals had to resist the temptation to remind their neighbors of the many punishments God had inflicted or was about to inflict upon the colony. The Evangelicals' opponents outlined their grievances in the *South Carolina Gazette*. They complained against Evangelicals, who without license missionized among slaves of different plantations. This, opponents argued, was dangerous, and could only lead to conspiracies among blacks. Furthermore, they would not tolerate unlicensed people prophesying to slaves the imminent destruction of the colony, and "filling their Heads with a Parcel of Cant-Phrases, Trances, Dreams, Visions, and Revelations."[61] Evangelicals may not have been happy with these attacks, but they did agree to alter their program of reform. The Bryans, for instance, gave up the conversion and education of neighborhood slaves but continued to hire missionary tutors for the instruction of their own bondsmen.[62] Each slaveowner was the sovereign of his own plantation, and therefore could do whatever he pleased with his slaves. Yet he could not gather slaves from different plantations for any reason, for the prospect of broad cooperation and socializing among slaves terrified many white Carolinians. Evangelicals would have to content themselves with reform by personal example. After

1742 Evangelicals of South Carolina and Georgia refrained from public denunciations of their societies. The open-air revival gave way to the establishment of new congregations and the capture of old ones.[63] The reform of slavery was no longer a goal to be pursued in a public forum, but, rather, privately on plantations and in the churches where the proceedings might be scrutinized and controlled.

EVANGELICAL SLAVEHOLDERS

Evangelicals did not give up their belief in the need for societal reform, but their agenda and methods changed. The Bryans remained active in the Evangelical movement and in the Christianization and evangelization of slaves. Johann Martin Boltzius discovered the paradigmatic slave society on the plantation of Jonathan Bryan in 1743. There Boltzius "found the most beautiful order in the housekeeping [by which he 'meant the entire economy of a household, especially the agriculture'] and among the Negroes, of whom several were honestly converted to God."[64] He believed that Bryan's slaves were so well treated that they loved their master, did not desire freedom, and performed their work well.[65] Bryan's plantation provided proof that slavery could be profitable, even though the slaves were treated humanely and were permitted Christianity. Boltzius defended Bryan's efforts to convert and to educate blacks in the face of social criticism: "Although the people in the land say that his Negroes do nothing but pray and sing and thereby neglect their work, this calumny is clearly contradicted by the very great blessing that he has just had in his fields. He and his Negroes are experiencing the truth of the words of Christ, 'But seek ye first the kindgom of God, etc.' "[66]

In 1743 the Bryans and many of their neighbors broke away from the Anglican church and formed an Independent Presbyterian congregation.[67] In contrast to the South Carolina Anglican church, here slaves were accepted as members.[68] The requirements for membership in the new church were a confession of faith and acceptance of the covenant written by its pastor, the former teacher of the Bryans' "negro school," William Hutson.[69] What membership encompassed is difficult to determine, but at least there was an implicit recognition that a regenerate slave was of God's elect and one of the visible saints. New members vividly depicted their "new birth," which was then inspected and judged by the saints. The subsequent granting of membership through the confession of faith and the candidate's acceptance of the covenant bound the elect together into fellowship before God. This denoted an equality of souls in the heavenly kingdom. Slaves who were accepted for membership in Evangelical churches enjoyed a dignity denied them in other congregations. Membership among the elect did not result in freedom, but at a minimum it signified that slaves possessed a commonality of the soul that bound people together, whether black or white, slave or free.

Despite the zealousness with which the Bryans fought for their slaves' right to Christianity, it should be remembered that they never sought any radical change in the institution. Slavery was the basis of the Bryans' wealth, and they did nothing for slaves that risked their investment. Jonathan Bryan was extremely self-conscious of the tension between his materialist desires and his "most ardent wishes for an heavenly inheritance." He shared his thoughts with Henry Laurens, another great planter and slaveowner who wrestled with the moral questions of slavery. Laurens assured Bryan that materialism and Christianity "are by no means incompatible." As "Men know they must die," they should live their lives with thoughts of the thereafter. But "it is likewise their duty to remember that they may Live & that therefore it is encumbent upon them while they have day to continue working in the Vineyard . . . they may receive each Man his penny." The man who is "doom'd to Labour in the Planting & Watering, without hopes of reaping the Harvest" is the "most miserable of all Men."[70]

Neither Bryan nor Laurens was willing to free his slaves or to give up the wealth that he had accrued from slave labor, but both did make alterations in their viewpoints of slavery and slaves. Laurens ceased participation in the slave trade and in later years denounced slavery. The legacy carried into the next generation. Laurens's son John promoted the arming of Georgia and South Carolina slaves to fight for the patriots in the American Revolution in exchange for the granting of freedom.[71] Bryan's sons Josiah and William both freed slaves, as did his son-in-law John Houstoun, the future governor of Georgia. Bryan continued to enslave blacks but possessed no illusions concerning the source of his wealth. Many years later he would write: "'The clothes we wear, the food we eat, and all the superfluities we possess are the produce of their labors, and what do they receive in return? Nothing equivalent. On the contrary we keep from them the key of knowledge, so that their bodies and souls perish together in our service.'"[72]

Bryan's realization did not result in freedom for any of his slaves, but his words provided a far more accurate description of reality than those utilized by George Whitefield in the 1750s when he became an advocate and apologist for the legalization of slavery in Georgia. During his many revivals, Whitefield collected money for the Bethesda Orphan House. Although slavery was illegal in Georgia, Whitefield received permission from local officials to have South Carolina slaves carry provisions for the orphanage into Georgia. By 1745, under the influence of the Bryans and William Hutson, Whitefield seriously considered illegally employing a slave in Georgia, presumably as his personal valet. After initially agreeing to break the law, Whitefield decided to confer with his friends in South Carolina before making a final decision.[73] Apparently, Whitefield decided not to use slaves in the colony (although they did continue to deliver provisions), but he agreed to become a slaveowner.

In 1747 Whitefield reported to correspondents that by the bounty of his South Carolina friends he now owned 640 acres in that colony of prime land, with sixty acres already "cleared, fenced, and fit for rice" and corn. The land had been owned by the Bryan family and was surrounded on two sides by their plantations.[74] The Bryans agreed to oversee the plantation's operation. All that Whitefield had to do was to claim ownership. For the evangelist, the plantation would provide provisions for the maintenance of the Bethesda Orphan House. For the Bryans and the other South Carolina Evangelicals it would provide incontrovertible proof that they supported the institution of slavery. It was not enough for South Carolina Evangelicals to affirm that they already supported slavery because they owned slaves—indeed, they had been slaveholders when pursuing their ostensibly radical reforms. But to have George Whitefield, the institution's greatest public foe become an advocate of slavery *and* a slaveowner would convince all but the pertinacious. The minister who had so cogently condemned slavery as practiced in the southern American colonies became a leading apologist for the institution and a strong proponent for its legalization in Georgia.

Whitefield felt compelled to write to the Trustees of Georgia, to persuade them to allow slavery in their colony. He had become convinced that the colony could not prosper without slave labor, for "hot countries cannot be cultivated without Negroes." Whitefield offered the Trustees his own personal experience with slavery as proof of the money to be saved by employing black labor. Although he had "only eight working hands" on his South Carolina plantation, he estimated that "there will be more raised in one year, and with a quarter of the expense than has been produced [by white labor] at Bethesda for several years past." He continued, "This confirms me in the opinion I have entertained for a long time, that Georgia never can or will be a flourishing province without negroes."[75]

Whitefield's orphanage was the largest civil employer in Georgia. He provided work for many of the colony's tradesmen and artisans. This gave him leverage with the Trustees, which he used to threaten them with the consequences of not allowing slave labor. My "chief end in writing . . . is to inform you . . . that I am willing as ever to do all I can for Georgia and the Orphan House, if either a limited use of negroes is approved of, or some indented servants sent over. If not, I cannot promise to keep any large family, or cultivate the plantation in any considerable manner. My strength must necessarily be taken to the other side [of the Savannah River?]." Whitefield coupled his threat to abandon Georgia with an offer to further the colony's development. If black labor was permitted in the colony and if he received more land, he would not only make the orphanage a refuge for parentless children "but also a place of literature and academical studies."[76] This letter had its intended effect: Whitefield achieved fame as an apologist for slavery.

When at last slavery was legalized in Georgia, Whitefield was effusive. He wrote Hugh Bryan: "Thanks be to God, that the time for favouring [Georgia] seems to be come. I think now is the season for us to exert our utmost for the good of the poor Ethiopians." Yet, his elation was coupled with doubt concerning both the morality of slavery and his role in bringing about its legalization in Georgia.[77]

Whitefield was positive of the "lawfulness of keeping slaves . . . since I hear of some that were bought with Abraham's money, and some that were born in his house." He admitted that blacks "are brought in a wrong way from their own country," and that the slave trade was "not to be approved of," but he rationalized, "it will be carried whether we will [it] or not; I should think myself highly favoured if I could purchase a good number of them, in order to make their lives comfortable and lay a foundation for breeding up their posterity in the nurture and admonition of the Lord." Thus, Whitefield believed that transporting Africans thousands of miles from their home and enslaving them was worthwhile, as long as they were provided Christianity.[78]

Whitefield mitigated his guilt and abrogated responsibility for the legalization of slavery by insisting that "I had no hand in bringing them into Georgia; though my judgement was for it." The act was done, he urged the Bryans; "let us reason no more about it, but diligently improve the present opportunity for instruction."[79]

Boltzius opposed Whitefield's schemes from the start. He first reminded Whitefield of the lack of Christianity among white farmers in Georgia and then asked him how much more difficult it would be for ministers to convert people who "take Advantage of the Poor Black Slaves." Boltzius suspected that Whitefield held ulterior motives for wishing slavery introduced in Georgia. Sarcastically he told Whitefield that if a minister desired "to imploy his Strength & time to Convert Negroes, he has in Carolina a Large Field."[80]

The fear of many Carolinians that Evangelicals intended a social and racial revolution had proven unfounded by the mid-1740s. Many did not agree with Evangelical reforms of slavery, but they would tolerate change as long as Evangelicals did not seek to force the issue in public debate. Evangelicals had learned that South Carolina's dominant political elite was too strong to attack from without. They determined to use the tools of persuasion to reform society and by personal example exhibit the value of regeneration and the efficacy of slave conversion.

The Evangelicals' attempt to reform slavery tells us much about slaveowners but little about slaves. There is a paucity of primary source materials on eighteenth-century South Carolina slaves. We can infer, however, some of their reactions to the attempts to convert them. Some slaves rejected Christianity while others adapted it to their own particular needs. There were advantages to be attained by a slave showing interest in religion. For example, the meeting of slaves from other plantations, a social outlet ordinarily denied blacks, was made available by attending church or interplantation prayer meetings. Slaves may also have been induced to attend church by a reduction in work days from seven to six per week. Since many Evangelical masters felt a moral duty to convert their slaves and to "dispel their darkness," bondspeople gained an important leverage in their relationships with slaveowners. They gave their assent to their masters' religious ethic in exchange for privileges. Thus the orderliness and bounty of Jonathan Bryan's plantation was probably a result of the granting of privileges that slaves on other plantations did not enjoy. The bargaining was an ongoing process, because at any time slaves might backslide and abandon Christianity and the new behavior their masters hoped they would adopt.

Hugh Bryan was anxious about his slaves' continual vacillation: "my servants were called to prayers, but none came." In October 1751 he complained in his journal that the previous two weeks had "been a time of trial and uneasiness from the disobedience of servants, &c." He hoped Christianity would make his "people" better servants. In poetry he prayed:

> Direct me, Lord, to rule my house,
> In wisdom's perfect way;
> Thy truths may all our hearts espouse,
> Thy laws may all obey.[81]

Christianity did not create the perfectly behaved slaves for which their masters had hoped, but it did provide a basis for bargaining between the slaveholder and the enslaved. By accepting these privileges, which later bondsmen assumed were their rights, slaves confirmed their masters' claim to be moral Christian planters. This was the first step in the development of a paternalistic relationship.[82]

The introduction of evangelism to slaves on the Bryans' plantations was a seminal moment in the spread of Christianity among Afro-Americans. Jonathan Bryan not only sought the conversion of slaves but also was one of the first southern planters to promote their evangelization by black preachers. In the 1780s Bryan's bondsman, Andrew Bryan, preached to large congregations of blacks and was twice imprisoned and tortured for it. He proudly "told his persecutors" that he "*would freely suffer death for the cause of Jesus Christ.*" Jonathan Bryan interceded on behalf of his slave and obtained his release. Chief Justice Henry Osbourne gave Andrew and his fellow slaves "liberty to continue their worship any time between sun-rising and sunset; and the benevolent Jonathan Bryan told the magistrates that he would give them the liberty of his *own house or barn.*" Andrew Bryan preached at Brampton Plantation until Jonathan's death a few years later.[83] With the loss of Jonathan's protection, many local citizens complained about Andrew. Jonathan's son William stepped forward as the patron of Andrew and the black Christian community. In October 1788 a Grand Jury Presentment was made against William Bryan "for permitting negroes to assemble, in large bodies, at the plantation called brampton, within this county, in violation of the Patrol Law." The Grand Jury believed that the assemblage of blacks "under pretence of religion, by which that holy institution is not only become a mere mockery, but a cloak for every species of blasphemy, theft, and debauchery."[84] Andrew and William fought to retain the rights of blacks to hear Christianity from black preachers. They eventually prevailed and in 1791 opened the first Baptist church, black or white, in Georgia. The First African Baptist Church provided the foundation for the growth of the Baptist movement in the lower South. How Andrew and William persuaded the authorities to allow them to open a church is unknown, but after obtaining his freedom, Andrew became a slave-owner himself, which might have signified to the white community his support for the system of bondage.[85] By 1792 Bryan's church had 235 members and 350 converted followers, "many of whom had not obtained permission of their owners to be baptized." Andrew Bryan remained minister until his death in 1812, at which time his church had 1,500 members and had mothered two additional churches. White ministers from Baptist and Presbyterian churches were among those who spoke at Andrew's funeral, which was attended by more than 5,000 people. After Andrew's death, his nephew Andrew Marshall became minister and the congregation grew to over 2,400 members by 1830. On several occasions Marshall and his congregation successfully resisted pressure from whites to compromise their theology and church independence.[86] Under the tutelage of Jonathan Bryan and Andrew Bryan, the spread of Christianity among Savannah-area slaves led to the creation of the most important institutional structure in Georgia's Afro-American community.

Evangelicals were correct in their assumption that slavery was at the root of South Carolina's ills. They felt guilty enough to introduce reforms of the system, but they sought no radical change. They did learn, however, to rationalize the system: they were raising Africans from their heathenish condition and introducing them to Christianity. Conversion of slaves was central to their self-images as Christian slaveholders. They rationalized the brutality of slavery by believing that however horrible a slave's existence in this world, he or she might, if saved, find bliss in the more important afterworld. Evangelical religion swept the South as new generations of slaveholders adopted and perfected these thoughts on the slave system. Men like Jonathan Bryan proliferated in the South of the nineteenth century; antebellum Evangelicals allowed their slaves Christianity and then congratulated themselves that they, as benevolent masters, treated their slaves with great humanity. The utilization of religion as a form of social control had long been in use in South Carolina and Georgia when it was discovered by slaveholders elsewhere in the 1820s and 1830s. What began as a chilling experiment on the plantations of Jonathan and Hugh Bryan ended as an essential element in the ideology of the southern master class.

3

FROM ONE FRONTIER
TO ANOTHER

The Assumption of Political Power

Carolinians' preoccupation with the Evangelical movement and the security of the colony against black rebellion led the government to ignore the pleas of Georgia for assistance against the Spanish. Even if it had not been so preoccupied, it is questionable whether South Carolina would have helped Oglethorpe after the failure at St. Augustine. When the long-expected Spanish counterinvasion came in the summer of 1742, the Georgians were left to their own devices. By the time assistance arrived from South Carolina, Georgia troops under Oglethorpe had turned back Spanish forces. There was little time for celebration, however, for war broke out between Great Britain and France, and South Carolina again was threatened by land and by sea.[1] The French fleet menaced the South Carolina coast and their attacks upon British sea-lanes disrupted the flow of goods to and from the colony. This exacerbated the economic depression which had struck South Carolina in 1740 and led Jonathan Bryan to take an elected position in the South Carolina Commons House of Assembly.

POLITICAL SOLUTIONS TO FRONTIER PROBLEMS

South Carolina's government reacted differently to the French threat from the way it did to the Spanish. Whereas South Carolina had refused to help Oglethorpe defend the southern frontier against the Spanish, the government took protective measures when war broke out with France in 1744.[2] A permanent garrison was stationed at Port Royal to patrol the southern border. Cannon supplied by the king were utilized to fortify Charlestown harbor, and the people of St. Helena were mollified by legislation to build a fort at Port Royal as a refuge for the populace in case of attack.[3] These and other measures evinced government interest in appeasing the southern constituency.

The government confirmed its interest when a new parish, Prince William, was erected out of the Indian Land in St. Helena Parish.[4] Since parish divisions formed the political units of the colony, inhabitants of the Indian Land received two representatives in the South Carolina Commons House of Assembly. This increased the political voice and clout of the Bryans and their neighbors, who had good reason to take advantage of the newly created seats: the economic depression of the 1740s proved especially debilitating in the southern parishes. Frequently, these parishes used Charlestownians to represent their interests in the Commons House, but in 1746 the voters felt it necessary to elect local men.[5] Thus, Jonathan Bryan and his brother-in-law, Nathanial Barnwell, were selected to serve from Prince William and St. Helena parishes, respectively.[6]

Bryan's tenure in the assembly was short. In fact, the first session lasted only seven days before the legislators adjourned for the autumn harvest. During that session Bryan took his oath, delivered a message from the house to the governor, and received appointment to committees on trade and on Indian affairs.[7] When the legislature resumed in November Bryan enjoyed an active schedule. He received several assignments, including membership on committees to respond to the governor's speech, to inspect laws expired or near expiration, and to investigate debtor relief.[8]

Bryan also served on committees to resolve specific local and special-interest problems. Perhaps as a result of his association with Evangelical groups, he became the first-named member of a committee to settle a dispute between the Antipaedobaptists and the "General Baptists."[9] Likewise, his involvement in the reform of slavery probably led him to take part in the bill he carried to the governor and council that granted freedom to Arrah, a South Carolina slave who had escaped from Puerto Rico and returned to the colony. In addition to Arrah's freedom, this notable bill provided freedom to "all Negroes and others, who have been or shall be Slaves to any of the Inhabitants of this Province . . . [and who] shall hereafter make their Escape from his Majesty's Enemies and return back to this Province."[10] Bryan must have taken great pleasure in this legislation, for it represented the kind of reform that he and other Evangelicals had been advocating. By rewarding Arrah, South Carolina slaveowners illustrated to their bondspeople that extraordinary acts of loyalty could result in special treatment, perhaps even in freedom. The reward of freedom allowed the slaveholders to feel better about themselves; their institution, they might have argued, had civilized the heathen Arrah by inducing him to return to his rightful masters. Perhaps other slaves would drink from the same cup of duty and loyalty.

The main thrust of Bryan's legislative activities in 1746 was directed at developing, diversifying, and rejuvenating the southern economy. Bryan had a hand in several pieces of special-interest legislation for his constituency. He and four other southern representatives sponsored a bill to provide a paid pilot for Port Royal Sound. The southern parishes were willing to pay the pilot and only requested House authorization to tax themselves.[11] The bill passed in the next session and received further government support by enactment of a bill "for building and keeping in repair a pilot boat to attend the bar of the harbor of Beaufort."[12] Improvement of Port Royal harbor seemed essential if southerners intended to bring long-term prosperity to the region.

To strengthen Port Royal further, Bryan and Anthony Mathews of St. Helena presented the governor in council with a bill to erect a fort in the Creek Nation.[13] The fort would improve settler safety and redirect a portion of the colony's Indian trade from Charlestown to Port Royal. Increased trade might invigorate the region's economy, and the placement of a permanent garrison would provide more opportunities for the Bryans and their neighbors to supply provisions for the troops. Thus, it seemed as if the South Carolina government had taken a sincere interest in both the defense and economic development of the southern parishes. Part of the reason for the northern parishes' willingness to help the south could be found in the growing realization that the planter elite of both areas shared similar economic and political interests. Both inhabited low-country lands and depended upon the world market for rice and the English market for indigo. Their wealth and their social position were mutually based upon the exploitation of black labor. The major source of contention between them had been outlays of government money for defense of the southern parishes. By agreeing to support the southern parishes' need for security and regional economic improvements, the northern parishes hoped to stabilize the colony by resolving the issues that had divided them since first settlement. In a show of benevolence, the northern-dominated government granted impoverished Purrysburg, located on the southern frontier below Prince William and St. Helena parishes, representation to the Commons House in 1747.[14] The largest of the northern parishes, however, did not appease all southerners. Long-term measures eventually worked to heal the enmity between north and south, but in 1747 the immediate economic plight of southerners went unresolved by the South Carolina government. The two sections could not agree upon debtor relief.

Debtor relief may well have been the major reason the southern parishes elected local men to represent them in the Commons House in 1746. Charlestown merchants, who ordinarily represented the parishes, were disinclined to support legislation that favored debtor interests. During Jonathan Bryan's term in the Commons House, the inhabitants of Prince William and St. Helena parishes, Colleton County, Craven County, Edisto Island in St. John's Parish, St. Bartholomew Island in Colleton County, and Wadmelew Island in St. Johns Parish, sent to the house nearly identical petitions begging for relief. The petitions read: "the general Calamities and Misfortunes of this province . . . the Produce . . . having fallen so low in Value . . . renders many of the Petitioners unable to pay their Debts at present, which Debts, were contracted when the Prices were much higher." The petitioners claimed there was a shortage of currency in South Carolina "in Proportion to the Trade and Number of Inhabitants," and that interest rates were "so excessive high that many industrious and well disposed Persons and their Families are and must be reduced to extream Poverty and Want." The result "in most cases" was arrest, which doubled the debt.[15]

"The petitioners are willing to pay their just Debts, but find it impracticable by the Scarcity of Currency," the large sums owed, and the difficulty of "raising Money by their Produce." Several solutions were offered by the petitioners and discussed in the assembly. Among the resolutions proposed were acts to lower interest rates on all former debts to 8 percent and future debts to 7 percent; to accept indigo, clean cotton and dressed hemp as legal tender; and to prevent imprisonment of debtors.[16] These resolutions failed. The Charlestown merchants could not allow a reduction of interest rates, nor acceptance of crops as tender, nor leniency in the punishment of debtors, because they were creditors who believed these measures would harm their personal interest in particular and creditor interests in general. The only debtor-relief measure enacted into law was an act, sponsored by Jonathan Bryan, to relieve southern debtors of having to travel to the colony's courts in Charlestown in debt cases of moderate value. His bill "impower[ed] two Justices and three Freeholders, or a Majority of them, to determine in actions of Debt . . . Trespass . . . Trover . . . Scandal or Defamation, and in all other Actions where the Debt, Damage, or Matter in dispute doth exceed twenty Pounds Current Money and not more than seventy-five Pounds of like Current Money."[17]

This small victory did little to appease southern planters. French privateering, rising freight and insurance rates, and declining rice prices forced many planters to sell or mortgage their land and contract heavy debts. The distress of these planters is more easily envisioned when the size of their debts is considered. A rich man like Hugh Bryan accumulated over £30,000 (South Carolina currency) of unpaid debts from 1742 to 1747.[18] Few contracted such large debts, but even £5,000 was a great sum to a planter of middling rank. Failing to achieve their ends, some delegates, including Jonathan Bryan, did not return to the assembly in 1748, and several southern parish seats went unfilled. Bryan's own parish, Prince William, filled only one of its two seats; St. Helena, but two of three. St. Peter Parish sent no representatives, though writs of election were issued.[19] Alienated by the government's failure to provide substantial aid, a number of planters moved their operations to Georgia when the Trustees legalized slavery in 1750. One of them was Jonathan Bryan.

THE BRYANS' FINANCES IN THE 1740S

Not until the end of the decade did the southern parishes begin their economic recovery. Several of the smaller planters could not wait for better times and abandoned the colony mid-decade. Some migrated to Georgia, where land could be obtained by those willing to live within a subsistence economy.[20] Several historians have claimed that South Carolina's economic malaise, as well as increasingly restrictive economic and political opportunities, led well-to-do planters to follow small planters in an exodus to Georgia in the 1750s.[21] Jonathan Bryan was one of those well-to-do planters. To delineate the reasons for Jonathan's migration, we must examine his family's economic fortunes in the depression of the 1740s.

The evidence concerning Jonathan's and Hugh's finances in the 1740s is scanty, but enough can be deduced from extant probate, conveyance, and judgment roll records, and from other legal documents and letters to indicate the effect of the depression upon their estates. On the eve of the depression, in 1740, Hugh Bryan had accumulated a large amount of capital by selling over five thousand acres of land to Thomas Jenys. Yet, two years later he contracted a debt of £3,000 South Carolina currency.[22] Soon afterward, Hugh and his nephew, Stephen Bull, Jr., undertook a disastrous speculative adventure, whereby they purchased and outfitted a ship laden with rice and other articles bound for St. Christopher. In 1745, they abjectly complained that their ship's captain, Joseph Heath, had absconded with vessel and cargo. Whatever the actual cause of their loss, they had assumed great risk by outfitting a trading vessel in the midst of war with France. Not only was the danger of privateers prevalent, but the proprietors had failed to divide ownership among several investors, to lessen individual losses in the event of unforeseen disaster.[23] One month after Bryan and Bull filed suit against the captain of the *Elizabeth and Mary*, Hugh was forced to assume a debt of £1,300 sterling, an enormous sum, then equivalent to approximately £9,300 South Carolina currency.[24] As noted earlier, his total debt between 1742 and 1747 was above £30,000 South Carolina currency. He would have agreed with William Hutson's stoic assessment, that economic misfortune "might be wisely ordered for his spiritual Good."[25]

Hugh's ability to borrow large amounts of money during a currency-short depression is striking. It testifies not only to his resourcefulness but to the size of his estate, which had to be used as collateral. Most of his wealth was in land and slaves.[26] At his death in 1753, Hugh's personal estate, which included seventy-three slaves, was appraised at almost £20,000 South Carolina currency. His outstanding debts were in excess of £30,000. The debit of £10,000 was removed by sale of his land. Yet, despite the huge debt, Hugh's widow retained a sizable estate from her husband, which included his main plantation, his house, and a portion of his slaves.[27] Thus, even though he assumed a heavy debt load in the 1740s, it was not enough to reduce him to middling planter rank. He retained both his wealth and his social status.

Hugh was able to retain his sizable estate by diversification of his economic resources. The ferry he operated from Port Royal to the mainland was certainly profitable, as goods, soldiers, and other travelers utilized its service overland from Georgia to Port Royal.[28] He continued selling goods in the Georgia market and did not cease from pursuing his myriad economic activities, which included cattle ranching, merchanting, transporting foodstuffs, and filling government contracts.[29] The economic depression, in fact, led him to further diversification. In 1752 Johann Martin Boltzius noted the manner by which Hugh had survived the depressed agricultural market. Boltzius wrote that Bryan "has been using his Negroes on his low land in Carolina . . . for no other work than manufacturing shingles and boards . . . and by that he earns a great deal of money. In previous years he fell into considerable debt as a planter on his land, which is distant from the [Savannah] river yet very fertile. It appears that he found no other means to escape it than this profitable work." Boltzius exaggerated the extent to which Hugh devoted his work force to lumbering, but as an interested observer of the local economy—he produced for German immigrants several tracts on how to become a southern planter—the minister was intrigued by Bryan's resourcefulness and willingness to pursue other avenues to wealth than planting. Jonathan Bryan echoed his brother's sentiments. He told Boltzius that "if he did not have to plant rice and corn for his many Negroes and white people and also for his cattle, then he would rather use his Negroes (of which he has at least 100) in making shingles, which would bring him much more than planting."[30]

In contrast to Hugh, Jonathan did not suffer heavy losses in the 1740s. His debt accumulation was small, and he even lent money to others at the end of the decade. He was less prone to speculative adventures than Hugh.[31] Jonathan accumulated capital during the depression, and records indicate his having purchased seven slaves for more than £100 sterling, 1,000 acres of land for over £3,000 local currency, and his lending of more than £500 South Carolina currency to other planters.[32] Bryan, like most planters of middling to higher rank, withstood the depression by turning to new crops, such as lumber and indigo; by operating nearly self-sufficient plantations; and by relying upon the high value of his slaves and lands to provide capital.[33]

In the depression of the 1740s southern parish planters learned several valuable lessons. Diversification of economic interests lessened dependency upon an unsure world market. Rice continued to dominate the low country and cattle ranching retained its importance, but indigo, lumber, shingles, and the production of foodstuffs became a growing part of the economy. To members of the Bryan family, economic security entailed both diversification and accumulation of large tracts of land.[34] Slaves, too, were valuable. They were the greatest expense for new planters starting a plantation. Adult male laborers were appraised at £225 to £275 local currency, an amount equivalent to fifty to one hundred acres of land in Prince William Parish.[35] For the established planter, however, the value of a planter's work force was equal to approximately three-fourths the value of his plantation. The above ratio did not apply to the richest planters: there was a limit to how many slaves they could profitably employ. As Hugh and Jonathan Bryan learned, slaves could be a drain on the planters' resources unless they were employed both in producing food for themselves and in profit-making enterprises. The well-to-do required other areas of investment besides slaves. Both Bryans chose to place a large portion of their wealth in land, which could be rented, mortgaged, or developed with little concern that its value would diminish.

Jonathan soon became one of the largest landholders in the Deep South. His drive to accumulate land—as a source of economic security and for capital development—may have been the outgrowth not only of the depression of the 1740s but also of the earlier closing of the land office in 1719, which had denied his family the coveted Yamassee land. Bryan never seemed satisfied with the land he possessed, and for the remainder of his life he incessantly bought, traded, and schemed to accumulate new tracts. But after the depression of the 1740s he opted to base his operations elsewhere than in South Carolina. By 1750, he was making plans to move his family and his work force to Georgia.

THE MOVE TO GEORGIA

The migration of Carolinians to Georgia has attracted much attention among historians. As West Indies planters once brought plantation slavery to South Carolina, so, too, did Carolinians carry their bondspeople, their political economy, and their social ideology across the Savannah.[36] Jonathan Bryan led the Carolinian vanguard, finding fame and fortune by planting his crops and his ideas of politics and society in the rich Georgia soil.

By any standards, Bryan was a wealthy planter, but he was not a member of the South Carolina ruling class. The size of Bryan's landed estate and the large number of slaves he possessed were evidence of his economic worth. Approximately thirty other planters in St. Helena Parish commanded property on a nearly equal footing.[37] Together they comprised a local elite, but as they once again learned in the 1747 session of the South Carolina Commons House of Assembly, their power scarcely extended beyond the parish. The real political power lay in Charlestown and in the low-country parishes that surrounded the city, particularly to the north. Men from this area controlled both houses of assembly. A few men from the southern parishes made their way into the colony's ruling elite, but they often had extensive economic interests in Charlestown, usually as merchants. Jonathan Bryan had little chance of gaining entry into this elite group: his association with Whitefield as well as his close identification with the southern parishes' interests may have stood in his way.[38]

David R. Chestnutt believed that Jonathan Bryan was one of a group of Carolinians, who were

> just below the planting aristocracy of Carolina, . . . well above the middling rank of planters. Yet they held no major political offices, nor were they likely to. Although the Carolina economy was beginning to recover, there was little chance for these men to quickly advance far enough along the economic ladder to assume the mantle of responsibility and prestige of aristocracy. That this was one of the important reasons for their departure from Carolina was revealed by their subsequent careers in Georgia.[39]

The quickness with which Bryan was elevated to high political office in the "fledgling colony" certainly lends credence to Chestnutt's assurance that political opportunity spurred men southward.[40] We should question the value of attaining high political office in Georgia, compared with attaining mid-level positions in South Carolina. The overwhelming majority of Carolinians elected to pursue their opportunities in Carolina.[41] Despite the fact that Georgia altered its land and slaveholding policies to attract whites who wished to live as slaveholding planters, relatively few Carolinians were willing to emigrate. Georgia's great period of growth was in the nineteenth century, and its most significant spurt in the colonial period resulted from the migration of farmers from Virginia and North Carolina into the backcountry at the end of the French and Indian War. Well-to-do Carolinians remained at home in the eighteenth century because the negative factors involved in settling below the Savannah River appeared to outweigh the positive. Most Carolinians who moved southward from desperation and desire were the type of people who welcomed the challenge of an "uncultivated" and "uncultured" frontier.[42] Jonathan

Bryan, like his father, was of this type. The difference between Bryan and most other Carolinians who moved to Georgia was the former's possession of a great amount of property in land, labor, and tools, his extensive knowledge of southeastern topography, and his ability and ambition quickly to convert large areas of swampland into rice plantations.

Political and religious considerations were important in Jonathan Bryan's move to Georgia, but they were secondary to his economic motives. Harvey H. Jackson has incisively described the chain of events behind Bryan's migration southward. Jackson found that Bryan petitioned for land directly in the wake of the alteration of Trustee policies regarding land and slave ownership. Without a doubt, Bryan would not have moved to Georgia had slavery not been legalized and if land has not been granted in "absolute inheritance." Only when it was possible to build slave plantations akin to those he owned in South Carolina did he petition for land.[43] Bryan believed that his political, social, and religious objectives could *only* be satisfied in the context of his ownership of large plantations worked by slave laborers.

The process of transporting his plantation operations was slow. Bryan was unsure that moving to Georgia provided the best prospect for future advancement. He maintained plantations, as well as important political and religious ties, north of the Savannah River and did not move his family and a major portion of his work force to Georgia until December 1752, almost two years after he had received his first grant of land. Once Bryan realized, however, that he could accumulate wealth and power in Georgia, he wasted no time investing his money and effort in the colony.

NEW RESPONSIBILITIES

The Bryan family was largely responsible for the operation of George Whitefield's Providence Plantation in South Carolina, since Whitefield spent most of his time in Great Britain. They sold Whitefield the land, supervised the purchase of slaves, and oversaw its affairs from their own neighboring plantations.[44] When Jonathan moved to Georgia he persuaded Whitefield to sell this plantation and to begin another south of the Savannah. Like Providence, the new one was designed to provide income and foodstuffs for Bethesda and to bring Christianity to its slaves. Locating the plantation close to Bethesda would lower costs and allow Jonathan Bryan more easily to oversee its operation. Whitefield was extremely grateful for Bryan's help and begged, "My dear friend, do exert yourself a little more for me in this time of my absence, and I trust the Orphan-house affairs will shortly be ordered, that none shall be troubled about its affairs but my own domestics." The evangelist promised to send people to help Bryan in the arduous task of establishing the plantation and reminded him that "Bethesda's God will richly reward you."[45]

Bryan looked after Bethesda and its slave plantation through 1753, when he reported to the evangelist that "your new plantation is in a prosperous way." Fifty acres of land for corn and rice had been cleared, fences erected, and a brick house almost finished. Four sawyers were erecting a barn and two more would soon arrive, and he was awaiting word from William Brisbane as to the purchase of additional slaves. Bryan feared disaster if the slaves were not purchased in time for the summer harvest.[46] By July they had not yet arrived and Jonathan recommended the overseer be discharged, for there were too few hands to justify his further employment. Perturbed with Brisbane's failure to obtain slaves, Bryan's service to Whitefield's plantation and Bethesda began to diminish by year's end.[47]

Bryan and Whitefield infrequently corresponded in the next two decades. The Bethesda Orphan House constantly drained the minister's resources, and Whitefield repeatedly urged its managers to reduce the number of orphans. In fact, it is questionable whether the slave plantation actually helped Bethesda. At Whitefield's death in 1770, the orphanage had seventy-five slaves and nine free employees but only sixteen orphans. Why the plantation could not support more children remains a mystery.[48]

By the end of 1753 Jonathan Bryan had little time to devote to Whitefield's affairs. Religious and social concerns remained important, but new responsibilities and opportunities demanded his attention. The drive to accumulate wealth and political power began to occupy a greater part of his life, and with his brother Hugh's death Jonathan found himself the patriarch of a large extended family.

Hugh Bryan died of unknown causes on New Year's Eve of 1753. To Jonathan he left a mourning ring, and to his wife, Mary, and his friend John Smith he left the task of administrating his estate, which was so debt-ridden that he provided no one should be paid until two years after his demise. This allowed his executors the chance to place the estate in order.[49] Though not an administrator, Jonathan became deeply involved in the division of property. Claims against the estate resulted in the sale of Hugh's land, which was then bought at auction by various members of the Bryan family.[50] Confusion over land jointly owned by Hugh and Joseph Bryan entangled Jonathan in a series of lawsuits with the executors of Hugh's estate.[51] Hugh's widow sued Jonathan as executor of his nephew Joseph; she in turn was sued by the executors of Burnaby Bull, another relative of the Bryans. The family's financial affairs appeared to have been settled amicably. They apparently used the court system to untangle the financial web in order to avoid any suggestion of malfeasance from the creditors of the respective estates. The most troublesome aspect for Bryan may have been the demand upon his time. Until the affair was settled in 1760, he had to devote great energy and effort to his dead nephew's estate. As administrator he had to make frequent trips to Charlestown and to Prince William Parish to oversee the sale of land and the continued operation of Joseph's plantations, pay debts, and arrange for his great-nieces' future.[52] Also, with the deaths of his brothers Joseph and Hugh, and his nephew Joseph, Jonathan was left with added familial responsibilities. Many members of the Bryan family followed Jonathan to Georgia and relied upon him in their economic and legal affairs. His own children numbered nine in 1755 and he had three more thereafter.[53] In addition, his slave "family" in Georgia numbered about sixty.[54]

We know little about Bryan's immediate family in the 1750s. In 1737, he had married Mary Williamson, the fifteen-year-old daughter of his brother Joseph's second wife, also named Mary Williamson.[55] Mary Bryan appears to have had little involvement in her husband's political and economic affairs except for the signing of releases of coverture when he sold parcels of land. A surviving letter from Mary to Jonathan displays the respect accorded patriarchs in many southern families: she addressed her husband formally as Mr. Bryan. (He addressed her as "Dear Wife.")[56] Mary's widowed mother followed her daughter to Georgia and became a planter in her own right. Perhaps she wished her daughter could enjoy the same independence as herself: in her will, she provided Mary with property to be kept separate from Jonathan's, which gave her an income to do with as she pleased. This practice was not unheard of among the elite; Jonathan established a separate income for his daughter Mary in her marriage to John Morel. Except for specific provisions made in bequests or marriage contracts, a husband obtained all rights to his wife's property except for that portion specifically protected by coverture. Jonathan Bryan probably shared with his contemporaries notions of women as inferior to men. Nevertheless, he treated his two daughters that survived to adulthood, Mary and Hannah, quite differently. Whereas Jonathan selected Hannah's husband to represent her interests in the administration of his estate, he allowed Mary to represent herself. In additon, he made significant sales of land to Mary, but not to Mary and her husband. Transactions with Hannah were made to her and her husband. At the least, Jonathan recognized Mary's ability to handle her own financial affairs.

As might be expected, Bryan gave large financial gifts to all of his children and grandchildren; he wished them all to take places among the colony's elite. His female children were provided with handsome dowries. The boys were given assistance in becoming successful planters. Jonathan's relationships with his sons remains only slightly less obscure than his relationships with his daughters. The sons patterned their public lives after their father. William, Hugh, and James, for instance, all served by Jonathan's side in colonial and revolutionary politics. James and William assisted their father in negotiations with the Creek Indians; Hugh and William served with Jonathan in the rebel assembly that met in 1775; Jonathan and Hugh served as co-commissioners on public works projects; James replaced his father as a member of the state's executive council in 1783. Whatever the exact nature of their personal relations, the Bryan family formed a potent political bloc in colonial and revolutionary Georgia.

Georgia offered Bryan myriad opportunities to extend his estate and provide for his children. He recognized the colony's immense potential and wrote Whitefield of the colony's prospects in 1753. "Georgia thrives apace," Bryan declared, and it would continue to do so, for slaveholders arrived every day from Carolina and the West Indies with large contingencies of black laborers. He believed that the colony's trade would quickly increase, encouraged by its duty-free ports. Bryan would "be glad to have our ports kept as Open as possible," for there was "great advantage in having Negro's Imported free of Duty." Because the colony did not have import taxes, rum and sugar were being diverted from South Carolina to Georgia. Bryan predicted prosperity for Georgia if free trade could be maintained: what he feared was government. He argued that there was little need to employ a governor for

Georgia "while we have peace," as "we are free of Taxes and quitrent and any charge of Goverm^r." As long as "we have a Court of Justice I think we are very Happy." A few laws were needed, he conceded, to regulate the militia, the conduct and treatment of blacks and to govern the erection and maintenance of roads, "but what I fear is when we come to have a Gov[ernor] and Assembly we shall be too fond of Making Laws and perhaps burthen our Selves with some unnecisary." He hoped that "the Lord has more than bare temporal blessings in Store for Georgia and that his Glory will be Seen in this part of America tho not perhaps with My Eyes (I am content with his promises), [but] perhaps My Children May See it."[57]

Bryan wished to maintain a free hand within the initial oligarchy of slaveholders. The lack of regulations and restrictions benefited the entrepreneur. Bryan's fears concerning the arrival of a governor would prove well founded, but they were allayed by his appointment to numerous important positions of power in the new royal government. Shortly after his letter to Whitefield, Bryan was given a seat on the council of Georgia.

One of the few talented men of wealth in the young colony, Bryan was called upon to perform duties requisite of a man of his station. Three things placed him in a position of power in Georgia. The most important was his ownership of a large number of slaves, which entitled him to extensive tracts of land, social prestige, and consideration for high political office. The second factor was Bryan's political and financial experience. His term in the South Carolina Commons House and his quick transformation of Georgia swampland to commercial rice production showed him to be a man of ability. Georgia magistrates certainly were impressed with his talents. When Bryan petitioned for five hundred acres of "Marsh and Swamp Land" it was "readily granted" because "this piece of Land cannot be cultivated without great Strength, which they know he is capable of performing."[58] The third factor in Bryan's selection to high office was his social network. His friendship with James Habersham, who held office under the Trustees and who also received selection to the council, and his association with Whitefield, provided him with influential friends who could both recommend and call attention to his talents and availability. In possession of the requisite accoutrements of upper-class leadership, Bryan assumed a wide array of political offices in the colony.

When the newly appointed councillor and attorney general William

Clifton arrived to establish a judicial system, he found only one lawyer in the colony.[59] This forced the governor to select as justices two of his councillors, Jonathan Bryan and Noble Jones, neither of whom had had formal legal training.[60] Bryan's multiple officeholding reflected a lack of experienced politicians in the colony rather than an attempt to create placemen. Besides his positions as justice of the General Court and the Court of Oyer and Terminer, and his council seat which entitled him to a seat in the upper house and numerous patronage positions, Bryan also served as justice of the peace and treasurer of Georgia. He may have been the only Georgian able to post the treasurer's £1,000 bond. He resigned several of his offices within two years, when other men were found to fill the positions.[61] But in 1754 and 1755 it was imperative that councillors perform functions for which no one, not even the councillors, were well qualified.

Bryan's most important political office was on the council. This body consisted of twelve men who were responsible for advising the governor and composed the upper house of the legislature. It had a veto over lower-house legislation and possessed sufficient influence, political know-how, and formal authority to assert itself actively into the executive decision-making process.[62] As a body, the "governor in council" conducted Indian diplomacy and was responsible for the granting of land from the public domain. Separately, the members acted as two of the three legislative branches of government. With control over the colony's administrative, legislative, and diplomatic affairs, Georgia's governor and council held more power over the lives of its citizens than the executive branch of government in any other of the original thirteen colonies.[63]

The man designated to establish royal government in Georgia was a naval commander, John Reynolds. He arrived in the colony in October 1754, displayed his commission and those of the council, and called for lower-house elections. The agenda of legislation which Bryan had recommended to Whitefield in 1753 was identical to the program proposed by the governor at the first meeting of the assembly in the autumn of 1754. Within six months of Reynolds's arrival, a flurry of legislation was passed to promote defense, protect property, and regulate the institution of slavery.[64]

The leading men of the colony initially supported the governor in his endeavors. Amity for Reynolds was displayed by individual councillors, like Jonathan Bryan, who resigned to Reynolds their grants on highly desirable Hutchinson Island.[65] Bryan later recounted that Governor Reynolds was received "with the greatest Satisfaction to the Inhabitants and had certainly the greatest prospect of being a happy Gover[nor]."[66] Both houses cooperated in passing most of the governor's proposals. Reynolds promised to support their petitions to the Crown for alteration of the land system the king had recommended and to apply for British aid for the colony's defense; these were the assembly's only grievances.[67] Likewise, the governor was pleased with the assembly; only in their provision for the judicial system did they fall short of his expectations. The assembly claimed that poverty was the source of their inability to meet the needs of establishing a judiciary. The governor accepted the excuse and iterated it to the Crown.[68] Nevertheless, both houses promised to make amends and to pass the necessary measures for raising funds in the next session.[69]

The harmony in the executive branch of government, between governor and council, was short-lived. The governor alienated the council when he denied its right to share in the executive decision-making process, specifically in the shaping of Indian diplomacy. Reynolds elevated his crony, ship's surgeon William Little, to a position as chief adviser. Little soon became Speaker of the house and from there attacked the power of the council as an upper house.[70] The council responded by enlisting the support of the lower house against the governor and Little.[71] Taking advantage of Reynolds's political ineptitude and growing lack of support, the council lobbied Whitehall for the governor's removal. Six of the seven councillors present in Georgia in the autumn of 1755 signed several remonstrances against the governor. Bryan, who was among them, resigned his seat from the General Court and was joined thereafter by Jones, who was removed by the governor. Bryan took it upon himself to report to the earl of Halifax, president of the board of trade, the "Declining State of this province," because "there have been no Representations Sent home by the General Assembly" since the governor had prorogued it. Bryan recounted how when Reynolds first arrived people had flocked to Georgia "fill'd with expectations of being Settled in a Country which has all the Advantage of Air & Soil and founded upon liberty." But expectations and the reality of life had altered. Few new settlers arrived and many "persons of property with their families are gon[e] out." The colony's trade had declined and Bryan feared that Georgia "will be reduced to as low an ebb as it was under the Late unhappy Constitution under the Trustees."

Bryan would not "presume to point out to Your Lordship" all the weighty reasons for this "ill turn of affairs," but he begged Halifax to "patronize this Colony," for then "I should Not Yet Dispair in a few Years to See it Vie with Its flourishing Neighbors."[72] The board of trade, in its report on Reynolds to the secretary of state and the king, expressed the opinions of the important men of property, that is, Bryan, James Habersham, Francis Harris, Clement Martin, Noble Jones, and Alexander Kellet. The board agreed with the Georgia council and confirmed that the governor had conducted his office incompetently. They declared that Reynolds should have conferred with the "Council in the most material points of Administration."[73] The governor was removed from office. The council's victory in the dispute was the single most important political event to affect the structure of the Georgia political system between the advent of royal government and the American Revolution. It paved the way for council power in Georgia as no other event or circumstance had.

THE POWER OF THE COUNCIL

Bryan served on the council from 1755 until 1770. Turnover during that period was slight. Power rested in the hands of an active core of just eleven men. Bryan, James Habersham, Noble Jones, Francis Harris, James McKay, James Edward Powell, William Clifton, and Patrick Houstoun were appointed in the 1750s and were joined by William Knox, Grey Elliott, and John Graham in the early 1760s. All eleven were men of substance, though three—Jones, Harris, and Habersham—had arrived in Georgia nearly penniless. Composing the council's inner circle, this entrenched group formed a ring of prestige and power around the office of the governor.

Checks on the council's power as an upper house came from several sources. One source was the lower house. In the first six months of its existence, the lower house established the exclusive right to initiate money bills, and periodically thereafter claimed or assumed rights it believed the prerogative of lower, or commons, houses throughout the British Empire.[74] Despite these occasional outbursts, the lower house was rarely in conflict with either the upper house or the governor before 1765. Unlike the appointed upper house, its membership was derived from election by all-white males aged twenty-one and over who possessed fifty acres of land.[75] This was a relatively wide-based suffrage, considering that all heads of household were entitled by freehold to one hundred acres of land. Theoretically, no free white males who claimed their freehold (and did not lose it) were denied the right to vote. The requisites for holding office in the lower house were not so easily met. Possession of five hundred acres was required for service in the lower house. Many white males were unable to meet this qualification, but cheap land was readily attainable in Georgia, ensuring that small slaveholders and even some nonslaveholders were able to meet the property requirements for officeholding. In comparison with South Carolina, where the value of a man's estate was adjudged at amounts which permitted only the well-to-do the opportunity of election to the assembly, it was infinitely easier in Georgia to fulfill the property requirements necessary for holding office. As more and more large slaveholders immigrated to Georgia the character of the assembly changed, with most seats going to the well-to-do. Retained, however, were both the relatively low suffrage requirements and the low property qualifications for election to the lower house.[76]

The lower house possessed the capability of becoming a dynamic force in Georgia but did not assert itself to any great extent until it became the center of colonial opposition to the Crown in the late 1760s. In the interim, the lower house relied upon the experience of the council and the direction of the governor for legislative programs. In addition, it looked to South Carolina for legislative precedents, especially in regard to its slave code and modes of taxation. The weakness of the colony's lower house in the prerevolutionary period vis-à-vis the governor and council was partly a result of Georgia's heavy reliance upon the mother country for appropriations.[77] The large subsidies provided by Parliament for defense and Indian diplomacy were placed in the hands of Georgia's executive. Moreover, the governor and council performed their duties so effectively that no concerted domestic opposition formed.

The potential animosity between the two houses was deflected in several ways. Small and large slaveholders shared many political goals in the early years of royal government. Both were interested in the enactment of a slave code, in making land both easily attainable and retainable, and in promoting a system of public works to ease the flow of goods to market.[78] There existed little cause for disagreement between the largest and the smallest slaveholders, or the lower and upper house, on laws governing slavery and land tenure. On the other hand, internal improvements might have become a source for dispute if locales competed for projects and men competed for the patronage of commissioner positions. With Georgia's white population huddled along the Atlantic coast and a few inland waterways, disputes arising over internal improvements remained infrequent until newcomers settled the backcountry in the mid-1760s. Slaveholders large and small raised the same crops and shared the same interest in maintaining Savannah's lighthouse, keeping select inland waterways free of obstructions, and constructing roads to facilitate the transportation of goods. All slaves worked the public roads, equalizing the burden on slaveholders, and commissioner positions were dispensed widely, particularly among the members of both houses. Jonathan Bryan utilized a position as road commissioner to his own advantage, and other colony leaders benefited the same way. Thus, most white Georgians reconciled themselves to royal government; certainly the slaveholders welcomed the public works projects, the establishment of a court system, slave code, militia act, and the creation of numerous patronage positions. With the Crown responsive to their needs and desires—it had removed Reynolds and provided substantial appropriations for defense and Indian diplomacy—Georgia slaveholders looked forward to an era of growth and prosperity.

THE COUNCIL IN ACTION

Tis done at Length the Tumults past,
The storm that Threaten'd us blown o'er;
R[eynold]S' Power had breath'd its' last
Littles' vile Threats are heard no more.[79]

Most Georgians were pleased to be done with Reynolds, but despite the odist's elegy, there was no insurance that his successor would prove any better. The new governor, Henry Ellis, arrived in Georgia in 1757. He had to reconcile the council to his leadership, secure Georgia's defense, improve relations with the Creeks, promote passage of numerous bills, and oversee the granting of the public lands. His prior experiences left him little prepared for the tasks at hand. In his youth, Ellis had traveled and, after publishing his observations on the northwest passage, had attained membership in the Royal Society, hardly adequate training for governing a frontier colony, but perhaps the board of trade had experienced difficulty finding a replacement: few Englishmen of talent and character would welcome the dubious honor of the Georgia governership.[80] The colony had achieved renown as a poor, hot, and unsophisticated place that obviously required great effort to live in, let alone govern. Only someone well connected but with little or no political experience would accept such a position; the politically aware knew better.[81]

A lack of political experience, however, did not prevent Ellis from capably performing his duties. His personality and his manner were well suited to the Georgia environment and helped him win the support of the colony's most influential citizens. The new governor applied himself diligently to his office and displayed an easy comprehension of Georgia's complex political situation. Cognizant of his limitations, he cultivated and solicited the opinions of those most familiar with the political realities of the colony, the council. He showered its members with "great deference and respect," and "was meticulous in consulting them on all matters of public interest." Ellis learned what Reynolds had not, that the council was "the governor's natural ally."[82]

Bryan welcomed the change in governors. The three years of Ellis's administration were Bryan's most politically active until the eve of the American Revolution. His attendance at council meetings rose from 58 percent in 1755 and 1757, and 25 percent in 1756, to 76 percent in 1758 and 71 percent in 1759, his highest rates of attendance in sixteen years of service.[83] Bryan's activities in the upper house also increased significantly and included committee work on land tenure, debtor legislation, and on bills to promote defense and to amend the Militia Act. In addition, Bryan served as commissioner on an array of public works projects; he assessed the needs of the lighthouse at Tybee, oversaw the construction and maintenance of roads in the northwest district, and performed duties as commissioner for the erection of several of the colony's forts.

Legislation and internal improvements, though substantial in Ellis's administration, were secondary in importance to the perennial task of Indian diplomacy. Keeping the peace with the neighboring Creeks was the foremost task of the Georgia government. No sooner had Ellis displayed his commission and administered the councillors' oaths than a delegation of Lower Creeks and Chickasaws arrived in Savannah wanting presents.[84] Over the next few months delegation after delegation arrived in Savannah to meet the new governor and to receive expected gifts. These parties had to be put off until autumn because no presents could be given until His Majesty's ships arrived. The interim allowed the governor and council time to assess the situation and to formulate a cohesive Indian policy. The executive council decided to invite all Lower and Upper Creek towns to a great conference at Savannah, where presents would be given and friendship renewed by treaty. The council, which frequently called upon Bryan's expertise for Indian affairs, designated him to visit the Upper Creeks to extend the invitation. Bryan played a significant role in the conference that took place in late October 1757.[85]

This conference was the most important between Georgia and the Creeks since Oglethorpe's parlay (with Bryan at his side) in 1736. In the midst of the French and Indian War, Britain had met defeat on virtually every front. It was imperative that Georgia secure her inland borders by persuading the Creeks not only to remain neutral but to prevent the French and their allies from crossing Creek territory. In return, the governor and council were prepared to promise fair resolution of all future differences and to reward the Indians with presents for past friendship and future good behavior.[86] In ordinary times the giving of presents provided the most important leverage for securing Creek cooperation. But these were extraordinary times and further measures were believed necessary to ensure Creek neutrality. The council deemed that a thinly veiled threat of military reprisal might convince the Indians that war with Georgia was suicidal. They would remind the Creeks that South Carolina and Georgia were as one in the event of attack. Not everyone, however, would be convinced of the value of that alliance, for in times past the two colonies had been slow in mobilizing their forces together for military action. Thus, the council elected to display Georgia's war-making prowess by opening the conference with a pageant displaying the colony's military might.

Bryan and Noble Jones, who had participated in Oglethorpe's pageant display of arms in 1736, used their martial expertise to help direct the proceedings in 1757. They orchestrated the pageant with military precision.[87] When a party of more than 150 Indians arrived several miles from Savannah, they were met by a troop of Rangers under Captain Milledge, who escorted them to an "Open Savannah about a Mile" from town. There they were met "by Captn Bryan with the Principal Inhabitants of the Town on Horseback," who "regaled them in a

Tent pitched for that Purpose." When the Indians were through dining, "the Cavalcade resumed their March—Captain Bryan at the Head of the Gentlemen led the Way, the Indians followed according to their Rank, and the Rangers brought up the Rear." The procession "advanced in this Order 'till they were in sight of the Town where they halted, and were Saluted" by sixteen cannon of four variously placed units. Bryan then led the procession to the town gate where he and his horsemen filed in military fashion to the right and left, forming two lines, through the middle of which the Indians marched. "They were next received by Colᵒ Jones at the Head of his Regiment of Foot Militia who conducted them with great regularity towards the Council Chamber." Passing the governor's house, the Indians were saluted by seven cannon, which were answered by cannon on the shore of the Savannah River and then by cannon on ships in the harbor. Just before the council chamber the foot militia divided into lines as Bryan's horsemen had done, and "the Indians marched through" and were "received by a Company of the Virginia Regiment of Blues." The Blues saluted the Creeks with a volley and "by a Particular Evolution formed two Lines extending to the Council House where the Indians were conducted and introduced to his Honour the Governor who holding out his Hands addressed them."[88]

Bryan and Jones, at the head of a troop of horse and foot soldiers, lent continuity to the proceedings for the Indians, many of whom had known these men for more than twenty years. Indian familiarity with Georgia leaders lent credence to the new governor's word in negotiations. At the same time, the sight of Bryan (reputedly one of the largest of men, tall in the saddle and at the head of a distinguished troop of horsemen) and of Jones (who in his youth led numerous patrols of the Georgia frontier and with Bryan had fought by the Indians' side against the Spanish) was a none too subtle reminder of Georgia's military prowess. The orderly procession and the carefully placed cannon implied a power to kill meant to intimidate as well as to impress. In one arm the Georgians bore gifts and in the other a sword. But on both sides the talk was of peace.

The conference was an unqualified success. A new treaty was negotiated reaffirming the peace and all previous treaties which existed between the Creeks and "the great Squire [Oglethorpe] or any other of the King's Officers, governors, councillors or beloved men." Future "difficulties and Dispute of what Nature so ever" were declared not to be just cause for war, but to be "amicably determined and adjusted at a Congress."[89] The Creeks and the Georgians, never the best of friends, held a healthy respect for one another, and more important, they were desirous of peace. The treaty made at the Savannah conference of 1757 was maintained through the vicissitudes of the French and Indian War.[90] It was severely tested when the Cherokees were at war with South Carolina from 1759 to 1761. That colony's preoccupation with the Cherokees was the perfect time for the Creeks to attempt a strike on Georgia, and depredations did in fact occur on both sides. But the tenuous peace was maintained, and it was in no small part due to the diplomatic efforts of the governor and council at the conference of 1757 and their determination to sustain the peace in the aftermath.

The success of their Indian policy raised the prestige of governor and council to new heights. With the colony at peace but with the threat of war always looming on the frontier, Georgians were willing to follow executive leadership in Indian affairs, and by extension to follow its lead in other areas of political decision making. The successful conduct of diplomacy allowed the government to devote its attention to other matters, such as legislation, public works, and the granting of the public lands.

The tasks a councillor chose to perform reflected his personal interests. This is evident by the rate of attendance at council meetings. Between 1755 and 1770 Bryan's attendance rate held steady at between 40 and 60 percent. Only during the years 1758 and 1759 when Indian affairs and the granting of public land became preeminent did Bryan exceed these figures, and only in 1756 during the last year of Reynolds's administration did he fall far below these figures.[91] Otherwise, Bryan's attendance displayed a consistent pattern. He could be counted upon to attend meetings important to the colony or himself, but he avoided council duties in matters of little interest to him. He was not alone. Other councillors behaved similarly. Occupied with diverse personal and economic affairs, most council members were selective in their attendance to council business.[92]

A few councillors attended the council with great frequency. In the five-year period of 1758–1762, William Clifton attended over 90 percent of the meetings for three years, William Knox for two years, and James Edward Powell for one year.[93] Each found fulfillment in the day-to-day tasks of executive administration. On those odd days when the governor called a meeting of the council to greet a party of Indians or to hear a report from the carpenters on the repair of a fort, these men were usually in attendance. They were professional politicians: Knox and Clifton had immigrated to Georgia in order to assume offices granted by the Crown. Their appointments, they hoped, were a stepping-stone to political advancement, one which Knox, for instance, readily followed to a position as undersecretary for the colonies.[94] The empire was the source of their position and indirectly of their wealth. A planter like Bryan or a merchant like Francis Harris had neither the time nor the inclination for a political career outside Georgia. Politics was not an end in itself to these men but the means by which they could perform public service for their neighbors while forwarding their own personal interests. They were provincials whose interests were colonial.[95]

Councillors pursued their interests in a variety of ways. Bryan elected to become involved in public works projects. Shortly after Ellis arrived in Georgia, Bryan informed the council of the "ruinous Condition" of the lighthouse at Tybee Island which guided ships into the Savannah River. Bryan volunteered with William Knox to visit the lighthouse with several carpenters and assess the need for repairs. When the work was done Bryan and Francis Harris visited the lighthouse to assess the quality of work. After reporting favorably to the council, Bryan recommended further improvements. He was designated to serve by legislative act as a public commissioner to oversee the repair and refurbishing of the lighthouse.[96] This work had its rewards. Only a few weeks after his initial offering to tend to the constant problems of the lighthouse, Governor Ellis, undoubtedly pleased that someone would undertake the tiresome task, rewarded Bryan by elevating him to captain of the Horse Militia.[97] Thereafter he was selected as commissioner for the building of a public magazine, for "Erecting a Fort Round the Magazine and Block Houses," for the "Erecting [a] Fort and Battery on the Island of Cockspur," and as a trustee of the Town Market.[98]

These appointments added to Bryan's prestige while allowing him the opportunity to dispense patronage. There were several commissioners or trustees for each project, so that Bryan could devote as much or as little time as he wished. If inclined, he could promote or hinder the economic interests of Georgians in the performance of his duties. Anyone desiring to sell at the public market, the only legal place to retail foodstuffs in Savannah, had to receive license from one of the trustees.[99] Bryan thus had a substantial amount of influence over the lives of truck farmers, butchers, and grocers. In the same way, Bryan achieved a modicum of influence within the community of white artisans of Savannah. Georgia enacted several laws to protect white labor in the colony because many whites believed that unfree labor filled jobs that should have been reserved for them.[100] Public works provided employment for a variety of artisans dependent upon the commissioners for work contracts. Bryan must have performed his duties as commissioner in an upright manner, for in 1770 the Union Society, a collection of skilled artisans and tradesmen, rewarded him for his public service by presenting him with an engraved silver tankard.[101]

LEGISLATIVE ACTIVITIES

At the end of Reynolds's administration Bryan had largely withdrawn from his duties in the upper house and on the council. His attendance at council meetings had fallen to 25 percent in 1756, the lowest level of his career.[102] The regularity of his attendance in the upper house was not recorded, but twice in 1756 he had been required by his fellows to appear.[103] Reynolds's removal led Bryan to increase his legislative activities.

Bryan devoted much of his legislative activities to bills regarding land tenure, internal improvements, and defense. He also looked after the interests of Dissenters, debtors, and landowners.[104] He preferred working on legislation beneficial to specific special-interest groups. Rarely did he become involved in legislation for the regulation of slavery, the protection of creditors, or the upholding of law and order.[105] The intensity of Bryan's political activity varied. After an initial assiduity paid to the important pieces of legislation in Georgia's formative years, Bryan refrained from participation in many of the legislative battles of the 1760s, when he became occupied with his personal fortune. In the 1770s he showed a renewed interest in politics with a brief but substantial interruption while he devoted his efforts to personal affairs. At no time were Bryan's politics completely divorced from his personal affairs, and frequently the two were thoroughly intertwined, but circumstances led him to give precedence to one or the other at various times.

The evidence is sketchy but it appears that Bryan cut a figure as champion of the Dissenter community in Georgia. Before the onset of troubles with Reynolds, Bryan helped frame a measure which would have earned the approval of many Georgians, particularly Dissenters. Along with James Mckay and Alexander Kellet, he initiated legislation "for the ease of Persons who have Scruples about the form of taking Oaths."[106] Bryan, who willingly took oaths for every office he held, was personally unaffected by the measure. Many Dissenters, Catholics, and the colony's small but significant Jewish population, however, welcomed this legislation. Because of Reynolds's prorogation of the assembly, the bill did not pass both houses and become signed into law until December 1756.[107] In the meantime, the upper house was forced to compromise, so that "ease of persons" taking oaths was altered to "Dissenting Protestants."[108] This excluded Jews and Catholics from the act, which, nevertheless, would have received warm approval from Georgia's Dissenters.[109]

Bryan also sponsored the emigration of Dissenters from South Carolina and France into Georgia, played a leading role in the establishment of an Independent meeting in Savannah, and promoted legislation "for keeping holy the Lord's day."[110] When the Puritan community at Midway was threatened by Indian attack, it was Bryan who warned the people.[111] He could not prevent the establishment of the Church of England in Georgia, a measure initiated by the lower house, but he may have been one of those who so limited church establishment that it had little effect upon the Dissenter community.[112]

The interest groups Bryan represented may be deduced from his committee work. The entire upper house comprised only twelve men, committees were small and members could choose those which they wished to serve upon. It should come as no surprise that in 1758 Bryan worked on the committee which originated legislation for the protection of imprisoned debtors.[113] The bill passed the upper house but not the lower house, and not until 1766 was substantial legislation passed to protect imprisoned debtors. Then, a most unusual bill proposed by the lower house was enacted into law.[114] It provided that creditors had to pay the maintenance of defaulted debtors if they insisted upon having them imprisoned. There is no evidence that Bryan had a role in initiating this legislation, but we may assume from his lifelong sympathy for debtors that he pushed for it in the upper house. Likewise, when a Committee of the Whole in the upper house met to consider the lowering of interest rates, the result was a reduction from 10 to 8 percent, exactly the same as the one Bryan had worked for in South Carolina in 1747.[115]

Bryan's sympathy for debtors was based upon more than personal economic interest. Planters were notorious for their indebtedness, but Bryan appears to have avoided it through diversification of investments. Credit to Bryan by Savannah merchants was a matter of convenience rather than necessity.[116] In only a small percentage of his land purchases did Bryan pay on terms; usually he remitted payment in cash with funds accumulated from the sale of his own land.[117] Rather than being a debtor, Bryan was a creditor. In both South Carolina and Georgia he loaned money to others and allowed purchasers of his land to pay on terms.[118] It is impossible to tell how many loans Bryan made, for they were intermittently recorded in the official records.[119] But from the records that survive it appears that Bryan's creditor activities were not intended as a means to increase his estate but as a way of extending a helping hand to less fortunate relatives, friends, and neighbors. Money was scarce in South Carolina and Georgia, and it was necessary to have the right contacts in order to borrow. Bryan, in his patriarchal role as a great planter and eminent member of the ruling class, lent money to others and established patron-client relationships which in turn extended his influence and good name through the colony.[120] He could promote debtor interests because creditor activities were not a major source of his income.

Bryan's political support for debtors was a natural outgrowth of his life in South Carolina. The extreme debt problems of Bryan's neighbors and brother Hugh had spurred him to action in the South Carolina legislature in 1747. Furthermore, as a child, political issues affecting the landed classes were discussed and acted upon in his home. When Bryan was eight both his elder brothers signed a petition to the king against the proprietors of South Carolina, and in 1724 Bryan's father was one of the petit jurors to request the king to hold hearings for the emission of paper money, a measure specifically designed to aid the plight of planters and debtors.[121] Agriculturalists often favored paper money because it provided the means for tax payments, promoted economic development, and fostered inflation, which reduced their debt load.[122] Virtually all commercial farmers were in debt to the merchants and their factors. Labor, seed, and implements were purchased on terms. For those planters able to borrow, the risks were well worth taking because of the high rates of return on investments. Contemporaries estimated that 20 to 25 percent yearly could be earned on a rice plantation.[123] But agricultural enterprises have always been subject to fluctuating conditions whereby a depressed market or extended periods of drought ruined many planters and farmers. People who derived their income from the land were sympathetic to debtor rights because they, their kin, and their neighbors were the most apt to fall victim to creditors and imprisonment.

Bryan's political support for the interests of agriculturalists was most pronounced in his work on legislation regarding land tenure. As one of the largest landowners of the colony, he possessed a personal stake in this legislation, but these bills benefited all landowners, particularly Georgia's squatters. Bryan directed legislation that limited the amount of time in which absentees could complete claims for lands granted by the Trustees. This would reduce the speculations of those who had no intention of cultivating the land and would help clear the confusion surrounding multiple grants. Land granting under the Trustees had become extremely careless, with the result that many claims conflicted because of duplicate surveys and the failure of colonists to register their claims. By limiting the time grantees' had to register their survey and make good their claim, those who had legitimately settled the land would be rewarded.[124]

Bryan further promoted the interests of Georgia settlers by initiating, with James Edward Powell, legislation for the "quieting of men's estates." This law stipulated that those who retained twenty years' "quiet possession" of a parcel of land had legal right over past and future claimants to purchase that land from the Crown. The benefits of this legislation were immeasurable to Georgia's squatters and others who were unaccustomed, or unable, to protect their lands in the colony's courts of law. Few would sue the poor landowner knowing that the law specifically protected them in their de facto possession of land.[125]

Bryan's political career was in no way solely devoted to the passage of legislation for the benefit of debtors, settlers, and Dissenters, but when occasion demanded, as it did during the depression years of the 1740s in South Carolina and in the formative years of royal government in the 1750s, he expended both energy and time to critical areas of political policymaking. His efforts earned him a favorable reputation among a wide spectrum of people. Henry Laurens, one of the richest men of South Carolina, who possessed several estates in Georgia as well, expressed admiration for Bryan, who in general was "esteem'd for integrity, Love of . . . Country, & usefulness in Society."[126] Bryan helped many Georgians both politically and economically. From the Salzburgers whose pain of removal to the New World he helped alleviate in the 1730s and 1740s, to the yeomanry whose interests he represented on landholding legislation, to the various Dissenters whom he helped emigrate in the 1750s and 1760s, Bryan earned a reputation as a statesman and a man of charity. Among Christians of all denominations he was known for piety and tolerance.[127] The tension within him, between his Christian desire to live a righteous life and his acquisitive spirit, spurred him to use his influence and power to help others but left him with many lingering doubts. He found it difficult to reconcile his "diligent endeavour to provide for family & to keep up a good understanding amongst Men," with his "most ardent wishes" for an afterlife. How Bryan succeeded in the eyes of his maker is unknown, but among contemporaries of similar social standing he retained an excellent reputation. He learned to heed the advice of his friend Henry Laurens: "Strip the Man who is honestly giving his daily Labour to the public for the good of rising generations, of his future prospects & you leave him the most miserable of all Men, doom'd to Labour in the Planting & Watering, without hopes of reaping the Harvest."[128]

4
LAND AND
POLITICS

Jonathan Bryan obtained lands by grant and purchase in Georgia and South Carolina in excess of 32,000 acres, on which he employed, at one time or another, more than 250 slaves. These possessions placed him at the very top of the small group of men who ruled Georgia during the quarter-century before the American Revolution. Bryan became one of the colony's richest and most powerful men because he understood every aspect of land ownership, from accumulation to development and sale. Aggressive and astute, he built an estate that can truly be termed a plantation empire. Bryan's use of political influence and economic calculation to create that empire illustrates the process by which the ruling class of colonial Georgia was formed.

ESTABLISHING A PLANTATION EMPIRE

Before examining how Bryan used his political offices and his varied skills in building his estate, we should trace the development of his plantation empire. Bryan began the accumulation of land in Georgia by petitioning the Trustees for 500 acres of rice land in 1750.[1] With forty to fifty slaves he settled the tract on New Year's Day, 1751, and moved his family there in August 1752.[2] The plantation, Walnut Hill, was located on the Savannah River, several miles below the capital. Almost immediately after he received this grant, Bryan began selling parcels of his land in Prince William Parish, though he retained the most valuable portion until 1757.[3] Although he valued Walnut Hill, he considered establishing his base plantation in several other areas. In 1752 he received from the Trustees 500 acres on the Little Ogeechee River, several miles south of Savannah.[4] He named this plantation Dean Forrest. An additional 500 acres contiguous to this land were granted in 1755.

In 1755 Bryan began petitioning for land on the Great Ogeechee, a freshwater river that many Georgians believed would replace the Sa-

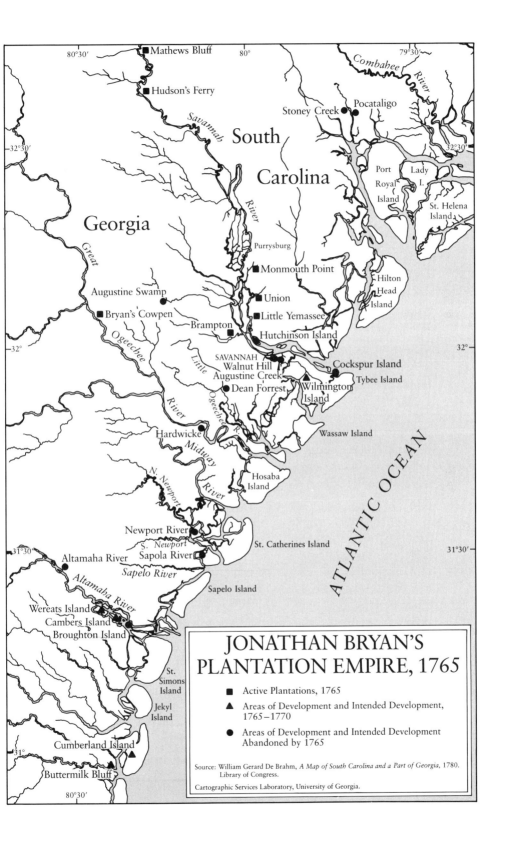

JONATHAN BRYAN'S
PLANTATION EMPIRE, 1765

■ Active Plantations, 1765
▲ Areas of Development and Intended Development,
   1765–1770
● Areas of Development and Intended Development
   Abandoned by 1765

Source: William Gerard De Brahm, *A Map of South Carolina and a Part of Georgia*, 1780.
Library of Congress.

Cartographic Services Laboratory, University of Georgia.

vannah as the colony's major waterway.[5] When the town of Hardwicke was laid out by Governor John Reynolds, who wanted to make it the capital, Bryan petitioned for and received 500 acres and a town lot. But his eyes continued to drift southward. In August 1755 he petitioned the council, "having Seventy eight Persons in Family, he was desirous of improving another Tract; and therefore pray[ed] for eighteen hundred Acres of Land on the Fort Swamp at the Head of Sapola [Sapelo] River."[6] Thus by 1755 Bryan had become engaged in establishing rice plantations on four Georgia rivers.

Bryan's tracts were too distant from one another for him to maintain effective control over them. Roads were few and rough: transportation from one plantation to another by water meant travel along the sometimes difficult coastal waterways. When it became apparent that the Atlantic trade would continue to flow through Savannah, Bryan began selling off or resigning lands that were not along the Savannah River.[7] Instead of becoming Georgia's capital, Hardwicke remained a small town of fewer than fifty people. Bryan sold his land there and disposed of Dean Forrest plantation to James Habersham. His claim on the Sapelo River was never completed because water from the river necessary for the flooding of the rice fields was found to contain salt.[8] Instead, Bryan determined to concentrate his holdings along the Savannah. In 1757 he began requesting land adjacent to Walnut Hill Plantation, which he supplemented with numerous tracts of "garden" and "farm" acreage on the east side of Savannah town. He also claimed 1,000 acres on Augustine's Creek, just below the town near Walnut Hill, and he sold his remaining acreage in Prince William Parish.[9] At this time Bryan probably increased his purchases and development of tracts on the South Carolina side of the Savannah River. He had begun settling land in 1752 at Monmouth Point in the township of Purrysburg, about seventeen miles northwest of Savannah. By the mid-1760s he owned from 4,000 to 7,000 acres on the South Carolina side of the river. The £864 he made from selling land in 1756–57 may have provided some of the capital for the purchase of those acres.[10]

One of Bryan's South Carolina plantations was at Mathews Bluff, about fifty miles northwest of Purrysburg on the Savannah River. This tract comprised between 2,000 and 3,000 acres and had an excellent harbor. Bryan described it in an advertisement as ideal for division into four tracts, the front two for producing indigo and corn, the back two for grazing cattle. He retained this land and willed it to his daughter Mary in 1783.[11] Twenty miles southeast of Mathews Bluff, on the Savannah by Hudson's Ferry, he secured another tract of approximately 2,000 acres. The land was probably similar to that at Mathews Bluff—the riverfront lots good for indigo, corn, and possibly rice, the back lots convenient for cattle. Mary bought this tract from her father in 1784 for £500.[12]

Bryan's most valuable plantation in South Carolina was located at Union, three miles south of Purrysburg on the road to MacKay's Creek. Easily flooded by a tributary of the Savannah, Union developed into one of the largest rice plantations in the area. There Bryan built a great house, which he and his children often used as their home. John Rutledge, Jr., attempted to buy the plantation in 1777, but Bryan refused and later willed it to his son William.[13]

The plantations at Mathews Bluff, Hudson's Ferry, and Union were not the only ones Bryan acquired in South Carolina along the Savannah. He also owned the Little Yemassee Plantation just below Union and many other tracts in and around Purrysburg on which he grew an array of crops.[14] All together, his holdings in South Carolina probably amounted to between six thousand and seven thousand acres, all selected because of their riverfront location. They were convenient to Savannah and to each other, and their crops could be shipped downriver. Not all land along the Savannah River was of good quality or easily reached. Much of it was worthless swamp. But Bryan selected parcels with good harbors and ones that his large labor force could turn to rice, indigo, and corn.

Bryan did not completely cease to settle land away from the Savannah, but clearly he wished to group his plantations along the major transportation routes. There was no logical reason for him to create rice plantations on the Little Ogeechee or the Great Ogeechee, since large ships did not serve these rivers, but he did acquire land on the Altamaha River about seventy-five miles south of the Savannah.[15] Although the Altamaha was considered by many colonists to be an excellent location for rice plantations, it was distant from Savannah and oceangoing transports. In 1758 Bryan petitioned for and received 900-acre Broughton Island in the river; he then exchanged this tract, along with 100-acre Doboy Island, for 1,000 acres on the North Newport River.[16] But he did not lose interest in the Altamaha. In 1760 he laid claim to 2,100 acres on the river about thirty-three miles from the coast, just above Fort Barrington.[17] He resigned this claim in 1765 for land on Cumberland Island near the Florida border but made further attempts to settle Altamaha land at the end of the decade.[18]

Why Bryan established a plantation between the North Newport and South Newport rivers in 1758 is unknown. It may have been an experimental plantation, for he raised a variety of crops and animals there. In an advertisement for the plantation's sale in 1763, he described it as good for corn, rice, and indigo and able to maintain horses, cattle, and other stock. He had built there "a good new framed barn, overseer's house, and negro houses." One hundred acres had been cleared and fenced, and he stated that the marsh land for the animals could be easily enclosed. Apparently, however, the local planters had difficulty attracting oceangoing vessels, with the result that the cost of transporting goods to market was raised. Bryan, at any rate, gave up: the result of his five-year development of land along the Newport rivers was a determination to leave the region to others.[19]

Bryan continued to develop Walnut Hill in the 1750s and 1760s. By grant, he added 600 acres of rice land and 300 acres of garden and farm lots in 1758 and 1762.[20] He referred to himself in legal documents as Jonathan Bryan of Walnut Hill, and he used the plantation as headquarters for his other operations. In 1758 he added to his holdings Cockspur Island, east of Walnut Hill, in the Savannah River. He also requested and received a wharf in Savannah and 300 acres above the town at Pipemaker's Creek.[21] At this time he also reconsidered settling land on the Great Ogeechee but in a location different from the one he had intended to settle in 1755. In 1759 he put in a claim for 250 acres, which he supplemented in 1760 with an additional 600.[22] This land, granted for a cowpen, was located about fifty miles from the mouth of the river. Bryan did not expect large ships to sail that far upriver, for settlement around the cowpen was very sparse. Instead, he could move cattle southward by water about fifteen miles to Fort Argyle, near the confluence of the Great Ogeechee and Cowanoochee, and run them overland from there to several of the colony's southern towns. Bryan desired a larger market for his cattle, one to be found only in Savannah, but had no way to get them there. In 1766 he used his influence to persuade the legislature to let him build a road that would connect his cowpen with the capital. His cattle could then graze on the excellent pasture land of the Great Ogeechee and be herded the twenty miles overland to the Savannah market. The legislature decided that he, his son Hugh, and five others serve as the new road's commissioners.[23] Many cowpens soon developed in the vicinity of Bryan's.

The cartographer William Gerard De Brahm, who immigrated to

Georgia in 1751, praised the quality of the colony's roadways but noted that they were seldom used for conveyance of goods because of the river system. De Brahm exaggerated the convenience of water carriage and underestimated road usage for the movement of goods. Neither his account of Georgia's road network nor his 1757 map of Georgia mentions the Newmarket road to Bryan's Cowpen, as it did not then exist. Subsequent editions of the 1757 map etched in two roads to the Great Ogeechee, the main highways to the south, but did not include the road to Bryan's Cowpen. Later maps copied De Brahm's, so that the only map of the period that includes the road is an obscure one made by a British army cartographer during the Revolution.[24] The Newmarket road was not important to Georgia mapmakers because few slaveholders used it. We know the road existed, for the colony's official records frequently mention it. Bryan's Cowpen became a major landmark on the Great Ogeechee for upcountry settlers, who signified the location of their land by reference to it. The men who sat on the council were unfamiliar with the area, so these backwoods farmers gave the location of their claims as "about Ten Miles above Bryan's Cowpen" or "within three Miles of Jonathan Bryan's Cowpen."[25] In the 1770s factions argued over where to continue the road. The upcountry won out, and Bryan's Cowpen then marked the terminus for a new highway that extended one hundred miles into the Georgia interior to the backcountry settlement of Queensborough.[26]

After fifteen years in the colony Bryan finally had arranged his plantations to allow easy access from one to another. In 1762 he began to consolidate his holdings by selling all of his land below the capital on the Savannah River. He resigned his tract at Augustine's Creek and in 1763 sold Walnut Hill Plantation.[27] Bryan determined to build a new homestead west of the city at Brampton, where Pipemaker's Creek flowed into the Savannah. This locale was considered one of the best rice-producing areas of the colony. Fields were easily flooded by both the creek and the river, and goods could be readily conveyed downriver for export abroad. Bryan's original grant on the creek was for 600 acres in 1759. He added 250 acres in 1765 and 350 more in 1770.[28] Brampton's location was excellent for both business and politics. It enabled Bryan to attend to his affairs in Savannah and gave him easy access to his South Carolina holdings along the Savannah. He need travel only a few miles by piragua to reach the road to his Union and Little Yemassee plantations: both were also approachable by water.[29]

(Reaching these same plantations from Walnut Hill meant an additional ten miles of travel upstream.) Furthermore, Brampton lay close to the terminus of the Newmarket road at Pipemaker's Creek. Cattle could be run directly there from his cowpen, whereas they could not have been run to Walnut Hill. Though Bryan continued to consider establishing plantations in other areas of the colony, for the remainder of his life Brampton and his plantations along the Savannah formed the central component of his economic empire.

COUNCIL CONTROL OVER THE PUBLIC DOMAIN

Bryan was able to build his empire largely because of his position on the executive council, which regulated Georgia's land system through legislation and careful control of the distribution of land in the public domain. Control over the public lands was the major source of the council's economic and political power. Although the rules governing the land-granting system appeared to be equitable (all free white males were entitled to receive a portion of the public domain), the formal entitlement to land was of negligible importance in obtaining a valuable parcel. The council held final say over who got which tracts. Since the Trustees had severely restricted landownership and little land had been ceded by the Indians, much of Georgia's chartered domain had yet to be granted when royal government was established. Thus it fell to the council to distribute most of the land that came under cultivation in the late colonial period.

Under the system established by royal officials, each head of household was entitled to one hundred acres for himself and fifty acres for every member of his household, including slaves. Among the slaveholders themselves, those who possessed influence on the council were most likely to receive the best land—freshwater swamp located along transportation routes and cultivable by the tidal-flow method. Although rice could be produced inland, planters who obtained land affected by the Atlantic tides, whereby fields could be easily flooded and drained, enjoyed a distinct advantage. This land lay above the saltwater line in an area ten to twenty miles wide along the coast.[30] Eighteenth-century maps reveal the result of the colony's land-granting system: a small group of land barons monopolized Georgia's premier rice lands, while the rest of the population became dispersed throughout the colony.[31]

The most important aspect of council control over the public domain was the consideration of petitions for land. Anyone wishing a grant presented his or her petition in person to the governor and council.[32] This gave the council direct contact with virtually every landowner in Georgia and provided occasions for it to display its "apartness" and majesty to the populace.

Petitioners ordinarily appeared before the council on "land day," the first Tuesday of every month.[33] They were required to swear to the number of persons in their households and to designate the location of a desired plot of land.[34] The council then accepted, rejected, or postponed action on the petitions. Successful claimants had six months to obtain and register a survey, upon the completion of which they received a signed grant from the governor. Requests for land averaged 359 per year from 1755 to 1769, and well over 500 in the last four years of that period.[35] The political importance of these petitions was reflected in higher than usual rates of attendance of councillors on land days.

Councillors attended land days to promote their interests and those of their clients. From 1755 to 1760, those interests focused on the valuable lands of the low country. After 1760 councillors continued to attend land days with great regularity because of the paucity of good land. They intently followed the petitions of newcomers who were extending settlement to the west and south. Learning from these petitions new locations of valuable land, they used this knowledge to submit petitions for land they had never seen. If the land was subsequently found unsuitable, they resigned the claim and submitted another. Jonathan Bryan resigned approximately 40 percent of the land that he claimed from the public domain before completing possession.[36] His son Hugh followed suit, resigning three successive claims, having found upon inspection that they were not as valuable as he had been led to believe.[37]

In the period of royal government, the council granted approximately one million acres.[38] The percentage of petitions granted was high.[39] In the most competitive period, 1755–1760, 1,406 of 1,785 petitions, or 79 percent, were accepted, at least in part. From 1761 to 1769 the yearly figure was over 80 percent.[40] These statistics appear to illustrate the ease with which Georgians acquired land, but they can be misleading. What they do not show is that sponsors often were needed for the granting of land and that many who hoped to obtain a portion, particularly of the valuable low-country swamp or marsh, had little chance of success without a friend on the council. The case of Mark Noble illustrates the importance of council patronage.

Noble's case does not enter our statistics because his petition was never officially adjudged by the council in session. He was the overseer of Henry Laurens's Broughton Island plantation. Laurens became furious when Noble, without his approval and "under the sanction of Jonathan Bryan, Esquire, . . . petitioned for a Warrant to Survey a parcel of that Marsh Land adjoining to the College Land and pretending that he had eight or ten Negroes."[41] Laurens made his displeasure known to James Habersham and other council members. In behind-the-scenes maneuvering Laurens was able to prevent his overseer from receiving the land. From the particulars of the case it is evident that both Noble and Laurens realized that council patronage was necessary for the overseer to receive the desired land and that politicking members of the council could promote or hinder a claim.

Requests for land were presented with or without a sponsor, but petitioners' chances for success certainly improved if a councillor verified their claims and vouched for their character. Otherwise, there was the distinct possibility that action on a petition would be postponed or rejected. The number of postponements averaged between 10 and 20 percent per month for all petitions presented.[42] Judgment often was postponed until the petitioner moved with his family to the colony, usually from South Carolina. Other reasons for postponement included possible conflict with an existing claim, vagueness in the description of a desired tract, and lack of proof of the size of a claimant's household. Perhaps half of all postponements were de facto rejections because the petitioner was never able to answer the council's objections.

A significant number of petitions were rejected outright. This was most apt to occur in the early years of royal government when planters scrambled for the best land. From 1755 to 1760, 17 percent of all petitions presented and not postponed were rejected. All told, the council postponed or rejected 21 percent of the petitions in that six-year period.[43] No reason was given for rejection in a majority of cases. The stated reasons included doubt of a claimant's intention to use the land or capability of developing it. Some petitions were rejected because the same piece of land had been granted earlier in the session. Accordingly, it was especially important to have political influence on the council, so that one's petition would be presented first. Thus Archibald Bulloch's petition for 2,000 acres on Cumberland Island was rejected in 1767 because Jonathan Bryan's claim to the same tract had previously been granted in the same session.[44] We may be sure that Bryan placed his petitions for consideration before those of his competitors. Petitions could be arbitrarily dismissed in the knowledge that appeal could be made only to the king and that few men possessed the means to pursue that course of action.

Bryan followed the granting of land with great interest. His attendance on land days was below 75 percent only one year during the period 1755–63 (excluding 1756, when land day was infrequently held), and in five of those eight years was above 85 percent.[45] One reason for this regularity was the steady stream of petitions he submitted on his own behalf, thirty-eight in all, over two-thirds of which were submitted between 1755 and 1764.[46] The thirty-eight were for over 18,000 acres plus wharfage and town and garden lots. Only two of his petitions were postponed and only one was rejected.[47] His completed grants totaled upward of 10,000 acres. This land formed the basis for several of his Georgia plantations, though he used a substantial portion for speculative purposes.

Bryan's council seat enabled him to obtain land not only of the best quality but in excess of what he was entitled to by freehold. Some Georgians were permitted to obtain public land by purchase. This allowed a privileged few to receive such land at minimal cost, once their freehold was completed. To purchase public land, planters had to swear that tracts would be developed and not used for speculation.[48] The council was the final arbiter of who could buy and who could not; thus Bryan was in an excellent position to have his purchase requests approved. For example, in 1760 he owned 113 slaves and had 8 children, entitling him to 6,150 acres. He then possessed 4,575 acres by freehold and sought an additional 2,100 acres on the Altamaha River. This would have placed him 525 acres over his entitlement. The council, however, agreed to Bryan's request and sold him 525 acres at ten shillings per 100 acres.[49] The cost was so low that, in effect, the land was granted gratis. In June 1767 Bryan also bought from the government 1,570 acres on Cumberland Island.[50] He would have purchased more had it not become apparent to the council that he obtained the land only to sell it. Prohibited from making any more purchases from the government, in October 1767 he had to turn instead to the private sector.[51]

Bryan had made intermittent purchases from private individuals in the 1750s, but not until 1764 did he begin buying large tracts in Georgia. Extant evidence indicates that he bought approximately 22,000 acres in both Georgia and South Carolina.[52] These sales were expedited by a legal fiction designed to circumvent England's Statute of Enrollments, which provided that the sale of freehold estates must be written, officially sealed, and enrolled at designated public places. To circumvent the law, a system of "lease and release" was used in England and the colonies for conveying land. This system permitted colonists to record land transactions at their leisure.[53] Bryan was expert at composing the necessary documents. Typically, the seller leased a parcel of land to the buyer for a period of one year for the nominal sum of five shillings. A day later, the seller signed a release, by which he resigned his right to the reversion of the land when the lease expired. In other words, the release was a promise by the seller not to take back his land. The buyer had the convenience of not having to take actual possession of the land as required in a common-law sale. Moreover, no one was the wiser of his financial affairs. Several of Bryan's purchases remained unknown to the public until years later, when they were recorded as sold to a third party. In a colony that had no lawyers as late as 1755, practical knowledge of the law provided one with a great advantage over one's neighbors.

THE SELECTION AND DEVELOPMENT OF LAND

Bryan's selection of land was based upon familiarity with Georgia topography acquired through years of travel and experience. He was expert in the native plants of the Southeast and an excellent assessor of soil for crop production. James Habersham recommended Bryan to naturalist John Ellis as one who possessed "a general knowledge of this Province and South Carolina, and of its many unnoticed, tho' useful Plants—both medicinal, and ornamental."[54] The naturalist William Bartram also testified to Bryan's horticultural talents. Bartram visited Bryan at Brampton Plantation in 1776, where he found a beautiful "villa" in "a very delightful situation." He was impressed by Bryan's "spacious gardens, furnished with a variety of fruit trees and flowering shrubs."[55] Benjamin Franklin learned of Bryan's talents and from England sent to him for experimentation some "Upland Rice, brought from Cochin China." This experiment failed but another succeeded: Franklin sent seeds of the Chinese tallow tree, which Bryan and a few others germinated so successfully that the tree soon spread through the Southeast.[56]

Bryan understood maps and surveying. He learned from his surveyor brother Hugh the art of surveying, and, though he rarely practiced it, when occasion demanded he made his own surveys.[57] He became familiar with the topography of the Southeast through his brother's maps and those of De Brahm.[58] Bryan befriended De Brahm when the latter led a large migration of Germans to Georgia in 1751.[59] We may assume that it was Jonathan who provided De Brahm with Hugh's maps, for Hugh received credit in the title of De Brahm's most widely circulated map of Georgia and South Carolina.[60]

Bryan's knowledge of Georgia geography extended to an appreciation of the important modes of transportation. When Bryan was twenty-seven years old, James Oglethorpe attempted to induce him to build a road from the Savannah River to the Great Ogeechee.[61] Bryan shrewdly stipulated that the eighteen laborers he was to be provided first be used to extend a road from his own plantation in St. Helena Parish to the Savannah. This road would have made his plantation on the Pocotaligo River a major terminus between Charlestown and Georgia, but the project was not undertaken.[62] Later, Bryan promised the Trustees' assistants in Georgia that if they granted him land in the Savannah River on Hutchinson's Island, he would build a road through the swamps on the north side of the river to facilitate travel between South Carolina and Georgia.[63] His offers to help improve Georgia's road system were accepted when he was made a commissioner of the roads for the northwest district, shortly after the establishment of royal government. Bryan utilized this position to his advantage. Thirty years after Oglethorpe had approached him, he built a road from the Savannah to the Great Ogeechee River, at the terminus of which was located his own cowpen.[64]

One area of opportunity that sparked Bryan's interest was investment in the islands of Georgia. He made a fortune buying and selling several islands in the early 1770s. His advertisements of them usually included a description of the soil, wharfage facilities, and accessibility by water. The results proved well worth the effort. From the sale of four islands in 1770–71 Bryan grossed over £2,300, with a net profit well above half that sum.[65]

Buying and selling islands took a great deal of energy. He had to visit the islands, assess their quality, and in at least one case make his own survey. His purchases and grants were often distant from Savannah and required travel over difficult terrain. But Bryan was among the most physically fit of men, with the stamina not only to visit the far reaches of Georgia but to develop much of his land into plantations.[66]

Bryan understood the characteristics that made a tract valuable: good soil, location along the lines of transportation, and utility for intended purpose. He purchased 650 acres on Wilmington Island in 1764 and 1765 at the very low price of £145 for land that was worth at least three times as much.[67] This tract became the family homestead for his son Josiah and his grandson Joseph.[68] Likewise, Bryan spotted several bargains on the Altamaha River, where land was inexpensive until, in the late 1760s, planters became willing to move far south of the main settlements about Savannah. He purchased 1,670 acres on two islands in the Altamaha River for £330 in 1767; the property's value increased 231 percent in four years, and he sold it for £1,092 in 1771. Ordinarily, it was very difficult to find planters wealthy enough to spend over £1,000 for a tract, especially one distant from a major port; most sales of this size were to merchants, not to planters. John Hall, a London merchant, purchased Bryan's islands in the Altamaha; Miles Brewton, a Charlestown merchant, paid Bryan £1,400, in the form of thirty-three slaves, for Walnut Hill Plantation in 1763. Ten years later, Brewton purchased 450 acres from Bryan, 100 of which were on Hutchinson Island, for the steep price of £1,100. In addition, South Carolina merchants Thomas Lynch and Alexander Mose paid him £1,100 for 10,870 acres on Cumberland and Little Cumberland islands. These islands were close to the Florida border, far from Savannah, and the land was unsuitable for rice production. The proprietor needed access to seafaring vessels to transport the islands' produce. The market for this land was therefore limited, but Bryan found purchasers and made approximately 100 percent profit from the sale.[69]

Sales of land, both developed and undeveloped, assisted Bryan in capitalizing other enterprises. The thirty-three slaves he received from the sale of Walnut Hill probably were used at his new homestead, Brampton Plantation, where he built the villa admired by Bartram. He operated so many plantations that he constantly required new labor. At any given moment in the 1750s, 1760s, and 1770s he had five or more plantations in production. The total number of slaves employed is unknown but may be estimated at about 250 in 1763. In Georgia alone, Bryan held 66 slaves in 1755, 94 in 1760, and 125 in 1763.[70] In South Carolina he possessed numerous plantations, totaling about 7,000 acres in the 1760s and 1770s; Union Plantation alone comprised 2,000 acres, was highly developed, and may have employed 100 or more slaves.

Access to capital was the key factor in obtaining slave labor. Because there were few shortages of black labor in Georgia and South Carolina between 1755 and the Revolution, men who possessed credit or cash could easily buy blacks, especially when, like Bryan, they had close business contacts with Bristol and Charlestown merchants.[71] Bryan had no difficulty stocking his plantations with laborers; he was able to provide ten slaves to each of his children when they came of age.[72]

Establishing a plantation took large amounts of capital. De Brahm estimated the cost of creating a rice plantation at £2,476. This sum purchased 200 acres, a barn, slaves, oxen and horses, two carts, tools, provisions for one year, and clothes and medicine for the work force; it also paid an overseer's wages. The greatest single expense which De Brahm calculated was £1,800 for the purchase of forty seasoned slaves. He estimated return on the first year of investment at £700.[73] This would pay a quarter of the planter's debt with interest. An overseer or tradesman who earned £50 per year could hardly expect to procure a £2,500 loan. Even a plantation of ten slaves was beyond the means of most men, given the scarcity of capital. Thus most white Georgians did not own slaves. A recent estimate by Betty Wood suggests that "by the early 1760s at least 5 percent of all white Georgians, and probably not less than a quarter of all households, held at least one slave." Most of these were concentrated in the tidewater area.[74]

The value of rice plantations varied greatly. When De Brahm calculated the costs of planting he did not mention the 2,000 acres a slaveholder was entitled to by purchase of forty slaves. That was because most of the good rice land was taken by 1760, and De Brahm made his estimate sometime after 1765. He also greatly underestimated the cost of improved rice land. On the Savannah and the freshwater creeks that fed the river, good land sold for much more than the ten shillings per acre he calculated. On Hutchinson Island in the Savannah, Bryan bought and sold land in 1773 valued from £2 10s. to £6 per acre, or 500 percent to 1,200 percent higher than De Brahm had figured. The value of acreage on the island rose greatly in the next decade.[75] Across from Hutchinson Island Bryan added a 250-acre tract to his holdings at Pipemaker's Creek. He paid close to £1 5s. per acre for this land.[76] In 1768 he sold the 450-acre Little Yemassee Plantation on the South Carolina side of the Savannah for £450. Only fifty acres were cleared for rice, while on another fifty to sixty were knolls of corn; the plantation also had an overseer's house. Little Yemassee was not a major plantation, at least not to Bryan. He had purchased the tract five years earlier for about £150. But the few improvements he made and the value of the rice land, which was excellently located, increased the plantation's value by 200 percent, despite the fact that 300 acres of the tract were uncleared.[77] De Brahm, though expert in topography, was not a great planter and did not understand how to use slavery and land to gain riches as Bryan did. Thus we must revise his estimate of the cost for establishing a plantation of forty slaves from £2,476 to between £3,000 and £3,600, with the latter the closer figure when prime rice land was purchased.[78]

There are few records of how Bryan operated his plantations. We do not know whether he utilized his sons, slave drivers, or paid overseers to direct his work force. He recognized the family unit among his slaves, twice directing in his will that, if at all possible, families should not be broken up in the settlement of his estate.[79] Johann Martin Boltzius asserted that his plantations were run in an orderly manner. Boltzius reported in 1742 that Bryan's slaves were well treated and, as a result, were contented and worked efficiently. Unlike most slaveholders, who denied their bondsmen the privileges of reading and of practicing Christianity, Bryan actively promoted the education and Christianization of his slaves in South Carolina and Georgia. Cornelius Winter, an Evangelical who attempted to instruct Georgia blacks in the precepts of Christianity, testified in 1771 that many of Bryan's laborers knew Christian prayers by heart. Later in the decade, as noted earlier, Bryan took the unusual step of permitting one of his slaves, Andrew Bryan, to preach. Bryan's treatment of slaves with a respect ordinarily denied them may have contributed to the great success of his plantations.[80]

Bryan's laborers performed a variety of tasks. They were cowboys, field hands, carpenters, sawyers, and house servants. Those skilled in woodwork produced lumber and shingles for market and built barns and slave quarters.[81] Thus with great speed Bryan cleared tracts and erected the buildings necessary to begin plantation operations; he then developed the land or sold it as a fully functioning plantation. It appears that the latter was his intention or at least the result of his efforts in the sale of Little Yemassee, Dean Forrest, his plantation on the North Newport River, and possibly those on Wereats Island and Cambers Island in the Altamaha River.

Bryan's plantations were largely self-sufficient. Not only did they produce their own food, but his laborers' skills made him less dependent upon hired labor than most planters, thus minimizing cash expenditures. When cash was needed, he could sell slaves, plantations, or undeveloped land, but his credit was always good and we may conclude that his notes were taken everywhere. Though he purchased clothes and miscellaneous household items from the Georgia merchants, his major transactions appear to have been with the merchant Edward Lloyd of Bristol, with whom there is record of correspondence in both 1765 and 1772.[82] With a reliable factor in England to handle his affairs, and in possession of nearly self-sufficient estates, Bryan was able to devote much of his time to the development of new land. By the mid-1760s he had built no less than a plantation empire.

DREAMS ALONG THE ALTAMAHA

While Bryan perfected his Savannah River plantation network his political activity declined dramatically. Bryan's rate of attendance at council meetings fell from its high of 76 percent and 71 percent in 1758 and 1759 to 52 percent in 1760 and 49 percent in 1761.[83] Except for an increase to 61 percent in both 1762 and 1763, his rate of attendance never again rose above 50 percent. This declining rate of attendance only begins to tell the story of Bryan's waning interest in political affairs: his committee membership in both the council and the upper house became negligible after 1760, and he accepted fewer commissioner positions. (The decline in political activity has been graphed in appendix 5.) Bryan's waning interest was not the result of age and lost vigor, but other factors, including the development of Brampton Plantation and the personal tragedy that struck the Bryan family in 1761 and 1762. In the space of two years three of Bryan's sons, Joseph, John, and Jonathan, Jr., all of whom were nineteen to twenty-one years of age, passed away.[84] In the three-year period following their deaths Bryan's behavior suggested a father in mourning. He

steadily withdrew from public life until he failed to attend a single
council meeting from May 1764 to April 1765.

Shortly after his sons' deaths Bryan sold his Newport River plantation and the family homestead at Walnut Hill.[85] This completed the
consolidation of his plantations along the Savannah River west of the
capital and permitted him the luxury of conducting his financial affairs
close to home. For the first and only time, Bryan devoted his attention
strictly to the development of property he already possessed and refrained from beginning new projects. Not only did he stop attending
council (including land day), but he abstained from both the buying
and selling of land.[86] Instead, he became absorbed in the building of a
magnificent villa at Brampton Plantation, a monument to himself and
a statement to his neighbors of the man he had become.[87]

During Bryan's political hiatus Georgia underwent many changes. A
vast population increase stretched Georgia's boundaries west and south
and altered the demography of the colony. Many Virginians migrated
down the piedmont and settled the backcountry. Soon they were followed by North and South Carolinians who fled their colonies as a
result of Indian disturbances, of the failures of the Regulator movements, and of the promise of free land below the Savannah. This migration accounted for a large portion of the 50 percent increase in the
colony's white population from 1760 to 1766; the white population
increased again by another 50 percent from 1766 to 1772. Even more
remarkable than this growth was the increase of Georgia's slave population. There were only 3,578 slaves in the colony in 1760. That number
more than quadrupled by 1773, when it reached over 15,000.[88] The
increase was confined almost exclusively to the tidewater, sharpening
the distinctions between the colony's two geographic regions. The low
country was characterized by its large plantations, massive slave labor
force, and aristocratic society, while the backcountry was populated by
yeoman farmers who possessed very few, if any, slaves. The economic
interests of the two regions were very different but did not lead to the
violent political and class divisions that struck both Carolinas mid-
decade.[89] Georgia's new immigrants were preoccupied with establishing and maintaining their freeholds. They would not challenge the low
country's domination of the colony until the 1770s.

Several members of Georgia's ruling class recognized and accepted
the needs of the backcountry yeomanry. The building of the Newmarket road to Bryan's Cowpen not only advanced Bryan's interests

but those of a whole region of settlers, who now had an easy route to the capital. Low-country planters approved and promoted backcountry development because it cost little and afforded many benefits. The new settlements provided a buffer against the Creek Indians. Land for the settlers was provided by a cession of almost 2.5 million acres above Augusta by the Creeks in 1763.[90] This land was of minimal value to low-country planters because it could not be converted to rice production. Thus the council readily approved the backcountry settlers' petitions for land. By 1764 the percentage of petitions rejected and postponed by the council became negligible.[91]

Council members continued to attend land day with great frequency because their control of the public domain remained a source of patronage and prestige. A further reason for the councillors' high rate of attendance sprang from the hope that new areas would be discovered for rice cultivation.[92] James Wright, the new governor of Georgia, voiced the concern of many of the colony's rice planters when he reported to London that all of the good rice land between the Savannah and the Altamaha rivers had been granted by 1760.[93] The decline in the quantity of land requested by Bryan in the first half of the 1760s helps to substantiate Wright's claim. From 1755 to 1760, Bryan requested an average of 2,000 acres per year; from 1761 to 1766 that average fell 85 percent, to 300 acres per year. All of the grants which Bryan completed from 1760 to 1766 were appendages to his holdings; none staked out new territory for development.[94]

The paucity of unclaimed rice land in South Carolina had been a driving force in the emigration of Carolinians to Georgia in the 1750s. In the 1760s, the lack of unclaimed rice land in both colonies became a point of dispute between them. In 1763, a new area of the low country was opened for development between the Altamaha River, Georgia's southern border, and the St. Marys River, the northern border of Florida. This region became available for English settlement when the Spanish evacuated the Southeast at the close of the Seven Years' War. South Carolina claimed the land as its own, though it was not contiguous to its borders. On a spring day in April, South Carolina's governor, Thomas Boone, issued grants of 343,000 acres of Altamaha land. A month later he issued grants for another 200,000 acres.[95] Georgia bitterly contested and won jurisdiction to the area but was instructed by the Crown to accommodate South Carolina claims, though the manner was left undetermined. The Crown's refusal to settle the matter definitively, and its blocking of Georgia's attempts to do so, arrested the development of this highly desirable region for the expansion of plantation slavery.[96]

Jonathan Bryan long held an interest in this region. He had visited the area as a scout and as a member of Oglethorpe's force that invaded Florida in 1740. Bryan moved cautiously in making and developing claims below the Altamaha. He could not request land from South Carolina's governor because it would have alienated his colleagues on the Georgia council. Instead, his brother-in-law Stephen Bull became the first Carolinian to try to make good a South Carolina grant along the Altamaha. An agent for Bull appeared before the Georgia council to assert his claim to 7,500 acres by a grant from Governor Boone. Bryan was absent the day of the hearing. Bull's petition was rejected, setting a precedent for the rejection of other Carolinian petitions.[97] Most Carolinians gave up settling the region, but so, too, did many Georgians, for no one could be sure of their title south of the Altamaha.[98] Those Georgians determined to settle the region had to make sure that lands they desired were unclaimed in South Carolina. If they were reasonably sure the land was unclaimed (and no one could be positive), they were still faced with the task of establishing plantations in an area without a port. Jonathan Bryan adjusted his interests in the area to the exigencies of this tenuous situation.

Cumberland Island was the first area Bryan chose for expansion after the completion of Brampton. He resigned a grant to 1,500 acres along the Altamaha River and exchanged it for 800 acres of this large but distant island in the Atlantic, just north of the Florida border. He also received a grant to 1,600 acres at Buttermilk Bluff on the St. Marys River, across from Cumberland. But he resigned this grant, too, in June 1766, for a comparable amount of acreage on Cumberland. Why Bryan chose to settle land so distant from the population centers of Georgia and Florida remains a mystery, but in 1767 he again altered his plans, and instead of developing the island he accumulated tracts for purposes of speculation.[99]

Bryan tested the market value of Cumberland Island by advertising it for sale, while he systematically went about obtaining the remainder of the island.[100] He correctly surmised that the value of Georgia islands would increase dramatically in the next few years. Freshwater islands were in demand because the land was easily turned to rice production, but even those saltwater islands like Cumberland which contained a supply of fresh water and excellent harbor facilities were valuable for cattle ranching, shipbuilding, lumber, and corn. In addition, they were desirable as family homesteads. In 1767 Bryan increased his holdings on Cumberland Island with a 2,000-acre grant. Three hundred acres of the grant completed his freehold, and the council permitted him to purchase at minimal cost 1,000 acres for himself and 700 acres in the name of his son Josiah.[101]

With the completion of these purchases Bryan was unable to obtain any additional acreage on Cumberland Island from the Georgia government. Governor Wright was opposed to speculation and it had become apparent that Bryan had no intention of developing the island. Bryan was probably informed that future requests for acreage on the island would be rejected, for he found new and imaginative ways to obtain more land.[102] First, he recruited others to obtain Cumberland land for him. His brother-in-law John Smith applied for and received a 2,000-acre grant, which he gave to Bryan for the sum of £50. That the tract was meant for Bryan all along was made evident by the low selling price, the quickness with which the transaction was consumated after Smith received title from the government, and by Bryan's personal surveying of the tract.[103] The day before Smith's sale to Bryan, the latter's longtime friend James Habersham, who had requested and received a grant of 1,100 acres on Little Cumberland Island, had turned his grant over to Bryan for £50. These transactions were followed by Bryan's purchase of 2,000 acres from James Bulloch in September 1768, and 1,500 acres from James Cuthbert in January 1769. He then had an aggregate total of 10,870 acres on Cumberland and Little Cumberland islands.[104]

In addition to his Cumberland Island holdings Bryan also purchased valuable acreage on islands in the Altamaha River. From John Wereat he purchased Wereats Island and from Thomas Camber and Francis Joffe he obtained Cambers Island in 1767. These islands were bought inexpensively. Bryan paid less than seven shillings per acre for Wereats Island and between four and five shillings per acre for Cambers Island.[105] In less than four years the value of these islands increased 330 percent, although only 30 acres had been cleared by his slaves.[106] He complemented these purchases with a 400-acre tract on the Altamaha, which he obtained from John Callwell in 1767 for between six and seven shillings per acre.[107] Initially, Bryan intended to settle these tracts and had formulated grandiose plans for the development of the whole Altamaha region. The scope of his plans was such that he might have been intending the removal of his operation from the Savannah. In the late summer of 1767 he wrote Henry Laurens of the Altamaha's prospects. Laurens agreed with Bryan to promote the region's development. They envisioned the construction of a great port that would one day surpass both Savannah *and* Charlestown in the value of exports, basing their beliefs (and hopes) on the quality of the region's land. Laurens recommended the establishment of a Customs House and noted the necessity of a lighthouse. He agreed to approach his old friend Governor Wright about appointing civil servants to the area. He further assured Bryan that he could personally command vessels to pick up their goods on the Altamaha, but it would be better if they could encourage traders to appear on their own accord. This could be accomplished, he believed, by creating a port where captains would be "sure of free access, good company & civil treatment." The success of their plans was dependent upon government cooperation, a settlement of the problem of land titles, and upon the attraction of planters from the Savannah River to the region.[108]

Laurens and Bryan were men of business who understood the ins and outs of large financial projects. Laurens was an extremely successful merchant of the Atlantic trade and one of the region's largest planters.[109] Bryan's business experience was more provincial but varied and had included participation in the establishment of ports at Port Royal and Savannah. While Laurens was, perhaps, the richest man in South Carolina, Bryan was one of the two or three wealthiest in Georgia. Together, they had as much capital and political influence as any other two men in the Deep South. They possessed the wherewithal, the knowledge, the political clout, and the vision to attempt a transformation of the Altamaha into a thriving commerical region. But they did not succeed. Within two years their dreams faded. By 1769 Jonathan Bryan had become disenchanted with the Altamaha project. The inability of South Carolina and Georgia to settle their land dispute hindered immigration to the area. Georgia passed a law that would have settled the matter of titles, but it was rejected in London.[110] Several planters moved to the Altamaha, raising the property value of Bryan's islands high enough to make him a fortune from their sale, but the dream of a great port fell by the wayside. The region had proven a disappointment and there was no other land in Georgia which he considered for the development of new plantations.

LAND, POLITICS, AND FAMILY POWER

The worldly rewards Bryan obtained from his plantations and his council position did not inspire an unwavering loyalty to the colony or its government. Bryan's behavior was directed by the dictates of his Christian conscience, which placed service to God and loyalty to family, friends, and self above affiliation with any institution. Bryan's break with the Anglican church in 1743 provided the precedent for his future relationship with institutional structures. Instead of switching his allegiance to another denomination, Bryan helped found an "Independent" congregation, which utilized the Presbyterian name but was in no way connected with the synod. After moving to Georgia, Bryan then played a major role in the establishment of another Independent congregation.[111] Opposition to institutional forms led Bryan to oppose mandatory oath-taking. It also became a lifelong tenet lauded by the author of his obituary: "Zealous in the cause of Christianity, [Bryan] considered modes of worship but as secondary, whilst a great first principle with him in all true religion was universal charity."[112]

Bryan interpreted his Christian duty as providing him the right to accumulate land, wealth, and power for use in promoting the well-being of his fellow man. Thus Bryan rationalized the exploitation of black labor by providing his slaves with Christianity. Bryan's political genius lay in the ability to pursue goals that simultaneously benefited himself and others. Who in the backcountry would fault the building of a road from Savannah to Bryan's Cowpen, when that road was a boon to all who lived along the Great Ogeechee River? The most spectacular example of his genius lay in the future, when Bryan convinced many members of the Creek Confederacy that leasing him four to five million acres of land in Florida was in their own best interests. Bryan understood better than most men that politics was a matter of give and take, that negotiation with clients, competitors, and dependents usually provided the best road to personal advancement.

Bryan's power in negotiations stemmed from his wealth and his political offices. His connection to the royal government allowed him the best possible position from which to improve his standing. In the eighteenth-century British political system, men expected private gain as a reward for public service. Whether conscientious servants of the king or placemen, they took for granted the enjoyment of privileges attached to their position. Jonathan Bryan was no different. He performed a flurry of legislative and administrative activities from 1755 to 1760, a critical period for the colony, when men of talent and political experience were scarce. He undertook these jobs because he was needed, but understandably, he expected to be rewarded with favors, preferments, and appointments. Thus he received valuable parcels of land, was named captain of horse, and was appointed to numerous commissioner positions. When the critical early period of royal government came to an end in 1760, Bryan paid less attention to politics and more to reaping the benefit of office.

The rise of the patriot movement in the 1760s forced Bryan to reassess his loyalties and the value of his royal government connections. Preoccupied with building his fortune below the Altamaha, he studiously avoided taking a stand on the issues that divided Americans. Fortunately, other Georgia elites also remained silent, so that his own reticence during the period of the Stamp Act went unnoticed. Bryan's political position, however, was too important to allow him the convenience of straddling the political fence indefinitely. In 1769, no longer able or interested in obtaining Georgia public land, Bryan joined the patriot movement. He and many other elites based their position on the constitutional rights of Englishmen—Bryan earned renown as a man of "constitutional" and "revolution principles"—but each man held great personal stake in the dispute with Great Britain.[113] Though Bryan joined thousands of others who pledged "our lives, our fortune, and our sacred honor" to secure American independence, the ideas he fought for and against were directly related to his perceptions of provincial economy, local politics, and his own personal economic goals.

Bryan withheld public support for the patriot movement until the Crown showed itself unwilling to settle the dispute over the land south of the Altamaha River. Not only did the British Empire no longer provide assistance for the expansion of his estate, but it appeared to arrest economic development at every turn. Moreover, the empire had barred land-hungry Americans from settling the interior continent by the Proclamation Act of 1763, which prohibited white settlement west of the Appalachian mountains along a line drawn from Canada to Florida. Bryan challenged this and other imperial laws in the 1770s—no Georgian posed a greater threat to British land and Indian policy. The quest for land that had driven his father to disregard the laws that protected the Yamassee also drove Bryan to a position of belligerency against the Crown.

Bryan risked his political offices and challenged the laws of the British Empire because of his obsession to accumulate land. One might imagine that at the age of sixty and in possession of a vast plantation empire, Bryan would have been satisfied with his wealth and status. Such was not the case. His drive for wealth and power did not decline with advancing age. Bryan's most politically active years lay ahead of him, and his quest for land intensified. Bryan's contemporaries were no more informed than we are today as to the source of his insatiable land hunger, but we can place his drive in the context of the eighteenth-century South and his family's life experience.

The ownership of a large landed estate provided the wherewithal for operating independently of other men. It facilitated the establishment of patron-client relationships with lesser men and bolstered family power. Employment of a large unfree labor force for the production of staple crops provided unmatched political and social legitimacy. Rare was the southern merchant who did not turn his profits from trade into land. Many mechanics and artisans did the same.[114]

The desire to acquire land was not unusual, neither were the speculative schemes by which several colonials hoped to become great land barons.[115] The lengths Bryan traveled to fulfill his goals, his expertise, and his success differentiated him from most of his contemporaries. Perhaps his family's quest for land in South Carolina provided the initial psychological impetus for his intense land hunger. Bryan's father had put forth great effort to secure Yamassee land only to have the closing of the land office negate his efforts. He did not live to take ownership of the Indian land, and the family had to wait anxiously for more than a decade before the land office opened. They studiously prepared for the land-office opening by selecting tracts and establishing political connections. With Hugh's knowledge of surveying, cartography, and topography, the Bryans quickly became a great landowning family, and Jonathan inherited his family's accumulative spirit.

Henry Laurens referred to Bryan's quest for land as "a diligent endeavour to provide for your family."[116] Bryan possessed enough wealth to bequeath each of his children slaves, money, and a plantation, but division of his resources would leave none as rich as himself. With all of the quality rice land in Georgia taken, Bryan's children could not expect substantially to increase their estates through agriculture. The family's difficult position was exemplified by the predicament of the eldest son, Hugh, in the late 1760s: he possessed the slaves necessary to operate a plantation but was repeatedly disappointed in

the acreage he had obtained by grant.[117] Bryan's other three sons were
of an age where they were almost ready to begin their careers. Josiah
was twenty-three; William, twenty-one; and James, seventeen. Bryan
had difficulty finding land for them. He did procure several parcels for
Josiah, but William forestalled becoming a planter for two decades and
instead practiced medicine in Savannah. Eventually he took over his
father's Union Plantation in South Carolina. James remained at home
with his father until the end of the Revolution.

Land was the key to power and social status, and the Bryans were
careful in the usage and disposal of it. When Jonathan Bryan arranged
his daughter Mary's marriage to John Morel in 1769, he concluded an
economically beneficial agreement by which no land was transferred to
the groom. In fact, if Morel died, Mary would receive one thousand
pounds sterling, for which Morel was forced to give her brothers 7,600
acres in trust on Ossabaw Island. In addition, Mary's slaves were to
work the island under supervision of her brothers, in order to provide
her with a separate income. If Mary died childless the slaves were to be
inherited by her sisters Hannah and Ann and not her husband, thereby
keeping them in the Bryan family.[118] How Bryan felt about Morel is
unknown, but he made sure that his children would be provided for,
that they would enjoy every advantage in marriage as well as in politics,
and that Bryan family property would not be diminished by marriage.

A man like John Morel understood what marriage into the Bryan
family meant. In addition to the value of Mary's companionship as
wife, this longtime resident of Georgia gained entrance into the upper
echelon of the colony's political elite. Two years after their marriage,
Morel was elected to the first of many terms in the Georgia Commons
House of Assembly.[119] The prestige of the Bryan name and the tie to
their wealth raised Morel's social status. Morel learned what Bryan
had long recognized: family name and great wealth led to the assumption of political power.

Jonathan Bryan realized that the family name was not enough to
maintain his children's status. Never one to wait for opportunities to
arise, in 1770 he began to lay the groundwork for a complex scheme
to procure the land necessary for providing his children with enough
to perpetuate family power. Bryan's public position, however, demanded that he also tend to affairs that affected the colony at large.
The growing dispute between Great Britain and her colonies beckoned
all men to take a stand.

5 POLITICS, 1761–1773

IMPERIAL POLITICS

The new imperial politics that excited American public opinion grew out of changes in the British administration of the colonies at the close of the French and Indian War. Incensed by American trading with the French and upset at the pecuniary stinginess of colonial legislatures in their contributions to the war effort, British politicians eclectically scrutinized life, politics, and economy in their North American colonies. The officers of empire learned from returning troops of American prosperity. The soldiers reported that Americans flaunted their privileged position in the empire and bragged that the colonies would soon surpass the mother country in trade and population. They disregarded the laws of empire, particularly regulations governing trade, and ignored the directives of monarchy and their appointed governors. Americans, it was argued, lived their lives as if they were independent of Great Britain. With British coffers in the red to the sum of 100 million pounds, a hue and cry was raised throughout England that the New World cousins living in splendor should help shoulder the empire's burdensome and unprecedented debt.[1]

The reorganization of empire that followed brought an end to the era of "salutary neglect." Salutary neglect described the treatment of the colonies by British imperialists before the French and Indian War, when Americans were permitted to run their affairs relatively free of London's interference. This policy had been more a matter of circumstance than choice. Enmeshed in global competition with France and Spain, British imperialists had little time to administer their North American colonies. The decisive victory over France and Spain in the Seven Years' War allowed Whitehall the opportunity to reappraise the relationship between the colonies and the mother country. The subsequent imperial changes affected Georgia differently from other colonies. For instance, the Currency Act of 1764, which severely restricted the colonies' control over their money supply, was a general cause for grievance in most colonies but provided little cause for complaint in Georgia until 1768, when a house request for emission of £30,000 was refused in London.[2] Likewise, the stationing of British troops led to resentment in Massachusetts, New York, and elsewhere but was welcomed in Georgia as protection from the Indians.[3] Georgia's position makes the development of a patriot movement in that colony all the more interesting.

Georgians shared with other Americans contempt for the Proclamation Act of 1763. They resented the British government's attempt to bring order to the frontier as an unwarranted intrusion in their lives. The government passed the act to placate the Indians, many of whom had undertaken warfare with the British colonies at the end of the French and Indian War. Frustrated with encroachments of American settlers on their land and fearful of the British monopoly over trade, Indian nations threatened white settlements all along the western frontier, from Canada to Florida. By prohibiting British colonial expansion across the Appalachians, the government hoped to set the minds of the Indians at ease. Troops were sent to occupy key western forts to maintain peace and enforce the act.

Thousands of Euramericans were unhappy with the closing off of western lands and the presence of so many troops in peacetime. Disgruntled murmurings could also be heard over the establishment of an imperial commission to regulate Indian affairs, the first real attempt to centralize diplomatic relations with the Indians since Edmund Andros's extension of the Covenant system with the Iroquois in the seventeenth century.[4] Theoretically, the new commissioners, one each for the northern and southern colonies, would assume powers previously held by the governors. The commissioners were to relate the home government's wishes directly to the tribes to avoid the cross-purposes that resulted from each colony's conducting its own Indian policy. Jealous colonial governors and assemblies worked hard to undermine the commissioners and reassert themselves into Indian affairs. They succeeded to a large extent. Americans found the Indian commissioners, the forts and the troops, and the Proclamation to be meddlesome interference that diminished profits from the Indian trade and crushed hopes for territorial expansion.

If other colonies had conducted Indian diplomacy as successfully as Georgia, the Crown might not have had reason or excuse for the administrative changes instituted at the end of the French and Indian War.

James Wright assumed the governor's mantle from the retired Henry
Ellis in September 1760 and maintained the peace his predecessor secured with the Creeks. Wright continued Ellis's policy of containing
settler abuses against the aborigines, particularly through the regulation of trade and by sending troops to the backcountry to remove frontiersmen from Indian land. His task was not easy. Georgia had no
control over other colonies' traders; unless permanently stationed,
troops could not keep once-departed squatters from returning.[5]
Wright had no great love for the Indians but recognized the expediency
of appeasement in light of Georgia's military weakness. Wright earned
the wrath of frontiersmen, who resented his defense of Indian interests
against their own. Since he also needed to placate the thousands of
whites who arrived in Georgia expecting free land, the governor helped
swindle the Creeks out of a large portion of their domain. Wright then
traveled to Great Britain to obtain government approval of the cession.
A devoted officer of the empire, the governor worshiped at the altar of
duty to his king and could be counted upon to secure every possible
advantage for British imperial interests in North America.

James Wright soon epitomized the kind of public servant many
Americans despised. The political culture of Americans underwent a
period of drastic change after 1740 as white colonials of all classes,
and particularly of the lower classes, became active in the political process.[6] Whereas Wright believed that he served the people best by serving his king, Americans had come to believe that public servants best
performed their duty by obeying the wishes of the people. Colonials
increasingly looked to their commons houses to provide direction in
public policy, and commons houses emphasized their peculiar qualifications for doing so. The growing prestige and power of commons
houses elevated the status of small propertyholders: elites had to seek
their votes for election. Quite often the appeals of elites were self-
serving, and many elected officials had no intention of conscientiously
representing the interests of those who elected them.[7]

The whole nature of the colonial political system was changing. The
ideology of republicanism espoused by American colonists in response
to British taxation measures reflected a substantial evolution in the
thought and manner of the body politic. As a matter of course, colonists expected elected officials to look after local interests before those
of the Crown across the ocean. The Regulator movements of North and
South Carolina showed what could happen when colonial govern-

ments became grossly unresponsive to popular opinion. Many local elites quickly learned to adjust to the exigencies of popular politics, but British officials, especially the governors, owed their power to the imperial connection and thus by the nature of their office had an increasingly difficult time earning popular support.[8] Moreover, many found it beneath the dignity of their office to bend to public favor. In several colonies these officers of empire were considered by the populace to be the dupes of British administrators in London.

Colonial resentment against Britain and British administrators was tempered in Georgia by an optimistic outlook among many whites for the colony's economic future. The first half of the 1760s held real and imagined promises of security and prosperity: new settlers and slaves arrived every day, stimulating the economy and giving evidence of growth and expansion. Yet beneath the veneer of projected prosperity lay evidence of discontent, especially among the lower classes, as witnessed in the popular outcry that arose against the Stamp Act. In other colonies, British officials claimed that demagogues riled the people against British taxation, but in Georgia no elites stepped forward to spur public opinion. The populace read in the *Georgia Gazette* of the more northerly colonies' opposition to the Stamp Act and perceived parliamentary taxes as a real threat to their economic interests. All legal documents, newspapers, pamphlets, and ships' clearance papers had to have stamps affixed to them, obtained by payment of a tax to the stampmaster. The tax fell directly on the merchants, editors, and lawyers, the three groups most able to articulate their protests through the written word. The tax itself was to be passed on to the common people, which would provide undue hardship in a currency-short province. Unlike local taxes, which could be redeemed in the colony's currency, the stamps had to be purchased with British money. Thus, the townspeople had little difficulty envisioning the threat of the Stamp Act. On the surface, the objection of backcountry farmers appears more difficult to understand. A tax on newspapers, pamphlets, and ships' clearance papers would not have been seen as threatening. Nevertheless, the tax appeared burdensome to the thousands of recent immigrants who were flooding the Georgia piedmont after the Seven Years' War. Their land grants now required a stamp. The free land of Georgia was no longer free.

Americans learned of the act several months before it was to take effect, time enough to organize a protest against Parliament's right to levy a tax on the colonies. Representatives of nine colonies met in New

York to discuss the form and substance of protest. Georgia sent no delegates to this congress, but several of her Commons House representatives notified the intercolonial meeting that the people of the colony would support whatever the congress resolved.[9]

In early November 1765, a gathering of townspeople in Savannah hanged the stamp master in effigy. A meeting at Machenry's Tavern followed, at which a group formed calling themselves Sons of Liberty. Willing to use extralegal methods for the protection of American rights, the Sons of Liberty unanimously agreed to threaten whomever arrived in Georgia as stampmaster. The resolve of the people, expressed in the streets and in taverns, led the lower house to vote their approval of the Stamp Act congress's petition of redress to king and Parliament. Thus far, events in Georgia developed along lines similar to other colonies. The people had displayed their disaffection for the Stamp Act with violence and threats against the stampmasters, the latter of whom often found their property destroyed.[10] Nowhere in the colonies were the stamps successfully distributed.[11] In Georgia, however, though no stampmaster had arrived, Governor Wright determined to enforce all acts of Parliament. Several merchants strengthened Wright's resolve by petitioning him to distribute the stamps so that their ships could leave port. A hostile crowd of people marched on the governor's house and demanded to know his intentions. He responded by lecturing them on the proper way to address their governor and dismissed them. Several hundred people then assembled to destroy the stamps. Wright gathered fifty men (most of whom were soldiers) and quickly removed the stamps to safe quarters and placed them under armed guard. The more rowdy and disrespectful the people became, the more determined was Wright to force the stamps upon them.[12]

George Argus, the stamp distributor, finally arrived on January 3, 1766, two months after the Stamp Act went into effect. An armed guard safely escorted Argus to the governor, who insisted he distribute the stamps. Argus complied, the port was opened, and sixty vessels legally were cleared. Rumors of a march on Savannah by backcountry farmers prompted Wright to remove the stamps from town to Fort George on Cockspur Island and then out to sea. Fearing an angry crowd, Argus fled for his safety into the countryside. As Edmund and Helen Morgan noted, Wright saved the stamps from destruction, but by removing them from circulation he fulfilled the wishes of most Georgians.[13]

Jonathan Bryan was conveniently absent from the council when the stamps arrived in December 1765. He remained absent the next two weeks, while the governor and council met regularly to adjudge the situation. Bryan returned to the council after the stamps were used to release the ships and then only to take his oath as a justice of the peace.[14] In the five months before repeal he attended only one council meeting, to hear the king's reaction to the Stamp Act disturbances.[15] Bryan's absence did not offend the governor and council, who approved his request for land on June 12, 1766, the very same day that news of the repeal of the Stamp Act arrived in Savannah.[16] His equivocation did not penalize him with the men of property who opposed the act, for none of them had yet mustered the courage to make a public display of their sentiments. Certainly many wealthy planters covertly supported the merchants' purchase of stamps, which allowed the ships to take the year's rice crop to market. Their support of or opposition to the Stamp Act remained a private matter. Public opposition to the act, according to the governor, could be found only among the lower classes. Their leadership, if they had any, remains unknown. As in several colonies, the common people were in the forefront of asserting American rights, while the men of property lagged behind waiting to see which way the political wind would blow.[17]

BRYAN BECOMES A PATRIOT

The controversy over American rights became in Georgia, as elsewhere, an intracolonial dispute between the branches of government. Not only was the power of Parliament questioned by Americans, but so was the respective rights of lower houses, upper houses, and governors. Colonial houses of assembly had come to view themselves as miniature parliaments, entitled to legislate fully within their jurisdiction.[18] The Stamp Act was opposed by the commons houses on the grounds that they, and not the British Parliament, held the sole right to raise a revenue from the citizenry. In defense of that prerogative, lower houses in virtually every colony became important centers for the expression of American rights. Not all Americans supported these assertions of power, even if they believed that the assemblies were constitutionally correct. In Georgia, for instance, the newly settled backcountry farmers became as opposed to low-country elites' domination of the Commons House as they were of British attempts at raising a revenue. Throughout the era of the American Revolution, the back-country remained wary of exchanging one master for another.[19] But until the eve of the American Revolution they played a small role in the battle that took place between the lower house on the one hand and the governor on the other. In that battle, the upper house briefly took a middle ground but soon fully supported the governor.[20]

After the Stamp Act, the next major issue to divide the governor from the lower house was selection of the colony's agent to Great Britain. In March 1767 the lower house peremptorily appointed Charles Garth as agent. The governor objected to this choice on two grounds. Since Garth also served as agent for South Carolina, Wright believed he could not fairly represent Georgia's interests. Second, Garth's selection by the lower house, according to the governor, made him the representative of that house and not the people of Georgia.[21] The upper house did not approve of Garth's selection but signed the tax bill that included provision for his salary and then appointed a committee to make a formal protest. Jonathan Bryan was not on that committee. Again he conveniently avoided taking issue on a question related to provincial rights. When the upper house appointed their own agent, William Knox, to "sollicit at the several Boards in Great Britain . . . in Support of the Rights and Priveledges of this House," Bryan joined neither the committee that addressed the governor on the need for this agent nor the committee that corresponded with Knox to direct his activities.[22] Again Bryan did not make known his position. He was in the midst of accumulating land on Cumberland Island and in the Altamaha River. Taking a public stand on sensitive political issues might jeopardize not only his receiving land grants but also government aid for establishing a southern port.

The dispute over Garth dissipated as another attempt at parliamentary taxation of the colonies rallied the defenders of American rights. In 1767 colonials learned of the Townshend Acts, a misguided attempt by the British ministry to raise a revenue to defray the cost of the colonies' civil list. Initially, public apathy prevented American radicals from instituting intercolonial action against the measures. Then the commons houses of Massachusetts and Virginia passed resolutions forwarded to other assemblies proclaiming the unconstitutionality of the duties and recommending that petitions be sent to the king for redress. Again, Americans argued that Parliament had no right to tax people unrepresented in their body. Charles Townshend, the king's minister of the exchequer, thought that Americans had objected only to internal taxes levied by Parliament and would have no reason to object to external taxes on goods shipped within the empire. Legislating for the empire had always been the prerogative of Parliament, so Townshend fully expected the colonists to accept the duties he proposed on colonial imports such as tea, paint, glass, and paper. Americans, however, were unwilling to accept any form of parliamentry taxation except for incidental revenue derived from the regulation of trade.[23]

The arrival of the Massachusetts circular letter in Georgia was publicized in the colony's newspaper by the Speaker of the lower house, Alexander Wylly. The circular was a statement of colonial rights produced by the Massachusetts Commons House that denied Parliament's right to lay taxes on Americans. The circular was sent to the colonial assemblies for endorsement, to present a united American front to Parliament. Wylly promised to present the circular to the Georgia Commons House when it met in November 1768. Governor Wright opened the legislative session with a speech warning the house that if the circular was considered he would prorogue the assembly.[24] Wright considered the circular insolent and intercolonial action to be conspiracy against the king. The Commons House believed it had the right to consider any measures it pleased and found no disrespect against the Crown in the circulars. Jonathan Bryan was on the upper-house committee that responded to the governor's opening address: its report made no mention of the circular or Wright's warning, presumably because this was an affair between the lower house and the governor.[25] Bryan's hand can be seen in the evasiveness of the upper house at taking a stand neither for nor against the governor in this matter.[26] He intended to place the upper house on a course independent of the governor, which isolated Wright in his opposition to the lower house. By occupying a middle ground and maintaining its independence, the upper house could lay claim to being a disinterested representative of Georgia's best interests. Only when the council ceased to take an independent line and followed the governor did the upper house lose any claim it had as a nonpartisan agency of the people.

The lower house postponed consideration of the Massachusetts circular until December 1768, after all other legislative business had been finished. The assembly then listened, debated, and resolved to remonstrate against the Townshend duties, as the circular had recommended. An unhappy Governor Wright prorogued the assembly.[27]

In August 1769, Georgians learned that the duties on paper, glass, and paints were likely to be repealed. Governor Wright doubted whether this would "answer any effectual purpose, . . . for the grievance complained of, whether real or imaginary, will still remain unredressed." It was too late for any new declaration affirming "the *right* of Parliament to tax Americans," and Wright was sure that force could not amend the situation. Americans, he wrote to the earl of Hillsborough, could never "be brought to change their sentiments or to acquiesce quietly under any tax or duty law." They were resolved to "observe strict economy and to manufacture everything they possibly can." The only solution, Wright believed, was "some alteration in the present constitution relative to America."[28]

The Savannah merchants agreed with Wright that repeal of the Townshend duties would not end American protests of parliamentry taxation. They also recognized that the general desire among the populace for an increase in American manufactures and a decrease in British imports constituted a threat to their economic interests. The merchants responded by instituting their own public opposition to the Townshend duties, intending to gain the leadership of the patriot movement, which they could then direct away from recourse to boycott. A group of Savannah merchants met on September 16, 1769, and passed their own nonimportation resolution. Citing the unconstitutionality of the Townshend Acts and the lack of specie in Georgia to pay the levied taxes, the merchants agreed not to import any item subject to British duties.[29]

Few Georgians were fooled by the claimed patriotism of the merchants. Three days after the merchants' meeting, a public meeting was held in Savannah with Jonathan Bryan in the chair. The public went beyond the insignificant resolve of the merchants, whose action boycotted only the importation of tea, and called for a general boycott of nonessential British goods. The "inhabitants of Georgia" had found themselves "reduced to the greatest distress and most abject condition" by the Townshend Acts and declared that "redress of these grievances have not answered the salutary purposes we intended." The people were "destitute of all hope of relief" and were resolved to take affirmative action to promote American manufactures and lessen colonial dependence upon English goods. At the meeting they agreed to encourage American production of cotton, flax, and wool, and to promote domestic spinning and weaving. In addition, they resolved to boycott all goods from England except those necessary for domestic manufacturing, drugs, books and pamphlets, "hardware of all sorts," guns and their accoutrements, inexpensive linen and shoes, salt, and "goods necessary for the Indian Trade." Furthermore, they determined to end the importation of slaves from Great Britain, the West Indies, and Africa. Nothing would be purchased from any merchant who refused to abide by the nonimportation resolves.[30]

When the governor opened the new assembly a few weeks later, no mention was made of the nonimportation meetings nor of the prorogation in January. Wright addressed the assembly on the need of legislation for increased government control of the Indian trade and for the protection of Indians in their land and hunting grounds. Furthermore, he informed the assembly of the king's suspension of several pieces of colonial legislation. These would have to be redrawn to the Crown's instructions. Finally, Wright mentioned the king's intention to reduce the "Taxes or Duties on America."[31] Jonathan Bryan and Grey Elliott were selected as a committee to respond to the governor's message. Their address affirmed that the upper house would support the governor "with peculiar chearfullness . . . in the framing of such Acts as may . . . remedy those Evils, and for the future prevent the too well founded, and repeated Complaints of the Indians." They also agreed to attend to a new law governing slaves, one that would meet with the approbation of the king.[32] As far as the "future Intentions of our most gracious Sovereign, and his present Ministers, with Respect to America," the upper house was pleased by "the taking off several Duties already laid on by Parliament" and was grateful for the "unsolicited, Encouragement given to the Productions of the Colonies" by bounties. The upper house was hopeful that "redress of such real Grievances as America may labour under, on the one Hand, and a Pursuit of Prudent, dutiful and cautious Measures by the Colonies on the other, will, under God, be the means of healing and composing those Differences which have unhappily and already too long subsisted."[33] This respectful reply to the governor and the king should have offended no one but those who believed that subjects should not petition their king. It was the last time that the upper house attempted a course independent of the governor. For in December 1769, the king, upon hearing from Wright that Bryan had chaired the September nonimportation meeting, suspended Bryan from his seat on the council.[34]

Without Jonathan Bryan the council became completely subservient to the governor. Lost was the one person willing to guide the council on an independent course. For the remainder of the colonial period the council gave to the governor unwavering support, but at a price. The council no longer had any claim as a viable representative of colonial interests. The dynamic council of 1755, which had successfully deposed a governor, was no more.[35]

Bryan's suspension made him a hero to many in Georgia and South Carolina. On March 12, 1770, a notice appeared in the *Georgia Gazette* from the Union Society, a social group of artisans and mechanics who accepted as members some professionals and planters. The society announced in bold letters its gratitude to the suspended councillor: "Unanimously Resolved That a handsome PIECE OF PLATE be presented to JONATHAN BRYAN, Esquire, as a token of the Sense we entertain of his *upright* Conduct as worthy Member of this Society, a real Friend of his Country in general, and the Province of Georgia in particular."[36] The *Gazette*'s reporter lauded Bryan as "a Gentleman of Revolution principles, and a person who has been greatly instrumental in the settlement of this colony."[37] The *South Carolina Gazette* also reported Bryan's suspension, asserting that the king himself and not the governor had ordered his removal: "We are assured, that Mr. Bryan has not betrayed the least sign of uneasiness upon the occasion: But as he always appeared, and was a staunch and jealous friend to liberty, upon constitutional principles, some there are, who cannot avoid looking upon this suspension as a Hint, what men of his stamp have to look for."[38]

Bryan, indeed, was not shaken, for the financial rewards of his patriotic politics were quickly forthcoming. In late March 1770, only a few weeks after news of his suspension reached Georgia, the Commons House of Assembly voted to build a road connecting the backcountry town of Queensborough with Bryan's Cowpen, which had been connected to Savannah by the road mentioned earlier that had been built by the colony in the 1760s. The road would lead all traffic to Savannah for one hundred miles along the Great Ogeechee to Bryan's doorstep, a location which could provide great rewards for the entrepreneur.[39]

Bryan's reputation as a friend of the opposition movement continued to grow. In June the "General Committee" in charge of nonimportation in South Carolina condemned the "People of the Colony of Georgia" for acting "a most *singularly infamous* Part . . . for the Preservation of *American Rights* . . . basely [taking] every possible Advantage of the more virtuous Colonies." Because of their failure to enforce non-importation, Georgia along with Rhode Island would "be *amputated* from the Rest of their Brethren" and no commercial intercourse would be carried on with either colony. The Carolina patriots made sure to mention that there were patriots below the Savannah true to the cause and let it be known that their condemnation excepted "Jonathan Bryan, and a few other Individuals."[40] And in July, the Club No. 45, "consisting of a great Body of the principal Inhabitants" of Charlestown, met at "Messrs. Dillon and Gray's Tavern, where an elegant Entertainment is provided for them," in celebration of the erection of a statue of William Pitt. Forty-five toasts were made on this festive occasion, to the ideas and men in America and England that spoke for American rights. Only one toast was directed to a Georgian—Jonathan Bryan.[41]

BRYAN IN THE HOUSE

The purpose of the public meeting chaired by Bryan after repeal of the Townshend Acts was to keep alive the spirit of dissent in the absence of overt acts of British tyranny. By promoting American manufactures, Bryan and his cohorts hoped to lessen the bonds of colonial dependence on Great Britain and create pride in locally made products. Once the duties were removed, however, the nonimportation movement fell apart, as did most efforts to promote colonial manufacturing. In each colony arose a small group of self-proclaimed watchdogs over American rights, who stood intent on diminishing British interference in colonial life. The removal of the duties left these men without a grievance to rally public opinion, forcing them to look elsewhere for examples of British tyranny. In most colonies these cadres formed "opposition" factions in the lower houses. Jonathan Bryan joined Georgia's opposition faction in the Commons House in 1771, when he won a special election to fill a vacant seat representing Little Ogeechee District. In two subsequent terms Bryan represented the town of Savannah.[42]

Governor Wright obliged the opposition with an issue to keep alive the specter of British tyranny by rejecting the house choice of Noble W. Jones as Speaker. The precise reason for Jones's rejection remains unknown, though it must have resulted from his opposition politics. The

governor ordered the house to select another Speaker. To Wright's cha-
grin, the house reelected Jones and declared the governor's action a
breach of Commons House privilege. Wright responded by dissolving
the assembly in April 1771.[43] For the next two years house business
came to a near standstill as the opposition faction refused to budge on
the right of the Commons House to select its own Speaker.

Governor Wright took a leave of absence in 1771 to visit London.
James Habersham, the colony's senior member of the council, performed duties as acting governor. Habersham informed Wright that the
opposition faction treated him coolly, "except Mr. Bryan . . . and we
both carefully avoid entering into Politics." In late November 1772 these
two old friends dined together at Habersham's. Bryan "dropt a Hint,
that [Habersham] should meet with no Trouble in [his] Administration." But the acting governor believed otherwise. He thought "these
Hints may be thrown out as a Pleasing Bait, and I cannot but consider
them, as tending to flatter me at [Governor Wright's] Expense."[44]

Habersham called a new assembly together, and the house promptly
selected Noble W. Jones, as Speaker. The acting governor rejected their
selection. The Commons House again selected Jones and again
Habersham rejected him. The third time Jones was elected he decided
to decline the post. Archibald Bulloch was chosen in his place. Habersham then called the assembly into session, and the house delivered an
amiable address to the governor. Later, Habersham perused the house
journal and learned that Bulloch was chosen only after Jones had declined election. The acting governor threatened the assembly that if the
third election was not expunged from the Commons House journal he
would dissolve the assembly. The house stood its ground and was prorogued. Public business again came to a standstill.[45]

The assembly was not called again to meet until December 1772,
when Jones once again was selected Speaker. He declined the office,
and William Young was chosen in his place. This time Habersham did
not interpret Jones's election as an insult to the Crown and to his office,
so he did not dissolve the assembly.[46] On the contrary, he hoped to
work with the new assembly and expedite public business. A dinner
held at the court house in honour of the king's birthday attracted all of
the representatives except "Doctor [Noble W.] Jones, Bryan, Bulloch,
& [William] Leconte," who refused to participate and honor the king.
For Habersham, "the day was spent with great good Humour," because he believed the celebration's turnout of a majority of representa-

tives an omen of good things to come.[47] He was correct. The opposition faction was again without an issue and could not command a majority in the new assembly. Bryan, Jones, Le Conte, and their confederates were hard pressed to promulgate the spirit of dissent in 1773.

The core of the opposition faction in the House of Commons was correctly identified by Habersham: Bryan, Jones, and Le Conte. Their allies included David Zubly, Benjamin Andrew, Thomas Carter, John Baker, Josiah Powell, and Henry Bourquine. Others, who were not a part of the Commons House in 1773 but who were in league with these men before and during the American Revolution were Archibald Bulloch, John Morel, John Houstoun, and Richard Wylly. Morel and Houstoun were sons-in-law to Bryan, and Wylly became one in future years. Although outnumbered in the Commons House of 1773 by the governor's men, the opposition faction stood steadfast in purpose and often attracted enough support to prevail on select issues.

Searching for an issue to rally support, the opposition pushed through a bill that required the recording and publication of representatives' votes in the *Georgia Gazette*. The intention of the bill's sponsors was to make representatives accountable for their political positions. This "republican" measure not only brought the workings of government closer to the people, it forced representatives to cast their votes in full knowledge that the public could construe their actions as indicating support for or opposition to the British administration of the American colonies.[48] Analysis of these votes reveals the nature of factionalism in the 1773 Commons House, one year before the opposition was provided with overt acts of British tyranny to rally public support. On the one hand a small group of men devoted themselves to combating the governor, and by extension, the British government. On the other hand a faction faithfully supported the governor and his policies. The governor symbolized British tyranny to the opposition; to his supporters he represented all that was good in the colony's relationship with the mother country.

Consistency of purpose in both the opposition and among the governor's men was evident on several house votes. The same men who voted against repairing the governor's mansion also opposed sending a delegation to welcome Wright upon his return to Georgia. Of twenty-one assemblymen who voted on both issues, only four split their votes. A similar pattern was evident on a resolution to offer thanks to George Galphin and Alexander McGillivray, for their role in negotiating a recent cession of land from the Creek and Cherokee Indians. The resolution was intended to diminish Wright's contribution in obtaining the land. Of the nineteen men who voted on this resolution and whether to repair the governor's mansion and/or welcome Wright on his return to Georgia, only four were inconsistent in their opposition to or support of the governor.[49]

The lines of faction also were drawn on a measure to appoint Grey Elliott as colonial agent to Great Britain. Elliott was a member of the colony's council, a leading upholder of the king and Parliament's prerogative in Georgia, and clearly the governor's man. All of the governor's faction in the assembly supported Elliott's candidacy. Two members of the opposition faction broke ranks and supported Elliott as well. Bryan, Jones, and Le Conte, however, the core of the opposition faction, opposed Elliott's nomination and were joined by additional opposition men in the final vote on his nomination.[50]

Representatives did not always divide strictly along factional lines. When the Commons House voted on whether to hold an election for the seat of the departing William Jones, three of the opposition faction joined the governor's men in negating the measure. Also, in a disputed election in the Sea Island District, Samuel Farley prevailed over Henry Yonge, a strong supporter of Wright, by winning several votes from the governor's faction.[51] Thus, personal loyalties and friendship could preempt straight party-line voting.

On some issues representatives voted in no set pattern. They supported or opposed the building of a new jail, the freeing of a prisoner, or the clearing of Savannah River obstructions based on judgments that had little or nothing to do with the governor or American rights. There were even large majorities on some issues. A vote to ban the practice of night hunting passed the Commons House eighteen to six.[52] All of the governor's faction supported the measure as did half of the opposition. The ban was intended to prevent "the dangerous practice of hunting by fire light in the night under pretence of killing Deer . . . by means whereof Cattle are frequently destroyed to the manifest injury of the owners."[53] The six opponents of the ban displayed great political foresight in the casting of their vote on this ostensibly nonfactional issue. Elite lower-house representatives were unhappy with the "common" practice of nocturnal hunting, whereby armed men roamed the countryside in search of food. Cattle and other property were fair game when the sun went down.[54] Many lived in fear of the forest fires caused by this manner of hunting. Elite backcountry representatives supported the ban, even though night hunting was an important means of obtaining food for their constitutents. Jonathan Bryan, as owner of the colony's most famous cowpen, ostensibly had every reason to support the ban yet he did not. Very much aware of the patriot movement's need to obtain political support out-of-doors, Bryan and five other members of his faction voted against the ban to court the great mass of white men who had populated the backcountry and whose support was necessary in the dispute with Great Britain.

It is difficult to predict a man's loyalties in the Revolution based upon his political stance two years before the outbreak of warfare in 1775. The Georgia Commons House of Assembly in 1773 was almost evenly divided between men who later supported independence and those who remained loyal to the king.[55] But the division between rebels and Tories in 1775 does not exactly replicate the factional division in the Commons House in 1773. Several future leaders of the American Revolution in Georgia were consistent supporters of the governor in 1773. John Adam Treutlen, Joseph Clay, and James Houstoun all played substantial if not major roles in the American Revolution.[56] As late as 1773, however, they had not altered their politics from dutiful loyalty to the governor. Clay, for instance, was hostile to the leveling tendencies of many patriots, but he risked becoming a rebel when war loomed on the horizon. Whether from principle or self-interest, he and others joined the patriots when there was no turning back—and they were welcomed into the movement for the prestige and skills they brought: each of the above-named men attained high political office in the new government. The lateness with which they made their transformation indicates that principle alone did not spur them, otherwise they would have stood up for American rights long before. More likely, they determined that the patriots eventually would prevail; better to be on the winning side with men whose political agenda did not reflect their own than on the losing side with men with whom they would have been more comfortable.

Other loyal supporters of the governor in the Commons House of 1773 also made the transition to the patriot side, though in a far less dramatic fashion than the above-mentioned rebels. Joseph Law, Stephen Millen, John Stirk, Thomas Young, and Thomas Netherclift were all strong supporters of the governor in 1773. Once the war began they juggled themselves on the fence of neutrality and remained there out of timidity or self-interest for as long as they could. Their initial hostility to the patriots did not lead them to fight for their king nor leave the colony like other Tories. Some made their peace with the patriots during the war; others had their property confiscated by the rebels but eventually regained their estates, ostensibly by not having taken an active role against the patriots.

Another group of men in the Commons House supported the governor consistently in 1773 and remained loyal to the king in 1776. This group included Sir Patrick Houstoun, John Jamieson, John Simpson, Henry Yonge, and William Young.[57] These men were not insensitive to the rights of commons houses, but their loyalty to the king, Great Britain, and the governor superseded all questions of constitutional theory or right. An important gentleman worth mentioning in this regard, who was not a member of the house in 1773 but a steadfast defender of the rights of American commons houses, was John J. Zubly, pastor of the Independent Presbyterian Church in Savannah. One of the great pamphleteers of the American Revolution, in the final determination Zubly could not make war against his king, and though he offered to take an oath to Georgia during the Revolution the rebels considered him a Tory.[58] Zubly's son David was a prominent member of the opposition faction in the house, but in April 1776 he, too, declared for the king. Other elites who initially gave their support to the American cause in Georgia but remained loyal to the king included Basil Cowper and George McIntosh.

The political activities of the opposition movement in the Georgia Commons House illustrate an important point about the nature of factionalism in 1773: the opposition faction lacked any positive program of action. Ever since the repeal of the Townshend duties in 1771, opponents of royal government were without a grievance to excite popular support. Only the duty on tea had not been repealed by Parliament, and the public was little interested in exerting themselves against the injustice of a single taxed item. The opposition was forced to adopt a policy of obstructionism. Thus when a motion was offered "that the House do resolve to provide for the expenses of government and the debts due" from the previous fiscal year, most of the governor's men supported the measure, while his opponents voted in the negative. The opposition had little reason to vote against settling the government's debts and the new year's expenses, except to display hostility toward the governor and the British administration he represented.[59]

We will never known all the personal reasons that drove Bryan and others to maintain their hostility to British interests in the early 1770s when there existed no overt examples of tyranny. These men were not satisfied to wait until Britain made another attempt to tax the colonies. Their emphatic opposition to Wright could be interpreted as a personal vendetta if not for the existence of similar cadres of patriots devoted to American rights in other colonies. Bryan, Le Conte, Jones, and their cohorts expected British tyranny to surface again, and they had every intention of being ready for it. They united in opposition to usurpation of American rights, but they also offered a positive program to strengthen the colonies: the development of the domestic economy through boycott of British goods and promotion of American manufactures. Alexander Hamilton noted in late 1774, that "if by the necessity of the thing, manufactures should once be established and take root among us, they will pave the way . . . to the future grandeur and glory of America, and by lessening its need of external commerce, will render it still securer against the encroachments of tyranny."[60] The opposition hoped to create a domestic economy that was not colonial but similar to that of nation-states. This was an arrogation of the mother country's traditional role as supplier of finished goods to her colonies in exchange for raw materials and staples. Whether or not the opposition realized the transforming power of their vigil, their defense of American rights was nothing less than an assertion of a new status for the colonies. They challenged the very concept of mercantilism on which the imperial connection was based. In effect, they argued that they were no longer colonials and that strict limitations existed on the power of the mother country. These colonists recognized and accepted their tie to Great Britain, but they rejected the mercantile proposition that colonies functioned in complete subservience to the mother country. British imperialists were right: in the traditional context of empire, the mother country made all the rules; the privileges a colony enjoyed could never conflict with the needs of the mother country. The advocacy of American rights and American manufactures was an act of rebellion, not of violence, but of the mind. In making themselves watchdogs over British tyranny, the opposition established themselves as the defenders of geographic entities that enjoyed legitimacy separate from Great Britain.

Jonathan Bryan, like his compatriots, had no idea that the road they followed led to independence and revolution. They knew that the old relationship could not return, but they did not anticipate the violence or the nature of the break with Great Britain.

6

DREAMS OF EMPIRE
Jonathan Bryan and the Creek Indians

Despite the quick development of Georgia's low country into rice plantations, the colony remained a frontier on the eve of the American Revolution.[1] New settlers flooded into the upcountry and practiced subsistence agriculture on a strip of land between the Savannah and Ogeechee rivers. This settlement extended approximately 100 miles to the northwest of Savannah. The vast stretch of territory to the west, south, and north, which would one day comprise most of the states of Georgia and Alabama, was the property of the Creek Confederacy. Also residing near the upcountry Georgia settlements were the Cherokees, with villages about 150 miles northwest of Augusta.

The close proximity of Indian, Afro-American, and Euramerican peoples remained one of the most prominent features of the region. The British colonial governments were preoccupied with keeping their formidable Indian neighbors at peace and in maintaining security over their Afro-American population. In the 1770s, the latter was more easily accomplished. Most of the black slaves were located on low country plantations. Their confinement along the coast made them relatively easy to manage. Slave patrols inhibited insurrection, and with St. Augustine in the hands of the British since 1763, there were few places to which runaways could flee. Collusion between blacks and Indians was not a serious problem for whites, as it had been before the Seven Years' War and would become again after the American Revolution. The major problem facing Georgia's government in the decade after the end of the Seven Years' War was regulating the interactions of Indians and whites.

Governor Wright and the Superintendent of Indian Affairs, John Stuart, worked diligently to contain abuses of the Indians by traders and to prevent white settlers from illegally squatting on Indian land. Wright and other officers of empire hoped to obtain new land cessions but not by force of arms. The Indians were deemed too powerful to conquer. The British coordinated their efforts and used connivance, negotiation, and extortion to fulfill their ends. They became much more adept in acting as a unit: the governors of Georgia, South Carolina, and the Floridas often were instructed by Whitehall to cooperate, particularly with the Indian Affairs superintendent. The Indians, too, attempted to work together to resist growing British power. The Cherokees and Creeks, and the Creeks and Choctaws, made significant attempts to overcome their ancient differences, but astute British diplomats helped keep them apart.

Ironically, as Great Britain increased its power over the diplomatic affairs of its colonies, the ties that bound the white colonists to the mother country began to fray. The patriot movement, in which Jonathan Bryan was a prominent member, became a potential fifth column. As he had done so often in his career, Bryan tied his political activity to his personal interest in accumulating large tracts of land. Only this time, instead of working with the powers that be, he formulated schemes with the potential of shaking royal government in Georgia to its core.

Bryan knew that for as long as the current administration was in power he would not receive any new parcels of land in Georgia from the public domain. He turned his attention to Florida and asked Henry Laurens to represent his interests for land during the latter's trip to London.[2] Florida's attractiveness lay in its superb land, excellent coasts, and sparsity of white settlers. A few large land grants had been made to individuals, and the speculative fever for Florida land quickly reached the highest levels of British government.[3] Bryan's politics precluded that he could ever win government favor, and if Henry Laurens could not obtain the land, it was likely that other prominent colonials would not receive grants either. Bryan logically assumed, given his own history of obtaining valuable land through his council position, that only those close to the reins of power in Whitehall would receive large grants in Florida. Thus Bryan determined that if he could not get land from London he would have to find another way. He turned to the Creek Indians.

For three years Bryan periodically traveled to Creek towns to obtain signatures on a lease of land in Florida. His fellow Georgians were unaware of what he offered the Indians, and many members of the house disapproved of his activities. As a leading obstructionist of royal government, his opponents could only conclude that Bryan was making an arrangement with the Indians that must bode ill for Georgia. When Bryan embarked on one of his trips to the Indians in July 1773, several members of the Commons House expressed disdain for his behavior. They were irate that Bryan had "some days since absented himself from this House without leave and having Yesterday Morning in a Contemptuous Manner departed from this Province without asking leave or even making his Intentions known." He was expelled from the house by a vote of eighteen to six.[4]

Over the next few years bits and pieces of Bryan's schemes came to public light. The general public learned that the Creek Indians had leased to Bryan an extremely large tract of land in Florida. Many assumed that this was but one of many schemes by white frontiersmen to defraud Indians of their land. Several British government officials also suspected fraud, but additionally, they had reason to believe that Bryan was trying to create a haven for disaffected Georgians outside the reach of the royal government. None of them apparently suspected that Bryan's machinations were not only meant to serve his own interests but to help the Creek Indians alter the balance of power on the southern frontier, which since the Seven Years' War had begun to tip heavily against them.

TWO CESSIONS OF LAND: ONE TO GEORGIA AND ONE TO BRYAN

The Creeks made up the most powerful Indian nation on the southern frontier. "For many generations," Verner W. Crane noted, they filled "the role of the custodians of the wilderness balance of power in the South."[5] They traded and conducted diplomatic relations with all three European powers, collecting presents from each. While the Creeks used the Europeans for their own ends in their ancient rivalries with neighboring aborigines, they, like other southern Indians, fell into a growing reliance upon European textiles, tools, weaponry, and alcohol. Forced into adjusting their lifestyles and diplomacy to maintain the flow of trade, they formulated strategies to obtain European commodities while keeping the imperial powers at bay. The Creeks recognized the expediency of "entangling alliances with none." By playing the Europeans against one another they kept their trade and their land.[6]

The conclusion of the Seven Years' War threatened their position. With the removal of France from Louisiana and Spain from Florida, the Creeks found themselves falling into a position of dependence upon

Great Britain. They could no longer set the Europeans against one another. Indeed, for the Creeks it was a world turned upside down. They had to seek new ways to procure trade, to lessen their dependence upon the British for European textiles, tools, and weaponry.

The British wasted no time flaunting their new position of strength. Large cessions of land in 1763 and 1773 revealed Indian weakness. The cession of 1773, known as the New Purchase, was particularly galling to the Creeks. Several Indian traders parlayed a Cherokee debt into a grant of land in what is now northern Georgia. Governor James Wright persuaded the traders to transfer the cession to the royal government. The Creeks claimed the Cherokee ceded land as their own but Wright was not to be denied the addition of so large a territory to his colony. He intimidated the Creeks into approving the cession, thus sparking the outbreak of warfare between the Indians and white settlers.[7]

To induce the Creeks into making peace, Governor Wright and Superintendent of Indian Affairs John Stuart closed the trade of Georgia, South Carolina, and East and West Florida. Wright helped formulate the British policy of withholding trade to force concessions. In November 1772 he urged the secretary of state for the colonies, the earl of Hillsborough, to send "Instructions to the several Governors to Unite and Co-operate in a partial, or total Stoppage of the whole Trade, as the Conduct and Behaviour of the Indians in any Particular Province may require." Since the Indians can "have no Supply or can have any of any Consequence but from the English, they may be reduced at any time to comply with all reasonable Demands, and do full Justice by a Stoppage of the Trade, or even by a Stoppage of Arms and Ammunition, as Occasion may require." The lieutenant governor of East Florida, John Moultrie, echoed Wright's sentiments, *"The Creeks in general know that it is from us alone* they can be well supplied with arms, ammunition, and other necessaries."[8]

Wright told the Creeks that they must accept the New Purchase cession or face dire consequences:

> the trade with you will be stopped from all parts, the people all round you now belong to the Great King George, and they will all take part with us and none of them will supply you with anything. And what can you do? Can you make guns, gunpowder, bullets, glasses, paint and clothing etc.? You know you cannot make these

things, and where can you get them if you quarell with the white
people and how will your women and children get supplied with
clothes, beads, glasses, scissors and all other things they now use
and cannot do without?[9]

Wright's threat did not prevent Creeks from attacking white settlers,
but the closing of the trade had its intended effect. George Galphin
reported that when a parcel of goods illegally arrived among the Upper
Creeks, "the Indians were flocking from all Quarters to Purchase
the . . . Goods." David Taitt reported that the Upper Creeks blamed
the Lower Creeks for all the "Mischief" against the Georgians and
begged "that they might have their Traders and pack Horses back to
their Nation, as they were now very poor for Goods, and the hunting
Season near at hand."[10] John Stuart noted that hunting was not the
Indians' only concern: "The Creeks are ill-provided with ammunition
and the Choctaws still continue a rancorous war against them . . . so
that I think it is probable that [the Creeks] will endeavor to make up
matters with us."[11]

The Creeks made peace with the British and realized that new
sources of trade had to be found. Thus they turned to a person whom
at first glance might be perceived as an unlikely source of help:
Jonathan Bryan. At the conclusion of the congress in Savannah where
the Creeks signed the treaty that reconfirmed the New Purchase cession, an agreement between the Creeks and Bryan was brought to public attention. In exchange for a ninety-nine-year lease to approximately
four million to five million acres in what is now northern Florida,
Bryan had offered the Creeks £100 in presents and a yearly rent of 100
bushels of corn. Contemporaries and historians have been unable to
fathom why the Creeks parted with so much to get so little. The transaction has been explained as a monumental fraud: Bryan must have
used alcohol to obtain the Indians' approval.[12] But the agreement between the Creeks and Bryan was far more complex than previously
realized. The Indians had much to gain. Their arrangement with Bryan
provides a key for unlocking the rationale, logic, and purpose of Creek
diplomacy between the end of the Seven Years' War and the advent of
the American Revolution. It also illustrates how far Jonathan Bryan
was willing to go to obtain the land necessary for perpetuating family
power.

Contemporaries' and historians' knowledge of the leases centered upon the testimony provided by a few Creeks in response to the governor's query. The executive council listened to and recorded the Indians' testimony, copies of which were printed in the *Georgia Gazette*. They reported that several of the Creeks "shewed much horror" when the lease was produced by Wright. The Creek headmen Taleeche, speaking for the other Indians, explained to the governor and his council that Bryan had come to him with some white men and an Indian woman named Maria, who served as interpreter. Bryan told the Indians that he desired some land to "settle a cow-pen and to raise some corn upon, [and] that he meant to come and live among them and settle a store." Taleeche noted "that he also understood the paper contained a good talk to the Nation. That he and the rest of them . . . put their marks to it, but told Mr. Bryan" that it had to be confirmed by the whole nation. This had yet to be done.[13]

Governor Wright also procured a deposition on the lease from Jacob Moniac, an interpreter to the Upper Creeks employed by John Stuart. Moniac testified that Maria had come to him the day after the congress in Savannah because she had been accused "by the Chiefs and Headmen of the Nation to have interpreted to have given away a large body of land," and she wished to be excused of all culpability. Maria asked Bryan to repeat to Moniac exactly what he had told her to say to the Indians in regard to the lease. Bryan replied that he had requested a body of land and the Indians asked him where he would have it, on the Altamaha or the Oconee. Bryan told them, "I do not want it in this province for the Governor of Georgia and I do not agree." It had to be at "a place where he could bring great boats up." The Indians then asked him what he wanted it for, and he told them "he had a great stock of cattle, and if they would give him a piece of land at the Appalachee Old Fields or the mouth of the Flint River, he would come and live amongst them and make a town larger than Savannah, and would get a great number of friends to come and live with him; but if it was not agreeable to the whole nation, men, women, and children, he would not insist upon it." Bryan then told Maria in the presence of Moniac, that "as long as I find it disagreeable to the whole Nation, I shall not trouble myself any more about it." Further he added, "the land is your own, it neither belongs to the King nor the Governor and you may do what you please with it."[14]

Bryan responded to the reports of the executive council in a subsequent issue of the *Gazette*. He questioned the motives of the government's officers, for if they had "really been very anxious to have ascertained the truth, nothing at that time was more practical." He was in town "almost every day when the lease was in agitation" but had not been called to the Congress, "whereby the matter might have been amicably understood and explained."

Bryan asserted that the Indians' apparent hostility to the lease was a staged reaction to the governor's proddings. They acted as they did out of "their tenderness and regard for me, fearing, from what was said, that I should suffer as an individual, if the lease was not destroyed." If anyone "should doubt the reality of this assertion . . . a little time will prove the truth of what I have said, and the honour, attachment, and steadiness of the Indians, in this particular."[15] He did not keep the public waiting. On their way home from Savannah, Taleeche visited Bryan at his cowpen and "drank a glass of wine" while twenty-one Creek headmen signed another lease for the very same land in Florida. Two weeks later, the *Gazette* reported that "Jonathan Bryan, Esq. accompanied by some Gentlemen from Carolina and this province, set out from his Cowpen on the Ogeechee, to take possession of a body of land at Lochua and the Appelache Old Fields, lately leased to him by the Chiefs, Headmen, and Warriors of the Upper and Lower Towns of the Creek Nation. They were escorted by two Headmen and a number of Indians deputed by the Nation to ascertain the boundaries, and to put him in possession of the premises."[16]

"BRYAN MUST CERTAINLY BE MAD"

The political intrigue over Bryan's lease had only just begun. It extended through three colonies, included two governors, a former governor, two chief justices and an associate justice, the Indian superintendent and his assistants, the councils of East Florida and Georgia, the secretary of state for the American Department in Great Britain, and other officers of empire. The episode was shrouded in confusion by the sheer number of interests involved. Jonathan Bryan utilized a lifetime of experience to attempt to build a new society south of Georgia, and in doing so he offered the Creek Nation the means by which they could attempt to counteract British power on the southern frontier. Bryan's own politics led him to undermine the British position. The king had expelled him from Georgia's executive council in

1770, and then he was expelled from the Commons House in 1773. Bryan had little political future in royalist Georgia. The opportunity to counter British strategy by supporting the Creeks must have appealed to Bryan as a wonderful method of revenge. Furthermore, he could elevate his own political status by opening a new area for settlement between the two Floridas, independent of British control. Thus, in exchange for a large tract of land, Bryan offered to provide the Creeks a steady supply of trade goods, "of a better quality and at a cheaper rate than any they were furnished at present."[17] Never again would the Creeks have to submit abjectly to the extortionist closing of their trade by British officials.

The persons who should have been in the best position to understand Indian motivations in leasing land to Jonathan Bryan were John Stuart and his assistant, David Taitt. Stuart "did not fail to upbraid [the Creeks] for having, contrary to their repeated promises and agreements, entered into negotiation of this sort with private persons and given away for such a trifling consideration a very large tract of country." He could not comprehend Creek behavior, for "upon every [other] occasion they either absolutely refused or with the utmost reluctancy ceded such small . . . parcels of land as had been asked of them by his Majesty's orders."[18] David Taitt at first thought Bryan's activities were meant as a "Bravado to perplex the Governor [of Georgia] but now I see that he is in earnest and it will certainly be the Cause of an Indian War." Taitt could do nothing to stop the cession until spring, when the men returned from their hunting. If war came, he warned Stuart, it would be worse for Georgia than the year before because the Indians now knew the white people's weakness. He adamantly told his superior: "Mr. Bryan must certainly be mad."[19]

Taitt, like Stuart, was unaware of the diplomacy involved in the Indians' cession. They found Indian behavior inscrutable. Both the Indian superintendent and his assistant sincerely wished to protect the Indians from land-hungry settlers, but they were utterly mystified by Bryan's actions. They were convinced that Bryan must have plied the Indians with alcohol to obtain their signatures. Stuart deluded himself into thinking that only seven or eight Creeks had signed Bryan's lease, even though he had been present at the congress and seen that twice as many had done so.[20]

To explain why the Indians signed another lease, historians have turned to testimony given by Samuel Thomas, John Stuart's interpreter to the Lower Creeks. Thomas informed Stuart's assistant that Bryan obtained the second lease by plying the Indians with alcohol. One Creek became so drunk, Thomas reported, that he fell ill and died. His relatives "blame[d] the White people for his death." Thomas's account provided evidence to both the Indian superintendent and historians that Bryan resorted to underhanded methods to obtain the lease.[21] But this second-hand report was highly unreliable and less an indictment of Bryan than an expression of Thomas's own self-interest. Thomas had informed his superiors that the Creeks were unwilling to grant land to Bryan but could be persuaded to make a cession to Georgia in exchange for the lives of Houmachta and Sophia, two Creek Indians who had murdered whites and whose execution was demanded by the government of Georgia. It was highly unlikely that the Creeks proposed this exchange and even more unlikely that the nation would have approved it. The idea originated with Governor Wright, who had already proposed it to his council as a point from which to begin bargaining with the Creeks for their land. Apparently, Wright induced Thomas to relay the proposal to the Indian superintendent as the Creeks' own offer: Stuart vehemently opposed Wright's efforts to press the Indians for land.[22]

Thomas's unreliability as a witness is evident on other particulars related to Bryan's lease. The Indians would not disclose to him the location of the land leased to Bryan. Furthermore, the Creeks never told Thomas why they had returned to Bryan's plantation. He was aware that Bryan had "sent for the Indians to his plantation . . . and those that were gone past were sent for back."[23] But Thomas, Stuart, and other British officials never thought of asking the Indians *why* they had voluntarily returned to Bryan's plantation, enjoyed his hospitality, and signed another lease, especially since it was alleged that he had insidiously deceived them on previous occasions.

Governor Wright orchestrated events at the Savannah congress to implicate Jonathan Bryan in fraud. He much preferred white expansion into his colony than into Florida. Wright called his council together at the conclusion of the Savannah congress and convinced them that if the Creeks were "disposed to give Lands [to Bryan] on that Ocassion, [they should] try to get the Lands to the Ocone River" for Georgia.[24] He desired new land for the colony for several reasons. Indian hostility and bureaucratic entanglements forestalled white settlement of the recently obtained New Purchase cession. Growing public dissatisfaction with the government's land policies led Wright to proclaim that tracts would be offered for sale as soon as possible, but the governor was too late to stem public disenchantment. It had recently been disclosed that virtually all of the southern portion of the New Purchase cession was useful only for grazing horses and cattle. Of 674,000 acres in this section only 31,000 acres, less than 5 percent, were deemed "plantable" by the council.[25] Governor Wright hoped to calm public discontent by obtaining a new cession of land. An urgency was added to his endeavor by the general public dismay over British reaction to the Boston Tea Party: the Coercive Acts made few friends for royal government in Georgia. In the winter of 1774–75, Wright not only needed to appease the populace but had to prevent Bryan from luring Georgians into removing to his leased land in Florida. The land Bryan procured from the Creeks was believed by the recently appointed governor of East Florida, Patrick Tonyn, and others to be the richest in America.[26] Georgia's governor feared, according to East Florida's chief justice, William Drayton, that Bryan's success would not only foil the attempt to settle the Oconee but would result in the depopulation of Georgia.[27]

Wright could do little to stop Bryan. That unenviable task fell on the shoulders of Patrick Tonyn, who arrived in the colony with little understanding of the colony, Indians, politics, or law. Tonyn knew of Bryan as a notorious opponent of royal government who could only harm Crown interests. His goal was to stop Bryan, and in the process to gain the ceded land for the Crown, thereby earning plaudits for his efforts in London. Tonyn wrote the earl of Dartmouth, secretary of state for the American Department, requesting that "every means may be thought of and adopted, every power of Law forcibly asserted, severely to reprehend Jonathan Bryan." He asked Dartmouth whether Bryan could be seized for trespassing on the king's land and assessed a fine; if Bryan succeeded in taking possession, he wished to know how to remove him. Tonyn asserted that land which the Creeks leased to Bryan belonged to the king because "the savages or Indians I hold in this view only. As wolves or wild beasts in a forest. They have no right in any land, the Spaniards called the Province of East Florida, which was given up at the treaty of peace to Great Britain."[28] Tonyn's assessment of the Indian right to land was technically incorrect. The British government recognized by treaty that it possessed only strips of land along the Florida coast; the Creeks retained ownership of the interior.[29] Despite Tonyn's ignorance of the treaties affecting his province and his prejudiced interpretation of the Indians' right to their land, he never-theless was willing to negotiate with the Creeks for a cession. The very day he wrote Dartmouth for advice on how to stop Bryan, he also wrote John Stuart for instructions on how to conduct a congress with the Indians in order to obtain their land.[30]

Stopping Bryan was no easy task. Dartmouth praised the governor for his efforts, but no new law could be passed which would provide punishment for those who illegally purchased land from the Indians.[31] The tenuous state of relations between Great Britain and her colonies prohibited the passage of new legislation effecting the latter, except that which was deemed absolutely necessary. Dartmouth tried to placate Tonyn by informing him that no court would uphold Bryan's lease. The reassurance was of little comfort. Tonyn then turned to his govern-ment's officers for help, but severe factionalism hampered his efforts. Lieutenant Governor John Moultrie headed one faction, while Chief Justice William Drayton and the former council member Andrew Turnbull headed the other.[32] Moultrie's group opposed Bryan but were not always helpful to the governor. Behind Tonyn's back they reported his every action to British officials, and some of them schemed to ob-tain Florida land for themselves. Tonyn believed "that one cannot let go ones breath in this place, that a report of it is not made, to the Rebel Councillors of Carolina and Georgia."[33] His words were also reported behind his back to the home government, the commander-in-chief of the army, Thomas Gage, and his predecessor, James Grant. In addi-tion, Chief Justice Drayton was a partner of Bryan and doing all that he could to prevent Tonyn from interfering with the lease.[34] Breaking the Drayton-Bryan partnership became Tonyn's major priority.

William Drayton had first met Jonathan Bryan in 1772, "in a Book-seller's Shop in Charlestown." Although he was personally unknown to the chief justice, Bryan was "an old aquaintance of my Father's, of my Grandfather's, & Uncle's (the late & present Lieutenant Governor of South Carolina)," William Bull. When their conversation touched upon the New Purchase cession, Bryan took Drayton aside and in-formed him "there was an opportunity through his means of adding as valuable a Tract to this Province; that the Indians were willing to yield it up to him in consideration of an old Aquaintance & of some Pres-ents." There was a problem, however, as Bryan did not have "any per-sonal Interest at Home [in England], by which he could hope to get that Cession confirmed by Government." If Drayton would help him he could have a share, the cost of which would not be above £100 (the whole expense Bryan estimated at £400). Drayton said he did not have much influence in England, but perhaps Bryan could approach Governor James Grant of East Florida. Bryan rejected the suggestion, for Grant would demand "very high Terms" and make "a hard Bargain with him." Drayton proposed instead that he approach Dr. Andrew Turnbull, who had "an extensive acquaintance with People in Power." Turnbull had been scheming to attain Indian land for some time and, according to Patrick Tonyn, had introduced to East Florida the notion of "Private Persons entering into a Treaty with the Indians for portions of land." Turnbull's interest in England was with none other than George Grenville, who had told him to "pay attention to procuring some of the Indian lands."[35]

Several years passed before Drayton again heard from Bryan. After receiving the second lease, Bryan informed Drayton of his plans to take possession. He assured the chief justice that "I shall & still may have from [the Indians] an absolute Grant or Conveyance of those Lands." He had left the first lease with the Indians so that it could be "publickly shewn to their People in all their towns for the approbation of the whole nation [and] to prevent any future Dispute about my Title to those Lands." The Creeks had since sent him word that the nation had approved the lease, and it would "be return'd by the first safe Conveyance to my Hands. But the late Disturbances in their nation prevented my receiving the Lease so soon as was intended." Furthermore, he added, at the "late Treaty with the governor at Savannah, he, by what means I will not say, got the lease out of their hands & by Menaces and Threats of stoping their Trade & their Fear of my being put to great Trouble, [they] tore off the seals & left the Lease in the governor's Hands." The Creeks assured Bryan that they would renew the lease, and they did. As a result, Bryan was on his way "to view those Lands in Company with some Gentlemen, Tom Grey [an interpreter] & two Indians, & if possible[,] to find some navigable Rivers fit for the Entrance of Vessels." Bryan promised to contact Drayton when he could and reminded the chief justice that "this may be made a great Acquisition to East Florida, & the whole Indian Trade may be carried on from one of there Rivers."[36]

As he departed for Florida, the citizens of three colonies—Georgia, East Florida, and South Carolina—wondered what was taking place between the Creeks and Jonathan Bryan. Everyone knew he wanted land in Florida, but confusion reigned over how much and to what purpose he intended to put his acquisition. Many of Bryan's contemporaries undoubtedly believed that these intrigues were merely the extension of his speculative spirit, and that he was but one in a long line of Americans who hoped to make a fortune from the sale of distant lands to unsuspecting settlers. Others assumed that Bryan's activities were the result of his enmity for Governor Wright and royal government.[37] Few, if any, learned the complete story, though not for want of interest. During the War of Independence, Thomas Brown, a leader of Florida and Georgia Loyalist troops, hoped to capture Jonathan's son William, "as perhaps Bryan may be capable of shedding some light on that affair respecting the lands."[38] The seeming ease by which Bryan received the several leases dazzled the public: what powers of persuasion did he possess over the Creeks? Many of his contemporaries did not know of Bryan's lifelong association with the Indians of the Southeast, of how he had traded with the Creeks in his youth, visited their towns as a scout, fought by their side at St. Augustine, negotiated with them for Oglethorpe and as a diplomat for the royal government. Sixty-five years of familiarity had given the Creeks a high estimation of Bryan's character and talents. They knew from experience they could trust him. Bryan only had to convince the Creeks that leasing him a large tract of land was in their own best interests.

THE LEASE

Jonathan Bryan asserted, and there was little reason to doubt him, that he could have had the Creek land in Florida by outright grant instead of by ninety-nine-year lease.[39] Bryan preferred a lease because he did not want to be in violation of the Proclamation Act of 1763, which prohibited private land purchases from Indians. The intention of the act was the protection of the Indians in their land, that they "should not be molested or disturbed in the possession of such parts of our dominions and territories as, not having been ceded to, or purchased by us, are reserved to them, or any of them, as their hunting grounds." Land could only be bought from the Indians at a congress, in the Crown's name, and by a governor or the commander-in-chief of the colonies.[40]

The tract of land leased by the Creek headmen had a roughly triangular shape, like a partially eaten slice of pie. The northern side of the wedge approximated the modern-day border between Georgia and

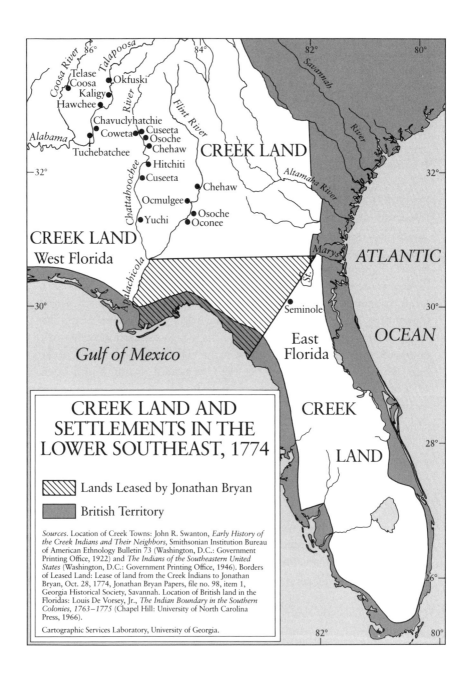

CREEK LAND

CREEK LAND
West Florida

CREEK
LAND

ATLANTIC

OCEAN

Gulf of Mexico

East
Florida

Seminole

Coosa River 86°
Talapoosa
84°
82°
80°
Savannah
Telase
Coosa
Okfuski
Kaligy
Hawchee
Coosa River
Alabama
Chavuclyhatchie
Coweta
Cuseeta
Osoche
Tuchebatchee
Chehaw
32°
Hitchiti
Cuseeta
Altamaha River
River
Flint River
Chattahoochee
Chehaw
Ocmulgee
Yuchi
Osoche
Oconee
Apalachicola
Marys
St.
30°
32°
30°
28°
26°
82°
80°

CREEK LAND AND
SETTLEMENTS IN THE
LOWER SOUTHEAST, 1774

▨ Lands Leased by Jonathan Bryan

▧ British Territory

Sources. Location of Creek Towns: John R. Swanton, *Early History of
the Creek Indians and Their Neighbors,* Smithsonian Institution Bureau
of American Ethnology Bulletin 73 (Washington, D.C.: Government
Printing Office, 1922) and *The Indians of the Southeastern United
States* (Washington, D.C.: Government Printing Office, 1946). Borders
of Leased Land: Lease of land from the Creek Indians to Jonathan
Bryan, Oct. 28, 1774, Jonathan Bryan Papers, file no. 98, item 1,
Georgia Historical Society, Savannah. Location of British land in the
Floridas: Louis De Vorsey, Jr., *The Indian Boundary in the Southern
Colonies, 1763–1775* (Chapel Hill: University of North Carolina
Press, 1966).

Cartographic Services Laboratory, University of Georgia.

Florida. Starting from where the Chattahoochee and Flint rivers run into the Apalachicola River, this line extended to the St. Marys River, the inland boundary for the new English settlement on the east coast of Florida. From there, the other, southeastern, side of the wedge extended in a line on a southwest course to the Gulf of Mexico. The curved crust of the pie, the western boundary of the leased area, was defined by the Apalachicola River, from the Chattahoochee to the Gulf of Mexico, and the bite in Florida's Gulf Coast known as Apalachee Bay formed the southern boundary, where the slice of pie appeared eaten. No Creek settlements were located within the leased area; their towns lay to the north and east (see accompanying map). The total area of the lease comprised the modern-day Florida counties of Gadsden, Liberty, Franklin, Leon, Wakula, Jefferson, Madison, Hamilton, Columbia, Suwannee, Lafayette, and Taylor, as well as parts of Baker, Dixie, Gilchrist, and Union.

A close examination of the leases reveals the widespread support which Bryan received from the Creeks. The leases were granted "in consideration of the sum of One Hundred pounds" Georgia money (which Bryan gave the Creeks in the form of presents), a yearly rent of 100 bushels of corn, and concluded "in Consideration of the great regard they bear to the said Jonathan Bryan."[41] To lessen in the public mind any question of malfeasance, James Adair witnessed the second lease. Adair, the renowned author of *The History of the American Indians,* had lived and traded with southeastern Indians for forty years and had frequently fought by their side against the French. Adair's presence, if publicized, would have muted suggestions of trickery.[42]

The Indians who signed the leases represented the several towns and tribal groups which made up the Creek Confederacy.[43] In the third quarter of the eighteenth century, the nation was geographically divided into two parts. The Upper Creeks resided in what is now northwest Georgia and midwestern Alabama, while the Lower Creeks were settled in towns along the Flint and Chattahoochee rivers in what is now southwest and south-central Georgia and southeast Alabama. Portions of the nation were beginning to migrate farther westward into Alabama, while another significant migration extended southward into Florida. The latter group of Indians acquired the name Seminole in the 1770s. Jonathan Bryan played a small but significant role in the events that led to the political division of this group from the main body of the Creek Nation.

The decentralized nature of the Creek political system has misled historians into thinking Creek politics anarchic. Yet, the nation's remarkable fulfillment of treaty obligations illustrates its ability to achieve consensus. An examination of the process by which diplomatic decisions were made will shed light on the Creeks' relationship with Jonathan Bryan. The Creeks lived in towns bound together by tradition and mutual interests into a confederacy. Each town possessed a large measure of autonomy within the confederacy: scholars have uncovered no mechanism of coercion by which the Creek National Council forced a town to act against its will. Nevertheless, the council successfully framed the nation's diplomacy through skillful negotiation, free discussion of the Creeks' needs in both the council and towns, and by the respect of the Indians for the decisions made by their headmen. For instance, before Jonathan Bryan asked Ohontholy to sign his lease, he recited the names of Creek headmen who had already done so. Thomas Grey, Bryan's interpreter, reported that the elderly Seminole responded that "if the head men of the nation had granted [Bryan] the land he supposed he must have it."[44] Respect for tribal leaders, however, could never completely ensure unanimous compliance with diplomatic arrangements. Creek leaders could not have concluded a treaty if a significant portion of the population did not approve of it. To prevent dissent, the people most affected by the nation's agreements were consulted. Thus, Taleeche had stipulated that his agreement with Bryan was invalid until all tribal groups had put their marks on the document.[45]

The most important factor overlooked by students of Creek diplomacy has been the individual Indians' knowledge of tribal politics. The oral communication of diplomatic information from tribal leaders to the rest of the community was an essential component of southeastern aboriginal culture. Cessions of land, trade agreements, and treaties had to be discussed and explained throughout the nation. The importance of communicating these decisions was illustrated by the widespread use of orators in public councils. Creek headmen almost always used *Henihas* and *Yatikas* to relay their thoughts.[46] Creek Indians understood the politics and political decisions of their nation better than the Euramerican population understood the rationale for political decisions in their own society.

The success of Bryan's plans depended upon receiving the approval of the great majority of Creek leaders; Bryan was too smart and experienced in Indian affairs to believe that he could build a port and establish a city without Creek acquiescence.[47] For three years before 1774 he had courted the Creeks on excursions to their towns. This resulted in his receiving approval from a wider and more significant range of Creek *mecos* and other headmen than Governor Wright had procured for his treaty with the Creeks in October 1774.[48] It was extremely important that Bryan obtain widespread approval of the lease: if a significant portion of Creeks were unreconciled to the agreement, Bryan could not people his colony.

Bryan's enemies argued that the leases he received from the Creeks were signed by only a few Indians, not the proper representatives of the Creek Nation. Evidence shows the opposite to be true. The first lease contained the signatures of fifteen Indians, representing both Upper and Lower Creeks. At least seven Creek towns or tribal groups can be identified on the first lease: Chehaw, Kaligy, Osoche, Okfuskie, Ocmulgee, Hitchiti, and Yuchi.[49] The second Creek lease did not replace the first one, it supplemented that lease with signatures from representatives of several towns and tribal groups that were unrepresented or underrepresented on the first lease. Twenty of the twenty-one parties to the second lease can be identified from this document, because their town or tribal group was listed. In addition, we can identify the offices of eleven of the signers, all of whom enjoyed high-status positions in their respective tribal groups. This information could have been used by Bryan to prove that he had received signatures from a representative cross section of Creeks.

The Indian parties to the second lease were as follows. Twelve of the signatories were Cuseeta Creeks, one of the major subgroups of Lower Creek Indians. Their towns were located along the Chattahoochee River about one hundred miles above the northern border of the ceded land. At least two Cuseeta mecos were among the signatories, one of whom had signed the treaty with Georgia in October. In addition, three Cuseeta *testanochies,* or head warriors, also signed the agreement.[50] Another major tribal group of Lower Creeks represented on the lease were the Osoches. Representatives from Osoche towns, which were located along both the Chattahoochee and Flint rivers, included a meco, and an *emahtla,* or a mid-level warrior.[51] The mecos of the Lower Creek town, Chehaw, and the Upper Creek town of Telase Coosa also signed the second lease.[52] Another Upper Creek signer was the emahtla of Tuchebatchee, who also signed the Creek treaty with

Georgia in October. Tuchebatchee was the leading town of the Upper Creeks and the most populous in the whole nation.[53] With Tuchebatchee Aletale Emahtla's signature, every major group of Creeks (except perhaps the Coweta) had signed Bryan's lease.[54] The only Indian party of which Bryan still required approval after 1774 were the Seminoles, and Bryan planned on visiting them next.

Bryan and the Creeks expected success from their plans.[55] The establishment of an illicit trade posed few problems. Bryan enlisted at least two South Carolina merchants to provide a steady supply of goods. Excited by the prospect of increased trade, Charlestownians John McQueen and John Smith traveled with Bryan to Florida intent upon preparing the way for a profitable business with the Creeks. While Bryan conducted further negotiations with the Indians, McQueen and Smith journeyed to St. Augustine to meet with Governor Patrick Tonyn. The merchants reasonably assumed that they could persuade Tonyn to approve of their operation for the right price—in 1773, Tonyn allegedly had participated in covert trading with the Indians.[56] The success of Bryan's plans, however, did not depend upon the governor's approval. Tonyn could do nothing to prevent Bryan from smuggling goods into the colony, and the governor possessed insufficient manpower for removing Bryan, his associates, and their followers once they settled upon Creek land.[57] The civil authorities held virtually no control over the two battalions of regulars stationed in East and West Florida, one at St. Augustine, the other at Pensacola. Even if the governor could obtain control over troop deportment, rampant desertion, low morale, and chronic illness left the soldiers ineffective. Officers balked when assigned to Florida, and the poor quality of living conditions led Commander-in-Chief Frederick Haldimand to comment that if the troops mutinied, they should not be punished. While regulars throughout North America concentrated on Boston to repress the population, the Florida troops remained at their station struggling to survive. With British military power focused upon Boston, the home government would be incapable of sparing troops for a Florida expedition in the foreseeable future. It might not have mattered. Once Bryan established his colony, Creek support would make Britain think twice before attempting to remove him from Florida. The British feared Creek military power and believed that cutting off trade was the *only way* to subdue the confederacy. When the governor of West Florida suggested that a preventive war be started with the Creeks, the earl of Shelbourne had him removed from office, claiming that anyone who could propose such a preposterous idea must be a "Perfect Madman."[58]

Bryan could assure his agreement's success by obtaining Seminole approval. He had to convince the Seminoles, as he had convinced their Creek brethren, that the lease promoted their best interests. The Seminoles migrated to Florida from Lower Creek towns after the Spanish evacuation in 1763. It was not unusual for Creeks to secede from one town to form another, but the Seminoles' choice of location set them apart. The very name Seminole, it is believed, means "those who separate," or "runaways." Despite their physical separation, the Seminoles continued to participate in Creek councils in the 1770s, but they were quickly developing separate political interests. They were much more oriented toward the government of East Florida than other Creeks. In fact, they may have chosen their location for settlement precisely because of its nearness to St. Augustine: they came to rely upon East Florida rather than Georgia for trade goods.[59] This reliance set them apart from the Lower Creeks in significant ways. The Lower Creeks maintained great distance—both physical and political—between themselves and the British. They retained a suspicion of the British which the Seminoles obviously did not share. The Lower Creeks may have hoped that ceding Florida land to Bryan would induce the Seminoles to move northward and rejoin them in Georgia. The promise of easy access to trade goods from Bryan could wean the Seminoles from the British. The Upper Creeks supported the Lower Creeks by sending one of their chief headmen, St. Iago, to convince the Seminoles of the efficacy of Bryan's lease.[60] With the support of the confederacy behind him, Bryan set out with a party of surveyors, interpreters, and Creek headmen to obtain Seminole approval.

INTRIGUES AND ESPIONAGE

Bryan and his entourage arrived in Florida in late November 1774. They proceeded to the main Seminole town, Alachua (near present-day Gainesville) only to find that the men had gone to war. Bryan left a message with Ohontholy that he wanted to "obtain his consent and the consent of the Cowkeeper and other head men of the Latchaway [Seminole] Indians[,] to grant him lands to erect a Town where large Boats and Vessels could come." Ohontholy agreed to the lease and received the customary presents in return. Bryan requested that Ohontholy tell Cowkeeper that he would return to the St. Johns River "in two moons with presents for the Indians in Boats which he would take care should be carried to Latchaway."[61]

While Bryan was visiting Seminole towns, Governor Tonyn learned of the Creek cession from Governor Wright. Immediately, Tonyn dispatched a messenger to the Seminoles to urge them against treating with Bryan.[62] Drayton tried to persuade Tonyn to cooperate with Bryan, but the governor refused. The chief justice suggested that Bryan might be moved to turn over his cession to East Florida if in exchange he received a reward of land. Tonyn thought the idea preposterous. Bryan's reputation as a foe of royal government, his failure to contact the king's men at an earlier date, and his outrageous assertion that the land belonged to the Indians and not the king made evident that he had no intention of working with the British government. Tonyn dismissed the possibility of ever working with Bryan and demanded that the chief justice provide his legal opinion on what charges could be brought against the Georgian for his trek through Florida, whether his actions fell "within the denomination of Treason," and if not, how should he be "proceeded against." Drayton informed the governor that no treason had been committed but perhaps Bryan could be apprehended for either "contempt of the King's prerogative," or for trespass on the king's land.[63]

On the evening of January 12, 1775, Tonyn received word that Bryan was on the St. Johns River. Tonyn sent a message to Drayton to issue a writ for Bryan's seizure. The chief justice informed Tonyn's messenger that a writ was improper and that he would come to town the next day to explain. An irate governor went to Drayton's home to demand action but was turned away by a servant: the chief justice had retired to bed.

The next morning Drayton visited the governor and promised to draw up the proper warrant. After placating the governor, he again tried to persuade Tonyn to allow "government to avail themselves of Mr. Bryan's interest with the Indians." Drayton explained that Bryan had meant to seek government approval of his actions but Governor Wright had stopped him out of self-interest. Tonyn, Drayton argued, now had the chance to obtain a great cession of land for East Florida, if only he would permit Bryan to proceed unobstructed. Tonyn wavered and informed Drayton that he would give him a decision the next day.

After all, he "did not mean to oppose Mr. Bryan or any man, but I meant to do my duty and what was right."[64]

Having made some progress with the governor, Drayton introduced him to the two South Carolina merchants Smith and McQueen, who had come with Bryan to Florida. Drayton went "into a long detail of encomiums on Bryan[,] of his being a very respectable man of great popular esteem in Georgia." Smith and McQueen later echoed these sentiments, that "Mr. Bryan was an American born, and stood up greatly for the liberties of America. [T]hat he was a very popular man and that half the settlers in Georgia would follow him into this Province." Tonyn stood his ground against Bryan and sent some men to the St. Johns River to arrest him.[65]

On January 17, Tonyn learned that Bryan had fled the province. Presumably, Joseph Penman had informed Bryan that the governor had sent a provost and a water baliff to seize him and his boat. Bryan returned across the Georgia border to Cumberland Island, where he awaited Smith and McQueen for the return trip north.[66] In St. Augustine, Governor Tonyn blamed Drayton for Bryan's escape. Drayton, Smith, and McQueen, however, blamed Tonyn for his departure: if the governor had not sent the provost after him, Bryan never would have fled. Bryan was a gentleman who did not deserve such shoddy treatment, least of all did he deserve a prison cell in the basement of St. Augustine's stone castle. Tonyn replied that any man who had set the government of Georgia and the congress at defiance, brought surveyors with him to mark the land, and "gone through all the Indian towns making them presents" must be guilty of some crime.[67]

In Bryan's absence from Georgia a Provincial Congress had been elected to remonstrate patriot grievances, but only five of twelve parishes elected delegates to the congress. The Provincial Congress's last act before disbanding in February was to select three delegates to represent the colony at the Continental Congress. In April, this delegation wrote the Continental Congress that they would not attend until the patriot cause received greater popular support in Georgia.[68] This added an urgency to the matter of the lease. Bryan visited Charlestown several times that spring, according to Governor Wright, to discuss the lease.[69] If the patriots could not obtain control of Georgia, then perhaps Bryan could lead the disenchanted to Florida. Certainly, it would not be safe for rebel leaders to remain behind. Bryan wrote to Cowkeeper in June apologizing for not returning to Florida when he had promised. He wanted "to bring with me people to make a settlement . . . in some place which you approve of where I can have the advantage of Planting in good lands and good navigation." He reminded the Seminole headman that he would "carry on a trade for the mutual advantage of both Indians and White people." Bryan hoped to see him in two and a half months and "sent small presents in Tobacco . . . in Love and Good Will."[70]

After the battles of Lexington and Concord, the fortunes of the patriot movement changed in Georgia and again Bryan had to put off his return to Florida. A new Provincial Congress was called to meet in July, and Bryan and his sons William and Hugh won seats.[71] Bryan sent first St. Iago and then Thomas Grey to treat with the Seminoles for approval of his lease. Learning of Grey's impending arrival, Governor Tonyn issued a proclamation against Bryan and dispatched constables to Latchaway with orders to apprehend Grey. The Seminoles were warned against cooperating with the patriots and urged to bring in Grey for questioning. In case they refused, Tonyn left men on the St. Marys River "to apprehend this Grey as he returns to Georgia. In short . . . I will do all I can to seize him."[72] Tonyn expected Bryan to follow Grey with a force of five hundred rebels, presumably to take possession of his land. The governor feared that if they achieved their purpose with the Indians they would attack St. Augustine. If they did not win over the Indians, "I should think the undertaking madness. But, indeed one should be mad, to know what Madmen would do."[73]

After Grey had been with the Seminoles for a day and a half, he was brought to St. Augustine. A "half-breed" whose mother was Creek and his father white, Grey possessed strong familial connections among the Seminoles and other Lower Creeks.[74] The turning over of Grey to the East Florida government was politically expedient for the Seminoles, and they undoubtedly did it with Grey's approval. The Seminoles guaranteed Grey's safety, and the governor promised the Indians that no harm would come to him. Thus, Grey agreed to make a statement to the governor of his activities with Bryan in full realization that Tonyn could do nothing against him. Grey volunteered to tell Tonyn precisely what he wanted to hear about the Indians, that they would not lease land to Bryan; he also told Tonyn what he wished to know about Bryan, that the Georgian used fraud in his dealings with the Indians. Tonyn was so hungry for evidence of loyalty in the Seminoles and of culpability in Bryan and Drayton, that he accepted Grey's testimony at face value. Tonyn was led further and further away from the truth and into a realm of delusion that colored his perspective and the performance of his duties as governor.

Tonyn wished to use Grey to implicate the chief justice in Bryan's "treasonous" activities. He had Drayton take Grey's statement concerning his recent visit to the Seminoles. Grey swore that he had only come to Florida to fetch some horses he owned, and that Bryan asked him to pick up some of his horses that had been left among the Seminoles the previous winter. Grey averred that he carried no message from Bryan and had no intention of talking to the Indians about approving Bryan's lease. On the other hand, Grey testified, he did overhear the Indians converse about Bryan and how the Georgian should not have come to their town in Cowkeeper's absence. Furthermore, Cowkeeper was upset that Bryan had "thrown Talks at a Distance to him." Grey said that in the course of his visit he had asked the Indians "whether they intended to grant those lands" to Bryan and they responded in the negative.[75]

When Drayton finished questioning Grey, the governor had Assistant Justice John Forbes take a second statement from the interpreter. This was a much more detailed exposition of Bryan's activities and was undoubtedly prompted by the governor's leading questions. Tonyn hoped that the differences in the two statements would provide proof of Drayton's complicity with Bryan. The governor suggested to his superiors in London that Drayton must still be in league with Bryan, otherwise he would have asked Grey more penetrating questions. But Drayton's performance had nothing to do with any present complicity with Bryan. He was embarrassed by the whole affair and wished to be dissociated from it. The escalation of the dispute with Great Britain had forced men to choose sides and Drayton decided for the king. Unfortunately for the chief justice, his cousin William Henry Drayton was a notorious South Carolina rebel and had written him a letter mentioning the confiscation of East Florida mail by Charlestown patriots. Added to his other "crimes," Tonyn believed that Drayton must be involved with his cousin and therefore was responsible for the "secret communication" that existed between East Florida and the rebels of South Carolina and Georgia. The home government, however, accepted Drayton's protestations of loyalty. They believed that greed and poor judgment had led to the chief justice's association with Bryan. But Tonyn persisted in hounding Drayton and became obsessed with proving his treason. This blinded the governor to the adept espionage of Thomas Grey, who earned the governor's sympathy by asserting that if his testimony were made known in Georgia, "Jonathan Bryan would make the mob tear him to pieces. . . . he had [only] narrowly escaped very bad usage . . . [for refusing] to sign the rebel association paper."[76]

None of Grey's testimony provided Tonyn with legal evidence of Bryan's having committed any crime, but his insinuations did win the governor's confidence. Although Grey depicted Bryan as having broken no laws, he alluded to the strong possibility that he used trickery with the Indians. This served the purpose of exonerating the Seminoles of complicity with Bryan and of confirming Tonyn in his belief that Bryan and Drayton were involved in fraud.[77] Grey teased the governor by suggesting that Bryan trespassed on the king's land but provided no proof that could be used in a court of law. He testified that Bryan's surveyors did not use their instruments but that they had kept a journal in which they made frequent notations. Tonyn had hoped on several occasions to find proof that Bryan had surveyed the land, but from Grey the only evidence he could obtain was that a single red oak tree had been marked with the date and Bryan's name. The tree, Grey reported in a vague way, was located about seventeen miles from Alachua. Thus, again, Grey showed Tonyn his willingness to cooperate without providing any usable evidence of Bryan's having committed trespass.[78] Grey promised that he would soon return to Florida with a letter from Bryan to confirm his guilt.

Grey returned to Georgia in October and immediately visited Jonathan Bryan. The latter "expressed great concern that [Grey] had met with hard usage at St. Augustine," but the interpreter explained that it was otherwise. Bryan took him to the Provincial Congress, "and introduced him to a large company of above forty Gentlemen." William Henry Drayton was permitted to address several questions concerning the examination of Grey in St. Augustine by his cousin, the chief justice. Grey informed the congress that he had divulged no information to Drayton about the patriot movement. He then was questioned "in a private room" by a committee. They requested that Grey return to St. Augustine, allegedly to learn whether an emissary from General Gage had arrived there, and if so, how he was to travel to West Florida. Then, "after injoining secrecy they informed him that they were to raise 500 men in Georgia" to descend upon the town of St. Augustine.[79]

Grey immediately returned to St. Augustine and fed Governor Tonyn this information. The rebel committee wanted the governor to believe that an invasion of Florida was imminent (and by the exact number of men which Tonyn feared would be sent, no less).[80] Grey also fed the governor false information concerning William Drayton. It appears that everyone but Tonyn knew the chief justice's true loyalties. The patriots decided to play on the governor's paranoia toward Drayton by implicating the chief justice in rebel activities. Grey informed Tonyn that "Mr. Bryan told him that Mr. Drayton was their particular friend, that he wished well to the cause i.e. to the American party, that tho' he was at St. Augustine his heart carried towards them." Moreover, Grey told Tonyn that he had learned from one of the rebels, "that they had very good information of what was doing at St. Augustine and that Mr. Drayton and Mr. Penman" were responsible. Armed with this information, Tonyn brought the chief justice up on charges before the council and preoccupied himself with chasing after shadows.[81]

Shortly thereafter, Thomas Grey was back in Georgia and in the employ of Jonathan Bryan. In March, many Indian headmen met at Bryan's plantation with Thomas Grey, "a favorite linguist" serving as interpreter.[82] These negotiations did not concern the Florida cession: the further escalation of warfare made the settling of a new colony irrelevant. While British agents worked tirelessly to enlist the Indians against the rebels, Georgia Whigs negotiated for Creek neutrality. Both Bryan and his son William conducted negotiations with the Lower Creeks.[83] George Galphin has been given virtually all the credit for winning many of the Lower Creeks to the patriot side, but historians have been unaware of Bryan's tremendous influence among the Indians.[84] In September 1776 Bryan wrote the Lower Creek headmen to remind them that "[I] am your Friend and Brother" and to persuade them to remain neutral in the dispute with Great Britain:

By the direction of the Great men of these Provinces of Carolina and Georgia I am directed to tell you that their desire is still to Retain and hold fast that love which has for many Years Subsisted between you and us, and to forwarn you of the Consequences of a Quarrel between [us, which] . . . must end in your own Destruction and Ruin. We therefore wish . . . that we may talk together to renew and Confirm that Friendship which has so long subsisted and have sent up our friend Thomas Grey to come down with

[your headmen. He] will also tell you of the unhappy war which
the Cherokee have brought on themselves by believing the Lying
Talks Given them by Mr. Stuart and His Men.[85]

Whether or not the Creeks would have permitted Bryan to establish his
colony amid the alteration in the balance of power on the southern
frontier which followed patriot victory in the Revolutionary War, his
relationship with the Indians influenced many Creeks who might otherwise have sided with the British.[86]

Circumstances, however, forced the Seminoles to throw in their lot
against the patriots. Dependent upon East Florida for trade and wary
of war with such a close and powerful neighbor, the Seminoles sided
with Great Britain in the American Revolution. It was not foreor-
dained. If Bryan had managed to start his colony before the war broke
out, the Seminoles would have been able to retain their neutrality in the
American Revolution. But the absence of patriot power in Florida
forced the Seminoles to side with the British. The only alternative was
to rejoin their kinsmen in Georgia, but once war began, southern Georgia became a vicious battleground for marauding parties of rebels, Loyalists, and Indians. The Seminoles participated in these encounters,
while knowing that their towns in Florida remained relatively safe. The
combination of all these circumstances led to the political break of the
Seminoles from the Lower Creeks.

The wisdom of divide and conquer provided the Creeks with the
only diplomatic policy that could allow them to maintain their relative
state of independence. No one doubted Creek power in the era of the
American Revolution; the confederacy still commanded fear and respect from its neighbors, both Indian and white. But the superior technology of firearms had created new dependencies among the Indians,
forcing them to work harder than ever to forge diplomatic ties with
rival groups of whites, so that much-needed goods would continue to
flow at competitive prices. On the eve of the American Revolution the
Creeks turned to their old friend Jonathan Bryan to help them restore
the balance of power which had been upset ever since the French evacuation of the Southeast. By establishing a new colony and an alternative source for trade, the Creeks expected Bryan to help them withstand growing British power. The war between Britain and her colonies
ended this scheme, and the former's defeat left the Americans to assume a position as the dominant power on the southern frontier.

7

THE WAR AND AFTER, 1776–1788

The American Revolution was a most unusual event: large numbers of conservative property holders risked their fortunes to bring about political change. Men differed in their definitions of change and their purpose in rebelling; each possessed his own agenda, goals, and understanding of the conflict. Some fought to effect radical democratization, while others hoped to reclaim rights believed to have been usurped. Still other men thought their best interests lay in supporting the king, while a significantly large group of individuals wished to remain neutral. Ultimately, all were at risk. None could foresee the full ramifications of his actions. Whether men made their decisions based upon self-interest or political principle, and for most it was a combination of both, few realized the extent to which sacrifices would have to be made.

REVOLUTIONARY ACTIVITIES

In 1775 Georgia's Provincial Congress selected a Council of Safety to conduct patriot affairs in the colony while the congress was not in session. Thus, the Council of Safety, and after the overthrow of royal government, the governor and the Council of Safety, directed Georgia's revolutionary activities. The council was composed of approximately fifteen members, with about nine making up the active core. Jonathan Bryan was among the latter. From 1775 to 1778 he was joined on the council at various times by his son William, sons-in-law John Morel and John Houstoun, and nephew Jonathan Cochrane. On several occasions the Bryan clan held a near majority. In addition, Houstoun served as governor in 1778 and 1784, and Jonathan served as vice-president and commander-in-chief in 1777. With the support of family members, Bryan wielded great influence in the day-to-day operation of rebel activities and was especially influential in the conduct of

Indian diplomacy, the recruitment of troops from other states for service in Georgia, and in planning military operations.[1]

In 1776 the Continental Congress sent General Charles Lee to Charlestown to put the defense of the southern colonies in order. Bryan, Houstoun, and Lachlan McIntosh visited the general in July to represent Georgia's interests. They urged Lee to undertake an invasion of Florida. Georgia was in a "weak and defenceless situation," and required immediate "assistance from the General Congress." Bryan, speaking for the delegation, informed Lee of "the intrinsic value of the lands, and other property in [Georgia] . . . its fine inlets, harbours, and rivers, and plenty of provisions, [which] make it . . . perhaps equal to any other [colony] . . . in the great cause of *America*." Georgia, he argued, must be defended "as a barrier to South Carolina," and for its valuable rice plantations, "thirty thousand head of black cattle . . . and hogs without number." The delegation recited the reasons for the colony's weakness by both land and sea. They complained of the threats posed by "the garrisoned Province of the *Floridas,* and the most numerous tribes of Savages in *North America;*" daily, British ships carried away Georgia slaves and cattle. Threatened by "upwards of one thousand *British* troops in *St. Augustine,*" fifteen thousand Indian soldiers, and "the vast number of negroes we have, perhaps of themselves sufficient to subdue us," the delegation made several recommendations. They asked General Lee to represent their situation to the Continental Congress, and to request six battalions, a grant to improve Georgia's fortifications and to build and outfit gunboats, and permission and reimbursement for the provisioning of Indians with cattle instead of ammunition and clothing (which "we have it not in our power to give them"). Cattle would not only win the Indians' gratitude and attachment but give them an "idea of property [which] would keep them honest and peaceable with us."[2]

What the delegation did not say in its official request was that Georgia desired the Continental army to invade Florida. These negotiations were conducted in secret with Lee. The general traveled to Savannah with five hundred men to assess Georgia's situation and ostensibly to lead the invasion. Upon arrival in Georgia, however, Lee decided against it. British setbacks in Florida had relieved pressure on southern Georgia, and the general believed there was "no possibility of transporting cannon, ammunition, provisions, or collecting a sufficient number of men for the Siege and reduction of St. Augustine." Lee asked the council to explain how an expedition could be supplied under the present circumstances, and what possible advantages could be attained by undertaking an invasion "to the general cause, or to this State of Georgia in particular, as to compensate for the trouble and expense." The council ordered Jonathan Bryan and Nathan Brownson to furnish a reply. The two-man committee informed Lee that "an irruption into the Province of East Florida" would be of "the most salutary consequences" to Georgia, "and of course, render service to the whole Continent." The plan of attack they proposed was nearly identical to that which Bryan had recommended to Oglethorpe almost forty years before: "if the whole country around [St. Augustine] is ravaged, the cattle on the east side of Saint John's drove off and the inhabitants obliged to evacuate their plantations and fly into the castle, [then] the scarcity of provisions and the want of fresh supplies . . . will of itself oblige the Garrison to submit to our arms." In other words, Bryan recommended to destroy the countryside and starve East Florida into submission. Moreover, if the fortress at St. Augustine did not surrender, the garrison would be so weakened as to become ineffectual and British troops would be driven from Georgia soil. This in turn would prevent slave desertion to Florida and "attach the Indians to our interest." Finally, "by carrying distress and war into" Florida, the latter's inhabitants would become "so much engaged at home, as not to be able to fit out Privateers against this Province."[3]

Bryan and Brownson were "inclined to think" that plunder would "compensate" the soldiers "for the difficulty and toil attending their march." They assured the general that troops could easily be supplied by a commissary north of the Altamaha River and that southward the men could live off the land. It would only be necessary to send the men by boat a quantity of rice for when they reached Florida.[4]

Lee acquiesced in the committee's recommendations and agreed to lead the invasion. Bryan and his nephew Jonathan Cochrane were appointed by the Council of Safety to cooperate with the general in preparing the expedition.[5] The Georgians, however, failed to supply the necessary equipment and provisions, and Lee complained about the government's inability to fulfill its promises.[6] Lee was recalled by the Continental Congress for service in the North, and his successor, Colonel William Moultrie, refused to lead the expedition until more troops were raised. Georgia had little choice but to postpone the invasion.[7]

The Georgia government believed postponement only a temporary setback. Invasions of Florida also were planned in 1777 and 1778, with the council inexplicably selecting the hottest months of the year for operations. Both invasion forces had command problems, with civilian and military authorities refusing to allow one or the other to possess overall control of the army. The invasion of 1777 ended in an aborted failure and resulted in the death of Georgia's governor, Button Gwinnett, who was killed in a duel by General Lachlan McIntosh. In the invasion of 1778, Governor John Houstoun—with the probable backing of his father-in-law, Jonathan Bryan—refused to give command of the militia to the Continental army. Houstoun insisted on leading the troops himself, though he had no military experience. The Continental army pulled out of the expedition and thus ended another attempted invasion. In a recent monograph on the tragicomic military activities of Georgia and Florida in the early years of the Revolution, Martha Condray Searcy has discussed Bryan's strategy for the reduction of St. Augustine (without naming him). The plan itself was sound, she concluded, but the Georgians were incapable of seeing it to fruition.[8]

The failure of the third invasion set the stage for the British capture of Savannah in late December 1778. Problems of command between the army, militia, and the governor again plagued the rebels and permitted the British easy entry into Savannah.[9] British naval forces were commanded by Commodore Hyde Parker, and the army was under the direction of Colonel Archibald Campbell. After easily subduing the capital, Parker dispatched men under Lieutenant Clark to pursue Governor Houstoun up the Savannah River. Arriving at Union Plantation, on the South Carolina side of the river, they failed to capture the governor "but returned with one [Jonathan] Bryan a notorious ringleader in Rebellion."[10] Bryan's son James was also captured. One of Bryan's daughters pleaded for her father's release but was rudely rebuffed by Parker.[11] Colonel Campbell, however, promised Bryan's wife "that every proper attention shall be paid to her Aged Husband."[12] After twenty-one days aboard the prisoner ship *Whitby*, the prisoners were put on a privateer and transported to New York. John Houstoun immediately wrote Henry Laurens, then a member of the Continental Congress, to effect a prisoner exchange: "I dare say his Age and your former Acquaintance with him will be sufficient advocate in his Favor to induce you to cause particular attention to be Paid to his Case."[13]

By June 1779 nothing had been accomplished, and once again Houstoun wrote Laurens. He and the Bryan family were satisfied "that nothing in your Power will be omitted to get [Bryan] exchanged and restored to his Country." Houstoun recommended that "since the Enemy make an Object of Resentment of him *We* ought in my opinion for the same Reason to make him an object of particular attention." Six months later Houstoun was forced to iterate: "I can't help thinking that that old Gentleman ought to have been more an Object of Exchange." He had no idea what "may have induced the Enemy to mark him out as so singular an Object of Oppression," but this was all the more reason to seek his release.[14] Whatever the reason for British vindictiveness, Laurens hinted at the reason why Congress took so long to attempt an exchange. He wrote General Benjamin Lincoln, that "I have done all in my power to serve my old friend Mr. Bryan . . . and his Son," but an exchange will have to be made "out of the common ro[u]tine, because Congress will not encourage kidnapping by Exchanging citizens taken in the manner those Gentlemen were captured."[15]

During his imprisonment, Bryan was allowed to send and receive mail. He wrote Laurens that he had been treated "with Civility and . . . with remarkable kindness but you must be Sensible how very disagreeable my Situation [is] . . . [considering I am] advanc'd of Seventy years [and] snatch'd from an [?] Family." Furthermore, Bryan was not accustomed to the "cold and inhospitable Clime" of New York, and he was "unknown without Fire[,] Money[,] Credit or a Friend." His only consolation was that it "happened by a divine permission and God's will must be done."[16]

Bryan's imprisonment on a ship off Long Island lasted far longer than anyone expected. After a year and a half he began to fear he would never again see Georgia. In May 1780 he wrote Houstoun of how he had received bills of exchange from Laurens and his old friends, Basil Cowper and John McQueen. Nevertheless, money was scarce and he also feared that one of his bills might be protested. Bryan was irritated at being "neglected as to hear nothing nor receive no Supplies from our friends in Carolina[,] especially as I & my Son are the only Captives here from that State." He was sure that if application were made to the South Carolina assembly or to John Rutledge that £100 sterling in specie could be procured for him. Bryan's appeal to South Carolina rather than Georgia was understandable: the latter was weak and in the hands of British troops; he still considered himself a son of the former.[17]

Bryan informed Houstoun he was "in a verry declining State of Health & think it verry uncertain of ever meeting again on this side of time." He repeated these sentiments to his wife. On June 2, 1780, Bryan wrote Mary a businesslike letter than instructed her to make arrangements for paying off debts he had accumulated in prison. The same day he dispatched this letter, he received another from her. The letter has been lost, but its contents broke Bryan's resolve to keep from Mary his fears, hopes, and anxieties. The next day he wrote Mary and apologized for her having to spend the "dregs" of her life "under a series of trouble" without him there to help her. Their separation caused him "great sorrow, on [their] being deprived of the happy seasons of bending our knees in union before the Throne of Grace. Our prayers are recorded in God's Book; our tears are preserved in His bottle and future destination is in His hands." Bryan's health was deteriorating quickly and he wrote, "I have no prospects of an exchange, and I know not how long I may remain in a situation where I am a burthen to myself and expense to you." He requested that she "Remember me to our dear children, and also to our poor slaves, if we have any left." He had "no account" of his affairs, "or whether any of our property yet remains in your hands," and hoped that God would protect her.[18]

Bryan's property was, for the most part, intact. Governor Wright had allowed Mary Bryan to return to Brampton Plantation (which was in her name), and many of the family's slaves remained with the Bryans throughout the Revolution. Several bondspeople and some of Bryan's property were sold during the war to pay off debts.[19]

Mary Bryan's letter may have provided the inspiration for Bryan to preserve his life and try to obtain his freedom, for two weeks after receiving her letter he wrote to Sir Henry Clinton, commander-in-chief of British forces, requesting a pardon for him and his son. Bryan informed Clinton that he "never bore arms or held any military office or commission in the present unhappy contest." (He did not mention that he had referred to himself as commander-in-chief of Georgia in 1777.) Bryan wrote that he was "both old and infirm [and] advanced to the very eve of Life being in the 73[d] year of age." He promised "on his Sacred Word of Honour most Strictly to adhear to any restrictions or limitations which your Excellency may think proper" and to use the "influence and authority of a Parent" to persuade his son to obey any restrictions placed upon him.[20]

On November 7, 1780, the Continental Congress, meeting in Philadelphia, made a resolution directing General Washington to insist upon an exchange of prisoners of war taken at the capitulation of Charlestown, "and also of Jonathan Bryan, Esquire and his son." The notation referring to Bryan, however, was crossed out in the journal because the elderly patriot and his son arrived in Philadelphia just as the resolution passed.[21] We do not know why the Bryans were released. The length of their imprisonment had been twenty-two months. They spent the next several months lobbying Congress for money to obtain passage home.

Bryan requested that the delegates of South Carolina and Georgia represent his interests, "having been alternately a Citizen of both" and from "having lost our Liberty . . . in the public service, and with it my fortune." Bryan believed he and his son had a rightful "claim to the public favour, at least for the pay & subsistence of militia men." But what he really desired was recompense for two of his boats that were utilized in the public service, and for $1,400 he had advanced to the state of Georgia. He realized that perhaps it was not the best time to request reimbursement, since Congress as usual had great financial problems, but it was impossible for him to return home without assistance—"from the indisposition of [my] Son, and my advanced Age, we cannot walk."[22]

Congress agreed to reimburse Bryan $1,400 and £43 10s. for half the value of his boats.[23] He used the money to purchase a "Light Wagon and Horses" but was unable to travel south because of the fighting in Virginia and South Carolina. Bryan returned to Congress in February and asked for the remainder of the money owed him so he could renew his journey. Congress approved the request and Bryan proceeded to Georgia, though it was over a year before he again saw Brampton Plantation.[24] His wife passed away as he left Philadelphia.

In August 1781 Bryan wrote General Nathanial Greene from Camden, South Carolina, requesting an escort to Augusta, where the Georgia government in exile was holding a state-wide election. Bryan received the escort and arrived in Augusta on August 27.[25] Immediately, Bryan was made a member of the rebel government's executive council.[26] Virtually all of the low-country patriot leaders were in hiding, in prison, or out of state; Bryan was the only member of the executive council to have been part of the Council of Safety during the early stages of the war. A new crop of men, many of whom represented backcountry interests, now stood in the forefront of the rebel movement in Georgia. They immediately welcomed Bryan into their ruling clique, not only for his lifelong advocacy of backcountry interests, the heroism of his imprisonment, and his reputation as a patriot, but also because he still was willing and able to work energetically for the patriot cause.

Bryan regularly attended the council and even participated in military activities. Steadily, the rebels pushed the British back to the Atlantic, and in the spring of 1782 patriot forces approached the capital. On May 21, rebel troops under General Anthony Wayne besieged the British garrison that remained in Savannah. David Ramsay, South Carolina's contemporary historian of the American Revolution, reported that "Mr. Jonathan Bryan, a respectable citizen of Georgia, though nearly eighty years of age, was among the foremost on this occasion and showed as much fire and spirit as could be exhibited by a young soldier in the pursuit of military fame."[27]

The British evacuated Georgia, and Bryan remained on the executive council until the military crisis ended in December 1782. He then retired from government and his son James took his place on the executive council and was appointed treasurer of Georgia. With Bryan's other son, William, elected to the state assembly and John Houstoun reelected governor, Bryan retained influence in Georgia politics.

In retirement Bryan played an active role in the Independent Presbyterian church and spent much of his time reestablishing his plantations on a profit-making course.[28] Also, he continued to promote the evangelization of blacks and, as noted earlier, he continued to permit his bondsman Andrew Bryan to preach to area slaves.[29] In early March 1788 Jonathan Bryan died at Brampton Plantation.

The obituary that appeared in the *Georgia Gazette* stated, "The many virtues which this gentleman possessed, both of a social and private nature, will not be readily forgotten." It was recalled how Bryan had "acquired a thorough and accurate knowledge of the country. This enabled him, and his generous heart always inclined him[,] to render that aid to the new settlers that he may be justly styled as one of the principal Fathers and Founders of Georgia." The obituary further recalled Bryan's religious zeal, tolerance of others, charity, devotion to the Revolution, and his lengthy imprisonment. "The strength of his constitution, and the unshaken firmness of his mind . . . rose superior to all difficulties. . . . Thus having spent a life marked with many private trials, [he] literally exhausted his days chiefly in the service of his country." The elegy closed: "he expired, or rather ceased to breathe without a pain, murmer or a groan."[30]

JONATHAN BRYAN
AND THE FORMATION OF A PLANTER ELITE

Jonathan Bryan lived a remarkable life. He rose from the obscurity of the southern frontier to become one of Georgia's richest, most powerful men. Along the way he met and befriended two of the most famous men of the English-speaking world, George Whitefield and James Oglethorpe. His life touched the lives not only of the rich and powerful but of the poor, and downtrodden, and the exploited. More than most of his contemporaries he sought to understand people of other races, social groups, and religions—and he profited from the knowledge thus obtained. An adventurous soul, Bryan not only explored the geographic areas that lay beyond the reach and understanding of most of his white contemporaries but experimented and contemplated religious, social, political, and economic ideas that many of his peers refused to consider. The slaveholding society with its basic conservatism considered virtually all new ideas to be dangerous, but Bryan recognized that what was new was not inherently bad. Many of his contemporaries as well as later generations of southerners profited by the new trails which Bryan and a few others blazed, but the later generations became increasingly disinclined to experiment and fell further into blindly accepting the paths followed by their fathers. Thus, the diversification of economic interests that protected Jonathan and Hugh during the economic depression of the 1740s was lost upon many antebellum planters. Likewise, the worship of agriculture as nearly the sole legitimate profession pursued by gentlemen had not yet hardened into unspoken law in Bryan's lifetime. Thus Bryan produced shingles for the West Indies market without suffering a decline in social status, and his friend James Habersham established his sons as merchants with little worry that they would be excluded from the political elite.[31]

Georgia was a rough-hewn frontier; a variety of factors were necessary for an individual to establish plantations and become a member of the planter elite. Capital was scarce but requisite for the purchase of slaves to clear the land, to erect the buildings and structures necessary for rice production, and to sow and harvest the crop. Ownership of slaves entitled an individual to large portions of the public domain, but political connections were needed for the procurement of the limited areas of low-country land that could be turned to rice production. Georgia's colonial ruling class understood the importance of political preferment and used their official positions to secure great personal advantages. The colony's executive council controlled the disbursement of land and adeptly used patronage and public works projects to maintain its political and economic dominance in the colony.

Georgia's ruling class, its planter elite, was formed by conscious decision of its members. The monopolization of land and offices, the granting of patronage, and the use of public works projects for personal benefit were predicated upon the close cooperation of council members. Without this cooperation the council could not have maintained its power.

The unity of Georgia's ruling class was most evident in the council's response to the patriot movement in the 1770s. All of the councillors except Jonathan Bryan remained loyal to the Crown that had nurtured their fortunes. Many of their children, however, did not feel the same loyalty. They inherited the practical politics of their fathers and looked after their own best interests in the dispute with Great Britain. They found British interference in colonial government a direct threat to their control over the economic and political life of the colony. James Habersham, Jr., Joseph Habersham, John Houstoun, James Houstoun, James Bryan, Hugh Bryan, William Bryan, Francis Harris, Jr., and Noble Wimberly Jones were councillors' sons who led the movement against Britain. From their ranks came four Speakers of the Georgia House of Delegates, one governor, three delegates to the Continental Congress, one postmaster general of the United States, and one treasurer of Georgia. Although the Revolution broadened the power base of the ruling class by adding to its membership, particularly from the backcountry, many of the colonial elite were able to pass the mantle of power, as well as their plantation estates, to succeeding generations.

Knowledge was power in this slaveholding society. The elite planters had to select the right land for development, supervise the construction of dams and flood walls for the cultivation of rice, familiarize themselves with the native soils and plants, and perfect the management of a large force of slave laborers. Additionally, in a colony of few lawyers, planters had to understand the local legal system, the complexities of financial transactions (for a poorly drawn document could lead to disaster), and the vagaries of the common law. Without this knowledge the prospective planter became dependent on the goodwill of the great men. Jonathan Bryan was one of the latter. He understood every aspect of agricultural production in Georgia, from the politics of land accumulation to the economic advantages to be reaped by development and sale of plantations. His large extended family relied upon him, as did a host of lesser men who looked to him for credit, guidance, and political patronage. He accepted his role as one of responsibility, one which he personally benefited from but also one from which he saw to the needs of others, whether squatters, Indians, slaves, orphans, or impoverished immigrants.

Bryan was an unusual slaveholder, and in the eyes of some contemporaries, a social radical. South Carolina slaveholders in the 1730s and 1740s appear to have treated their bondspeople with little humanity. A seven-day work week for slaves was the rule not the exception. A few masters, like Bryan, perceived the brutal treatment of bondspeople to be disadvantageous to both blacks and whites. Evangelicals perceived that whites were perverted by the heathenish influence in their midst and that by treating their slaves poorly, masters brought upon them the wrath of an angry God. Evangelicals beckoned slaveholders to treat their bondspeople as dependents who warranted not only status as members of the patriarch's family but preparation and guidance for a Christian afterlife. The masters' reward was not only the fulfillment of Christian duty but the expected earthly bounty that accrued from productive slaves happily working blessed soil.

Jonathan Bryan's political, social, familial, and economic goals could not be fulfilled in eighteenth-century Georgia with a free labor force. Alternative sources of labor did not exist which would have allowed Bryan to compete with slaveholding planters. Furthermore, it is questionable whether Bryan would have turned to inexpensive white labor if it had been available—nothing illustrated more an individual's devotion to the dominant society than ownership of black slaves. And if a man like Bryan owned slaves, a man who recognized that "the clothes we wear, the food we eat, and all the superfluities we possess are the produce of [black] labors," it is little wonder that the vast majority of Georgia and South Carolina slaveholders did not consider manumission of their bondspeople.[32]

Bryan's promotion of the evangelization and education of slaves was a heartfelt attempt to reform abuses of the existing system. While these reforms eased his conscience and made for greater profits, they also worked to the elimination of unnecessary brutalities and hardships. Bryan's own concept of bondspeople as family led him to respect the actual families formed by his slaves. He recognized the slave family unit—which many of his peers did not—and begged his heirs not to divide families in the settling of his estate.[33] Bryan's paternalistic ideology was transmitted to his kin, several of whom took the extremely rare step in eighteenth-century Georgia of freeing bondspeople. Two of Bryan's sons, Josiah and William, freed favored slaves, as did his son-in-law John Houstoun. Houstoun freed several bondspeople with cash bequests, which was all the more remarkable in light of the fact that prior to his marriage into the Bryan family he had been rebuked by a neighbor for beating slaves.[34]

In bridging the gap between slaves and Christianity, Bryan fulfilled the role of mediator.[35] Throughout his life he facilitated the exchange of ideas and goods between diverse groups of people. He understood the expediency of seeing to the interests of all parties in a relationship. Rewards for slaves may have eased his conscience for exploiting blacks while it also helped create profitable plantations; the Creek Indians thus were to benefit from access to trade goods, while he fulfilled his desire for more land. The mediation of interests between peoples and between himself and others arose from an "enlightened" understanding of exploitation: personal needs were best met by accommodation to the needs of others.

On the southern frontier of South Carolina Bryan learned the importance of accommodation and political patronage. In the Great Awakening he learned the limitations of both. The eccentricity of Jonathan and Hugh converting slaves to Christianity was tolerated to a point, but the brothers could not breach those boundaries which seemed threatening to the majority of slaveholders. The ownership of bondspeople was the dominant ethos of this society, and evangelical Christianity had to subordinate itself to that ethos. When evangelical Christianity was transformed from a competing ideology to a supporting exponent of the dominant order, the path was cleared of obstacles for its spread through the South.

Bryan's world view resulted only partly from religious influences: life on the frontier shaped the way he treated people of other religions, races, and social groups. The frontier was the classroom in which southern whites honed their racism toward blacks and Indians. From Virginia to

Georgia and west to the Mississippi, southern whites brutalized the native peoples, took their lands, and reduced them to slavery and death. Even after the American Revolution, as George Lamplugh has recently shown, Georgians debate not their right to dispossess southeastern aborigines of their land but the method of parceling the land to whites.[36] The South's legacy of violence can be traced to the treatment of aborigines and blacks as much as to any medieval code of honor.[37] The experiences of the Bryan family beckon us to reexamine the formative influence of the frontier on southern life. The brutality of Joseph Bryan and his neighbors toward the Yamassees was repeated time and again by other whites as the frontier moved. A pattern can be sketched: Indians were exploited in trade, bamboozled out of land, and defeated in warfare; whites then settled the region with large forces of unfree black laborers, who also faced brutal treatment; Evangelical religion then entered the region, the society was stabilized, and paternalism took root on plantations. Thus, Evangelical religion helped white southerners adapt to the frontier conditions of loneliness, hardship, and noninstitutional support while alleviating the guilt that arose from the inhumane treatment of Indians and blacks. The conversion experience allowed the southern slaveholder to rationalize that he was a completely new individual whose past life no longer mattered while allowing him the opportunity for repentance in the improved treatment of bondspeople. In their own minds white southerners effected a transformation from ruffian frontiersmen to benevolent masters of large and dependent families. But the brutality often persisted—with varying degrees of success, bondspeople were lashed to transform them into docile, Christian servants. Other slaveholders learned to use rewards—material inducements and special privileges—to lure their laborers into proper behavior. Both groups of masters slept better believing themselves the purveyors of Christian benevolence.

Jonathan Bryan's rise to wealth and power was in many ways typical of the small group of men who, in the quarter-century before the American Revolution, ruled Georgia. Their broad-based knowledge, ambitions, political abilities, and expertise in labor management helped them shape their society in their own image. They appropriated knowledge, adapted new techniques and concepts, and adjusted themselves to the changing social and economic system of revolutionary Georgia. Some did not adjust to the era's new politics, but many of their children perceived the importance of dropping their loyalty to the king and combining their interests with the new men of property in the back-country.

Jonathan Bryan's success can largely be attributed to his ability to adjust to changing social circumstances. From the frontier of South Carolina to the creation of large "Christian plantations," and from the council of Georgia to the towns of the Creek Confederacy, Bryan sought to understand his environment and formed strategies to fulfill his self-interests. His piety, manner, and strength of character earned the gratitude, cooperation, and admiration of others. He created an image as a Christian patrician who could be relied upon in both public and private affairs. Only by earning the trust of others did he succeed in earning a position as one of the most powerful men in Georgia.

Bryan's powerful combination of Christianity, wealth, and power was not lost on later generations of southern elites. The dominance of planter elites in antebellum southern society was predicated upon the Christian paternalist ethos that rationalized and justified not only the exploitation of black slaves but the right of elites to rule over other whites. Jonathan Bryan's life is a cogent reminder that elite dominance was maintained by bridging some of the gaps that existed between classes. By brokering patronage, Christianity, money, favors, and land, Bryan persuaded diverse groups of people to cooperate with one another. Yet the purpose behind his mediating remained the aggrandizement of his own wealth and power.

Appendixes

Jonathan Bryan's Attendance at Council Meetings

Year	Rate of Attendance (%)	Rate of Attendance on Land Day[a] (%)	Total Meetings (no.)
1755	.58	.86	81
1756	.25		43
1757	.58	.75	64
1758	.76	.91	33
1759	.71	.92	42
1760	.52	.58	61
1761	.49	.89	45
1762	.61	.75	36
1763	.61	.91	21
1764	.30 (1.00)[b]	.33 (1.00)[b]	20
1765	.32 (.44)[b]	.44 (.67)[b]	22
1766	.40	.40	15
1767	.50	.67	16
1768	.46	.67	28
1769	.42	.60	19

a. Computation includes only the scheduled land days on the first Tuesday of every month; land days were held infrequently in 1756.

b. Bryan was completely absent from council meetings from May 2, 1764, to Apr. 24, 1765. Figures in parentheses are the computed percentages exclusive of this lengthy absence.

Percentage of Petitions for Land Rejected and Postponed, 1755–1769

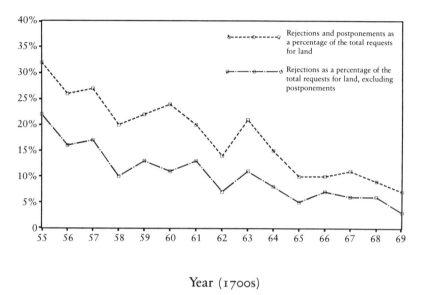

Year (1700s)

Source: Data compiled from *Colonial Records of Georgia,* vols. 7–12.
Note: Total requests, 1755–69 = 5,387; excluding postponements = 4,966.

Jonathan Bryan's Petitions for Land in Georgia

No.	Acreage[a]	Date of Petition[b]	Date Granted[b]	Location	Source[c]
1	500	9/26/50	9/26/50 10/31/53	Savannah R., Walnut Hill Plantation	6:333–34; 7:284–85; 27:84, 135; A78
2[d]	500	5/11/52	resigned 6/55	Hutchinson's Is.	6:369; 7:204, 284–85; 27:87
3	50	?	12/6/57	Savannah, 45- and 5-acre lots	7:685; 8:719; A602
4[e]	500	6/24/52	10/31/55	Little Ogeechee R., Dean Forrest Plantation	27:84, 135; A80; C15
5[f]	500	4/5/54	10/31/55	Little Ogeechee R., Dean Forrest Plantation	6:434; 27:135; A80; C15
6	Town lot	2/4/55	5/15/56	Hardwicke, Lot no. 47	7:103; 27:142; A145
7	500	4/4/55	10/2/59	Great Ogeechee R., Bryan's Cowpen(?)	7:154, 155; 8:155; B206
8	1,800	8/6/55		Sapelo R.	7:229–30
9[g]	300	2/1/57	2/19/57 3/28/58	Salter's Creek, Walnut Hill Plantation	7:468, 493, 698, 746; A601
10	Town lot	4/5/57	?	Hardwicke, lot no. 5	7:512; B55
11	135 [140]	7/4/57	3/28/58	Savannah, eighteen 5-acre lots; 45-acre Savannah town lot	7:609–10; 27:238; A600
12	1,000	11/1/57	resigned	Augustine's Creek	7:650–51, 702

(continued)

No.	Acreage[a]	Date of Petition[b]	Date Granted[b]	Location	Source[c]
13[h]	300	1/3/58	3/28/58	Salter's Creek, Walnut Hill Plantation	7:698, 746; A601
14	1,000 [900]	2/3/58	7/[?]/58	Altamaha R., Broughton Is.	7:702, 791; 28 (part 1), 238; A652
15	250	?	10/2/59	Great Ogeechee R., Bryan's Cowpen	8:155; B205
16	100 [83]	6/6/58	8/7/59	Altamaha R., Doboy Is.	7:776–77; 8:108; 28 (part 1), 321; B378
17	100 [150]	9/5/58	10/7/59	Savannah R., Cockspur Is.	7:809; B204
18	Lot	11/7/58	postponed	Savannah, town lot	7:837
19	600	7/3/59	8/3/62	Pipemaker's Creek, Brampton Plantation	8:67; 28 (part 1), 432; D149
20	Wharf	9/4/59	12/5/69	Savannah	8:125; 10:983; H30
21	300	11/6/59	postponed	Savannah R., Skidaway Point	8:181
22	90	11/6/59	rejected	Savannah R., Walnut Creek Plantation	8:184
23	600	6/3/60	8/3/62	Great Ogeechee R., Bryan's Cowpen	8:318, 719; 28 (part 1), 432; D150, D151
24	2,100[i]	12/2/60	resigned 1,500 acres, 12/[?]/65	Altamaha R.	8:439
25	150	2/3/61	8/3/62	Between North and South Newport rivers	8:480, 719; 28 (part 1), 432; D152
26	44[j] [144]	8/4/61	8/3/62	Savannah, eight garden lots	8:550–51, 719; D154

No.	Acreage[a]	Date of Petition[b]	Date Granted[b]	Location	Source[c]
27	45	?	8/3/62	Savannah	8:719; D153
28	37	11/2/62		Savannah R., is.	8:760
29	700	2/1/63		Branches of Augustine's Swamp	9:23
30[k]	Farm lot[j]	2/7/64	2/7/64	Savannah	9:127
31	800 [600]	12/3/65	4/7/67	Cumberland Is.	9:441; 10:60; 28 (part 2), 268; F158
32[l]	1,600	?		St. Marys R., Buttermilk Bluff	10:160
33	1,600 [1,500]	6/16/66	4/7/67	Cumberland Is.	10:160; F157
34	300	6/2/67	3/1/68	Cumberland Is.	10:189; G34
35	1,000[j] [870]	6/2/67	3/1/68	Cumberland Is.	10:189; G35
36[m]	700[j]	6/2/67	3/1/68	Cumberland Is.	10:190; G36
37	150	2/2/68		Altamaha R.	10:400–401, 975
38	100	2/2/68		Altamaha R., island near Camber's Is.	10:400–401, 975

Note: Total acreage requested was 18,456 acres, plus three town lots, one wharf, and a farm lot in Savannah that was probably about 45 acres. All but one town lot and 390 acres were granted. It is likely that Bryan submitted more requests for land, but because of the records being lost or never recorded they do not appear here. Bryan completed his grants for 9,682 acres, two town lots, one farm lot, and a wharf in Savannah. He actually settled some acreage in which he did not complete his grant. When he requested no. 36, he mentioned that he was already settling acreage by another grant on the Altamaha River, which referred to the 600 acres he had not resigned when he exchanged 1,500 acres of grant no. 23 for 800 acres on Cumberland Island. This was common practice in Georgia, especially in the 1750s, but Bryan was usually conscientious about getting full title to every piece of land he was granted or purchased and it is likely that he let the grants to land on the Altamaha lapse as there is no record of his disposing of the land by sale, gift, or inheritance.

a. Acreage is the amount requested; bracketed amounts are the acreage actually granted.

(continued)

b. Question marks indicate that no petition has been found though the grant was completed. All dates are month, day, and year, 1700s. Blank cells indicate that no date was recorded.

c. All numerical sources refer to the volumes of Candler's *Colonial Records of Georgia*. The letters refer to the grant books located at the Georgia Department of Archives and History, Atlanta.

d. Grant originally taken out in the name of Jonathan Bryan, Jr.

e. Grant originally taken out in the name of Joseph Bryan, minor.

f. Grant originally taken out in the name of Josiah Bryan.

g. Became part of a 600-acre tract with no. 13.

h. Became part of a 600-acre tract with no. 8.

i. 1,575 acres granted by family right and 525 by purchase.

j. By purchase instead of freehold.

k. The lot was first granted to Alexander Heron, 3/10/61, who died before completing the grant. Bryan purchased the right to the lot from Heron's daughter. The council approved the transaction and allowed Bryan the lot.

l. The only reference to this petition is in no. 33, where Bryan requested "that one thousand and six hundred Acres of Land be laid out . . . on Cumberland Island in Lieu of like Quantity heretofore ordered him at a Place called Buttermilk Bluff."

m. Grant originally taken out in the name of Josiah Bryan. As with nos. 1, 2, and 3, Jonathan Bryan petitioned for the land and controlled the land once granted. But unlike the other grants he actually recognized Josiah's ownership when he disposed of the land.

Conveyances of Land and Other Property to and from Jonathan Bryan

No.	Source[a]	Description	Conveyance	Date[b]	Cost (pounds)
1	SC Q, 301	700 acres on Pocataligo R., Prince William Parish	Hugh and Catherine Bryan to JB	7/7/36	1,400SC
2	SC T, 507	230 acres in Prince William Parish (see no. 16)	Wm. and Helen Trewin to JB	8/15/39	500SC
3	SC S-S, 115	1059.5 acres on Stoney Creek, Prince William Parish (see nos. 8 and 10)	Ann and Wm. Palmer to JB	7/1/48	3,240SC
4	JR, box 31B, no. 31A	Note	Wm. Palmer borrowed from JB	3/1/49	350SC
5	JR, box 31A, no. 58A	Note	James Hendrick borrowed from JB	3/22/50	240SC
6	JR, box 31A, no. 64A	Note	William Holman borrowed from JB	5/9/50	100SC
7	GA C, 33	50-acre town lot, Savannah	Maurice Anderson to John Smith to JB	10/20/50	50SC
8	SC R-R, 92	52 acres on Stoney Creek (see no. 3)	Mary and JB to John Smith	6/28/51	260SC
9	GA C, 32–33	200 acres on Savannah R.	Estate of George Philps to JB	10/21/51	150SC

(continued)

No.	Source[a]	Description	Conveyance	Date[b]	Cost (pounds)
10	SC V-V, 1	910 acres on Stoney Creek (see no. 3)	Mary and JB to William Simmons	4/10/52	3,600SC
11	JR, box 62A, no. 168A	Note	Elisha Butler borrowed from JB	5/8/53	480SC
12	GA R, 3–4	Bond, ½ due 1 yr., 3 slaves as security	Matthew Roche borrowed from JB	11/30/54	230GB
13	GA J, 261	Bond	Thomas Goldsmith borrowed from JB	1755	200GB
14	GA C, 133–34	500 acres on Hutchinson's Is.	JB resigned right to land to Gov. John Reynolds	4/29/55	
15	GA C, 184–90	1,000 acres on Little Ogeechee R., Dean Forrest Plantation (see app. 3, nos. 3 and 4)	JB to James Habersham	3/25/56	200GB
16	SC R-R, 62	230 acres in Prince William Parish (see no. 2)	Mary and JB to Ann Mathews	9/29/56	450SC
17	SC S-S, 120	700 acres on Stoney Creek, Prince William Parish (see nos. 1 and 3)	Mary and JB to Andrew Fesch and Peter Guinard	9/22/57	4,200SC
18	GA C, 989–90	1,000 acres: 900 on Broughton Is., 100 on Doboy Is., both in Altamaha R. (see app. 3, nos. 14 and 16; no. 53) 1,000 on North Newport R.	JB to Lachalan McIntosh Lachlan McIntosh to JB	7/16/58	trade
19	GA J, 289	Ten slaves	JB to son, Hugh	9/7/59	gift
20	GA S, 1	Savannah: lot no. 5, 2d tithing, Anson Ward;	Abigal Minis, from estate of Minis Minis to JB	11/8/59	30GB

No.	Source[a]	Description	Conveyance	Date[b]	Cost (pounds)
		Garden lot no. 7 west of town; 44-acre farm lot, lot no. 8, 2d tithing, Anson Ward (see no. 27)			
21	GA J, 499	Lot at Yamacraw	William Knox to JB, James De Veaux, and Matthew Roche in trust for William and John Roche	10/2/60	2GB
22	GA O, 341–43; D-3, 479	350 acres on Savannah R., Purrysburg, S.C., at Monmouth Point (see no. 26)	Robert and Margaret Williams to JB	9/12/61	200GB (1,400SC)
23	Duke University, Wright Papers	Bond of Samuel Miller to adm. estate of Robert Homer	Cosigned by JB, Samuel Miller, and Benjamin Baker	8/10/62	2,000GB
24	GA C, 807–12	1,400 acres: Walnut Hill Plantation and miscellaneous garden and farm lots (see app. 3, nos. 1, 8, 10, and 25)	JB to Miles Brewton	2/25/63	33 slaves valued at 1,400GB
25	*Georgia Gazette*	Plantation of 1,200 acres betw. North and South Newport rivers (see no. 17; app. 3, no. 25)	Advertisement, JB offered for sale	7/21/63	
26	SC B-3, 33	125 acres on Savannah R., Purrysburg (see no. 22)	JB to Andrew Hendrie and Hugh Burn	10/10/63	95GA

(continued)

No.	Source[a]	Description	Conveyance	Date[b]	Cost (pounds)
27	GA C, 776–77	Lot no. 5, 2d tything, Anson Ward (see no. 20)	JB to John Barnwell, trustee for Anne Green	10/14/63	trade
		Lot no. 1, Digby tything, Decker Ward (see no. 34)	John Barnwell, trustee for Anne Green to JB		
28	SC X-3, 213–23	450 acres on Savannah R., Purrysburg, and lot no. 119, Purrysburg (see nos. 47 and 48)	Executors of Charles Lowndes to JB	12/21/63	1,000SC
29	CRG 9:127	Farm lot no. 1, Heathcote Tything, Decker Ward	Martha Heron to JB	2/7/64	?
30	GA S, 12–13	450 acres on Wilmington Island (see no. 39)	William and Mary Dews to JB	3/7/64	100GA
31	GA R, 377	Lot no. 6, Digby tything, Decker Ward, and 45-acre farm lot, lot no. 1, Digby tything, Decker Ward (see no. 41)	William Bradley to JB	5/25/64	60GA
32	GA R, 83	200 acres, Wilmington Is. (see no. 39)	John Casper Beltz to JB	4/20/65	45GA
33	GA O, 380	Two bonds, 250 acres on Savannah R., Brampton Plantation (see app. 3, no. 19)	JB signed two bonds to Thomas Vincent; for accts. due to 1/1/65, including 312£ for a 250-acre tract	8/7/65	414GA
34	GA C, 1045–49	Lot no. 1, Digby tything, Decker Ward (see no. 27)[d]	Mary and JB to Francis Arwin	10/30/65	260GA
35	GA A, 145	500 acres on Great Ogeechee R.,	Will of Mary Bryan conveyed to	6/25/66	Gift

No.	Source[a]	Description	Conveyance	Date[b]	Cost (pounds)
		Bryan's Cowpen (see app. 3, nos. 16 and 23)	daughter, Mary Bryan, wife of JB		
36	*CRG* 10:370–71	500 acres on Great Ogeechee R. (see app. 3, no. 6)	JB to Elizabeth Butler	1767?	?
37	GA X-1, 493	400 acres on Altamaha R. (see no. 54)	John Callwell to JB	1767	120GA
38	GA Y-2, 471–75	Ten slaves	JB to Mary Bryan, daughter	1767	gift
39	GA DD, 114–15	650 acres on Wilmington Is. (see nos. 30 and 32)	JB to Josiah Bryan, son	1/10/67	gift
40	GA S, 365–71	350 acres on Altamaha R. (see no. 60)	John Wereat to JB	5/19/67	140GA
41	GA V, 254; X-2, 1017	Lot no. 6, Digby tything, Decker Ward and 45-acre farm lot (see no. 31)	JB to Alex Inglis and Nathanial Hall	7/29/67	120GA
42	GA S, 374	450 acres on Altamaha R., Cambers Is. (see no. 60)	Thomas Camber to JB	10/10/67	80GA
43	GA S, 439–41	Garden lot, lot no. 147	Robert Bolton and James Wright to JB, who gave lot to James Wright	10/17/67	3GA
44	GA S, 367	470 acres on Altamaha River, Cambers Is. (see no. 60)	Francis Joffe to JB	10/19/67	110GA
45	GA S, 366	1,100 acres in Atlantic Ocean, Little Cumberland Is. (see no. 58)	James Habersham to JB	10/24/67	50GA

(continued)

No.	Source[a]	Description	Conveyance	Date[b]	Cost (pounds)
46	GA S, 363	2,000 acres on Cumberland Is. (see no. 58)	John Smith to JB	10/25/67	50GA
47	*Georgia Gazette*	7,500 acres on Cumberland Is.; 150-acre Cockspur Is.; 450-acre Little Yemassee; 500 acres on Wilmington Is.; 2,150 acres at Mathews Bluff, S.C. (see nos. 28, 45, 46, and 48; app. 3, nos. 17, 31, 33–36)	Advertisement, JB offered for sale	2/10/68	
48	SC X-3, 213–23	450 acres in S.C., Little Yemassee; lot no. 119 Purrysburg (see nos. 28 and 47)	JB to Charles William McKennon	9/16/68	450GA
49	GA S, 360	2,000 acres on Cumberland Is. (see no. 58)	James Bulloch to JB	9/20/68	300GA
50	Chatham County Deeds, 1785–1910, 183–84	150 acres in Savannah	Mary and JB to Basil Cowper (for Cowper, Telfair and Telfair)	11/10/68	300GA
51	GA S, 357	1,500 acres on Cumberland Is. (see no. 58)	James Cuthbert to JB	1/3/69	275GA
52	Duke University, Georgia Miscellaneous Papers	Bond	JB cosigned for John Martin bond that he would settle tract of land with slaves	1/3/69	400GB
53	GA CC-1, 156–59	Doboy Is., in Altamaha R. (see no. 18; app. 3, no. 16)	JB to Lachlan McIntosh	2/16/69	trade

No.	Source[a]	Description	Conveyance	Date[b]	Cost (pounds)
54	GA X-1, 493	400 acres on Altamaha R. (see no. 37)	JB to James Spalding	4/14/69	120GA
55	Duke University, Telfair Papers	Bond	JB to Edward Telfair, given to attorney by Basil Cowper for immediate payment	7/30/69	280GA
56	*South Carolina Gazette*	Two islands in Altamaha R.: 1,600 acres on Cambers and 600 acres on Wereats; 11,750 acres on Cumberland Is.; 2,000 acres on Savannah R. at Mathew's Bluff (see nos. 42, 44–47, 58 and 60; app. 3, nos. 31, 33–36)	Advertisement, JB offered for sale	6/70–7/70	"moderate rates, credit available"
57	GA V, 351	700 acres on Cumberland Is. (see no. 58; app. 3, no. 36)	Josiah Bryan to Thomas Lynch and Alexander Mose	8/6/70	130GA
58	GA V, 290–92	10,870 acres on Cumberland Is. and Little Cumberland Is. (see no. 56)	JB to Thomas Lynch and Alexander Mose	8/7/70	1,100GA
59	GA X-2, 865	350 acres on Savannah R., Brampton Plantation (see no. 65)	Isaac Young to JB	11/30/70	500GA
60	GA V, 502	1,280 acres: 920 acres, Cambers Is.,	JB to John Hall	1771	1,092GA

(continued)

No.	Source[a]	Description	Conveyance	Date[b]	Cost (pounds)
		and 360 acres, Wereats Is. (see nos. 40, 42, and 44)			
61	GA X-2, 868	100 acres in Savannah R., Hutchinson's Island (see no. 66)	John and Francis Graham to JB	3/28/71	600GA
62	GA X-1, 100	Wharf no. 1, Savannah (see app. 3, no. 20)	JB to Peter Blyth	7/18/71	30GA
63	GA Y-1, 180	Five slaves	JB to Samuel Douglas	3/9/73	200GA
64	GA X-2, 856	100 acres in Savannah R., Hutchinson's Is. (see no. 65)	Lachlan McGillivray to JB	4/17/73	600GA
65	GA X-2, 856	450 acres: 100 on Hutchinson's Is.; 350 of "Brampton Plantation" (see nos. 59 and 64)	JB to Miles Brewton	4/22/73	1,100GA
66	GA X-2, 853	100 acres on Savannah R., Hutchinson's Is. (see no. 61)	JB to Lachlan McGillivray	5/11/73	600GA
67	GA HH, 24–25	Ten slaves	JB to James Bryan	9/22/73	gift
68	*Georgia Royal Gazette*	Ben and two children to be sold	Cowper and Telfair et al. vs. JB in attachment	2/15/81	
69	Chatam County Deeds, 1785– 1910; D75–77	Eleven slaves, including six given in trust with one progeny, 5/28/75, and four more	JB to John Houstoun and Hannah Bryan Houstoun	3/5/82	gift

No.	Source[a]	Description	Conveyance	Date[b]	Cost (pounds)
70	GA CCC, 22–23	Two slave girls	JB to Esther and Hannah Morel, granddaughters	1783	gift
71	Chatham County Wills, no. 14	Union Plantation; 2,000 acres at Mathews Bluff; two slaves; six carpenter slaves, their wives and children	JB willed to children and grandchildren	12/15/83	gift
72	GA H, 488–89	3,000 acres in S.C. opposite Hudson's Ferry	JB to Mary Morel, daughter	3/20/84	500GA
73	Chatham County Deeds, 304–305	One slave boy	JB to Richard Bryan Wylly, grandson	5/7/85	gift

a. SC = South Carolina Department of Archives and History, Conveyances, 1719–76; JR = South Carolina Department of Archives and History, South Carolina Court of Common Pleas, Judgment Rolls, 1703–90; GA = Colonial Records, Georgia Department of Archives and History; *CRG* = Candler, *Colonial Records of Georgia*. All other letters are book designations. Chatham County Records may be found at the Georgia Department of Archives and History.

b. Date refers to the actual transaction, not to when it was recorded; dates are for 1700s and follow month, day, year order.

c. All figures are computed in pounds and rounded to exclude shillings and pence. SC = South Carolina currency, GA = Georgia currency, GB = British sterling. In general, Georgia money was of only slightly less value than British money. South Carolina currency usually traded at approximately 7 to 1 for GA or GB.

d. Bryan obtained this lot for £30GB. He may have built a house on the lot he purchased from Abigal Minis (no. 20), then traded the house and lot in 1763 to Anne Green (no. 29), and moved his family to Green's house from Walnut Hill while he built Brampton. He sold the house when Brampton was completed.

Jonathan Bryan's Political Activity Compared

with His Requests for Land

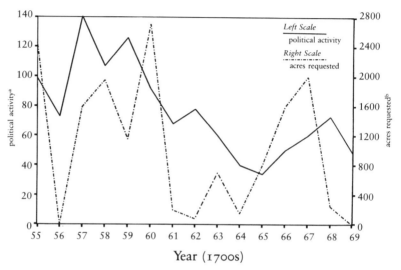

aPoints granted on the following basis: 10 for council membership; attendance at council meetings per year: 5 for 25 percent; 10 for 30 percent; 10 additional points for every 10 percent thereafter. Committee work given 4 points if of minor importance and 8 points if Bryan was a major contributor or if committee was of major importance. Appointments to minor political offices and commissioner positions awarded 10 points each. Twenty points granted for extraordinary political activity.

bAll grants documented in appendix 3. Town lots calculated as the equivalent of 150 acres.

Selected Vote Tallies Illustrating

the Factionalism of the Georgia Commons

House of Assembly, 1773

Representative	1	2	3	4	5	6	7	8	9	Political alliance after 1775
THE PRO-GOVERNOR FACTION										
Barnard, Francis	O		G	G	G			G	G	Tory?
Clay, Joseph			O		G	G	G	O	G	Rebel
Houstoun, James	G	G	G		G		G	G		Rebel
Houstoun, Patrick	G	G	G		G		G	G		Tory
Jamieson, John	G	G	G	G	G	G	G	G	G	Tory
Jones, William	G	G	G							Tory
Law, Joseph	G		G	G	G	O	G	G	G	Tory
Maxwell, Audley	G	G	G*	O	G	O	G		G	?
Millen, Stephen	G	G	G	O	G			G	G	?
Netherclift, Thomas	G	G	G		G	G	G	G	G	Tory
Shruder, Thomas	G	G	G	G	G	G	G	G	G	?
Simpson, John	G	G	G	G	G	G	G	G	G	Tory
Stirk, John	G	G	G	G	G	G	O	G		Rebel
Treutlen, John		O	O*	G	G	O	O	G	G	Rebel
Yonge, Henry	G		G*			G	O	G	G	Tory
Young, Isaac		O	G		O	G	O	G		?
Young, Thomas	G	G	G	G	G		G			Tory
Young, William (Speaker of the House)										Tory
OPPOSITION FACTION										
Andrew, Benjamin	G	O	G	O	O	O	O	O	O	Rebel
Baker, John	G	O		O	O	O	O	O		Rebel
Bourquine, Henry	G	O	O*	O	O	O	O	O	G	Rebel

(continued)

Representative	1	2	3	4	5	6	7	8	9	Political alliance after 1775
Brown, Francis	O	O	O	O	G	G		O		?
Bryan, Jonathan	O		O	O	O	G	O			Rebel
Carter, Thomas	O	O	G	O	G	O		G	O	Rebel
Jones, Noble W.	O	O	O	O	O	O	O	O	O	Rebel
Le Conte, William	G	O	O	O	O			O	G	Rebel
Powell, Josiah	G		O*	O	G	O	G	O	O	Rebel
Sallens, Peter			O*			O	G	O	O	?
Zubly, David	O	O	O	O	O	O		O	O	Tory

Notes: G = vote with the pro-governor faction; O = vote against the pro-governor faction; blank cells indicate that the representative did not vote; the Speaker of the House votes only to break a tie.

Vote 1: "Bill for the preservation of Deer and to prevent the Mischiefs arising from the practice of hunting and killing Deer by Night" 12/15/72. (Candler, *CRG*, 15:349–50).

Vote 2: Determination of "whether the election for the sea Islands [between Samuel Farley and Henry Yonge] be deemed an undue election" 1/21/73 (ibid., 359–61).

Vote 3: "An ordinance to appoint the Honourable Grey Elliott, Esqr to be the Provincial agent in Great Britain in case of Mr. Franklin's absence" 1/28/73 (ibid., 369). Those individuals whose vote has an asterisk did not vote on the initial confirmation. They did cast their vote, however, on Elliott's final confirmation on Aug. 6, 1773 (ibid., 485).

Vote 4: Determination of whether to appoint a committee "to examine into the State of the Governors House, and if any repairs be found Necessary to report the same" 2/9/73 (ibid., 381).

Vote 5: Determination of whether to appoint a committee "to wait on his Excellency Sir James Wright, Baronet, on his Arrival at the landing place, to congratulate him on his safe return to this province" 2/11/73 (ibid., 384).

Vote 6: Determination of whether to fill the seat of William Jones, who had left Georgia with no intention of returning 6/17/73 (ibid., 430–31).

Vote 7: Determination of whether "thanks of this House be given to George Galphin and Lachlan McGillivray Esquires for exerting their Influence with the Indians and being Very Instrumental in assisting the Governor to obtain the late Cession of Lands" 6/28/73 (ibid., 439).

Vote 8: Determination of whether the House should "resolve to provide for the Expences of Government and the debts due from the publick incurred between the 26th of April 1771 and the 21st of April 1772" 7/23/73 (ibid., 467).

Vote 9: Determination of whether "Jonathan Bryan Esquire having some days since absented himself From this House without leave and having Yesterday Morning in a Contemptuous manner departed from this province without asking leave or even making his Intentions known—be Expelled [from] this House" 7/30/73 (ibid., 474).

NOTES

INTRODUCTION

1. Frederick Jackson Turner, *The Frontier in American Society* (New York: Holt, 1920); Francis Jennings, *The Invasion of America: Indians, Colonialism, and the Cant of Conquest* (Chapel Hill: University of North Carolina Press, 1975), and *The Ambiguous Iroquois Empire: The Covenant Chain Confederation of Indian Tribes with English Colonies* (New York: Norton, 1984); James Axtell, *The European and the Indian: Essays in the Ethnohistory of Colonial North America* (New York: Oxford University Press, 1981), and *The Invasion Within: The Contest of Cultures in Colonial North America* (New York: Oxford University Press, 1985); Peter H. Wood, *Black Majority: Negroes in Colonial South Carolina from 1670 through the Stono Rebellion* (Chapel Hill: University of North Carolina Press, 1974), and "La Salle: Discovery of a Lost Explorer," *American Historical Review* 89 (Apr. 1984): 294–323; William Cronon, *Changes in the Land: Indians, Colonists, and the Ecology of New England* (New York: Hill and Wang, 1983).

2. Rhys Isaac, *The Transformation of Virginia, 1740–1790* (Chapel Hill: University of North Carolina Press, 1982): Allan Kulikoff, *Tobacco and Slaves: The Development of Southern Cultures in the Chesapeake, 1680–1800* (Chapel Hill: University of North Carolina Press, 1986); Edmund S. Morgan, *American Slavery, American Freedom: The Ordeal of Colonial Virginia* (New York: Norton, 1975); Wood, *Black Majority;* Verner W. Crane, *The Southern Frontier, 1670–1732* (Ann Arbor: University of Michigan Press, 1929; repr., New York: Norton, 1981).

3. Historical archaeology is rapidly filling the gaps in our knowledge of cultural interaction and adaptation. With the recent uncovering of the site of the free black community at Fort Mosa, we can expect to enlarge our understanding of cultural exchange well beyond what written documents alone have permitted. John H. Hann's recently published *Apalachee: The Land between the Rivers* (Gainesville: University Presses of Florida, 1988) successfully combines historical archaeology, anthropology, and history in a study of the long-neglected Apalachee. Several students of Charles H. Fairbanks have been painstakingly analyzing a variety of sites in and around St. Augustine. One of his students, Kathleen Deagan, has synthesized her work with others and disclosed patterns of adaptation among St. Augustine's different ethnic, social,

and economic groups, see *Spanish St. Augustine: The Archaeology of a Colonial Creole Community* (New York: Academic Press, 1983).

CHAPTER 1: THE SOUTHERN FRONTIER

1. Virginia, Maryland, Kentucky, Arkansas, eastern Texas, and western Louisiana properly belong in any discussion of the South, but I have excluded them in discussion of the Southeast because of their different colonial experiences. Unlike the southeastern colonies, the Chesapeake colonies did not face a strong Indian threat after the mid-seventeenth century. Virginia occasionally participated in the Indian wars of the Southeast and conducted offensive operations against aboriginal nations to the west, but it did not have to contend with powerful Indian neighbors like the European colonies to the south did. Virginia, moreover, was largely able to ignore the British, French, and Spanish competition in the Southeast until it threatened to hinder its own expansion into the Ohio River valley in the 1750s. Thus the dynamics of war, trade, and diplomacy differed in the Chesapeake from those in the Southeast.

The Southeast also was tied together by its Indian population. The Indians of the Southeast traded with the aboriginal nations to the north and west, but the former did not share with the latter a common political, religious, and cultural heritage. French and Indian interaction with the aboriginal nations of what is now Arkansas and eastern Texas had little bearing on the southeastern region.

2. Works on the southeastern Indians are too numerous to permit mention of all of them. Charles Hudson, *The Southeastern Indians* (Knoxville: University of Tennessee Press, 1976), provides a general overview and a good bibliography. The works of John R. Swanton remain the preeminent source for information on Indian life, language, and customs. Crane, *Southern Frontier,* is the best place to begin to examine the relations of the Indians to the Europeans, but also see Peter H. Wood, Gregory A. Waselkov, and M. Thomas Hatley, eds., *Powhatan's Mantle: Indians in the Colonial Southeast* (Lincoln: University of Nebraska Press, in press). Two recently published essays merit the special attention of scholars: Daniel H. Usner, "The Frontier Exchange Economy of the Lower Mississippi Valley in the Eighteenth Century," *William and Mary Quarterly,* 3d ser., 44 (Apr. 1987): 165–92; Patricia K. Galloway, "Choctaw Factionalism and Civil War, 1746–1750," in *The Choctaw before Removal,* ed. Carolyn Keller Reeves (Jackson: University of Mississippi Press, 1985), 120–56.

3. For the relationship between European stereotyping and dispossession, see Jennings, *Invasion of America.* Governor Patrick Tonyn of East Florida illustrated the viewpoint of many Anglo-Saxons when he wrote to the earl of Dartmouth: "The savages or Indians I hold in this view only. As wolves or wild

beasts in a forest. They have no right in any land, the Spaniards called the Province of East Florida, which was given up at the treaty of peace to Great Britain" (Tonyn to Earl of Dartmouth, Dec. 18, 1774, British Public Record Office, Colonial Office Papers [Great Britain], series 5, 556, pp. 171–72, Manuscript Division, Library of Congress, Washington, D.C. [hereafter cited as CO]). Usurping the Indians' land became the major political issue of the 1780s and 1790s: Georgians disagreed over how to distribute the land to white people. Apparently, there was no public discussion of whether it was morally or legally correct to take the Indians' land from them. See George R. Lamplugh, *Politics on the Periphery: Factions and Parties in Georgia, 1783–1806* (Newark: University of Delaware Press, 1986).

4. Pre-Columbian population estimates of the southeastern Indians, like population estimates of all pre-Columbian Indians, have come under radical review in the last two decades. For instance, many earlier anthropologists and historians grossly underestimated the aboriginal population of Florida as falling between 10,000 and 40,000. Although Dobyns's conclusions will be challenged, it seems clear that his estimates are much closer to the mark than those of his predecessors. Henry F. Dobyns, *Their Numbers Become Thinned: Native American Population Dynamics in Eastern North America* (Knoxville: University of Tennessee Press, 1983).

5. On English disrespect of Spanish boundaries, see Herbert E. Bolton and Mary Ross, *The Debatable Land: A Sketch of the Anglo-Spanish Contest for the Georgia Country* (New York: Russell and Russell, 1968); Herbert E. Bolton, ed., *Arredondo's Historical Proof of Spain's Title to Georgia: A Contribution to the History of One of the Spanish Borderlands* (Berkeley: University of California Press, 1925); John Jay Tepaske, *The Governorship of Spanish Florida, 1700–1763* (Durham, N.C.: Duke University Press, 1964), 125–30. For the boundary between the Indians and British colonies, see Louis De Vorsey, Jr., *The Indian Boundary in the Southern Colonies, 1763–1775* (Chapel Hill: University of North Carolina Press, 1966). The British superintendent to the southern Indians, John Stuart, commented in 1765: "The fixing and ascertaining a distinct Boundary between the Indians and all the Provinces is essential to the tranquility of this district; it is a point which greatly concerns them, and to which they are extremely attentive" (CO 5/66, p. 367, quoted in De Vorsey, *Indian Boundary,* 44).

6. British trading with Spanish colonies provided a major motive for the Spanish government to undertake war with the British in 1740. Less than five years after Spanish Florida had invaded Georgia, and seven years after South Carolina had participated in the British invasion of Florida, the South Carolina upper house rejected a bill to "prevent exportation of slaves from this province to his Majesty's enemies" (J. H. Easterby, R. Nicholas Oldsberg, and Terry W. Lipscomb, eds., *The Colonial Records of South Carolina: The Journal of the*

Commons House of Assembly, 13 vols. [Columbia, S.C.: Historical Commission, 1951–86], 7:260). See also Tepaske, *Governorship of Spanish Florida,* 42, 53, 71–76, 83, 88–91, 105.

7. See discussion of the Yamassee War below. The cessions of land wrested from the Creeks are discussed in chapter 6. On the role of the British traders in the Choctaw civil war, see Galloway, "Choctaw Factionalism and Civil War"; Wilbur R. Jacobs, ed., *The Appalachian Frontier: The Edmond Atkin Report and Plan of 1758* (Lincoln: University of Nebraska Press, 1967), 24, 72–73.

8. See, for example, "David Taitt's Journal of a Journey through the Creek Country, 1772," in *Travels in the American Colonies,* ed. Newton D. Mereness (New York: Macmillian, 1916), 493–565.

9. This remained a problem into the nineteenth century, for Americans could conquer the Creeks only by employing aborigine warriors.

10. Tepaske, *Governorship of Spanish Florida,* 113–15, 197. See also Charles H. Fairbanks, *Florida Indians III: Ethnohistorical Report on the Florida Indians* (New York: Garland, 1974), 19–20, 71–72.

11. An episode reported by André Pénicaut illustrates the flexibility and open-mindedness of the French compared with the British in their view of aborigines. When supplies were short and the French garrison at Mobile faced starvation in 1706, the French commander, Jean Baptiste Le Moyne de Bienville, permitted soldiers to live with the Indians until the food situation improved. In 1710, French soldiers were again forced to find subsistence by living with the Indians. British officers would not have allowed their men the liberty to join the Indians. The British found reprehensible the practice of whites joining Indian nations and forced hundreds of "white Indians" to return to Euramerican society (Richebourg Gaillard McWilliams, trans. and ed., *Fleur de Lys and Calumet: Being the Pénicaut Narrative of French Adventure in Louisiana* [Tuscaloosa: University of Alabama Press, 1953], 105–107, 114–15, 133; Axtell, *European and the Indian,* 168–206).

12. Wood, *Black Majority.*

13. Not all British people became involved in the plantation system, but this remained the predominant form of economic organization until farmers began inhabiting the backcountry in the early 1760s at the end of the French and Indian War. Those who made their wealth from the plantation system retained control over the political life of their colonies and then states through the colonial and revolutionary periods.

14. For the origins of South Carolina, see M. Eugene Sirmans, *Colonial South Carolina: A Political History, 1663–1763* (Chapel Hill: University of North Carolina Press, 1966), 3–18, 36; Wood, *Black Majority,* 3–9, 13–34, 65; Robert Weir, *Colonial South Carolina: A History* (New York: KTO Press, 1983), 47–59, 64; Edward McCrady, *The History of South Carolina under the Proprietary Government, 1670–1719* (New York: Macmillan, 1901); Crane,

Southern Frontier, 31, 162–63. For the history of the Port Royal region, see Lawrence Rowland Sanders, "Eighteenth Century Beaufort: A Study of South Carolina's Southern Parishes to 1800" (Ph.D. diss., University of South Carolina, 1978).

15. J. H. Redding, *The Life and Times of Jonathan Bryan, 1708–1788* (Savannah, Ga.: Morning News Print, 1901), 6; A. S. Salley, ed., *Warrants for Lands in South Carolina, 1672–1711,* rev. ed. (Columbia: University of South Carolina Press, 1973), 569; Memorials, Record Group (RG) 30, series 2, p. 262, item 2, South Carolina Department of Archives and History, Columbia (hereafter cited as S.C. Archives).

16. Clarence L. Ver Steeg, "Internal Politics in Proprietary Carolina: An Emerging Political Mosaic," *Origins of a Southern Mosaic* (Athens: University of Georgia Press, 1975).

17. Lewis Jones to David Humphreys, July 14, 1738, Papers of the Society for the Propagation of the Gospel in Foreign Parts (hereafter cited as SPG Papers), B7, 231, Manuscript Division, Library of Congress, Washington, D.C.

18. A. S. Salley, ed., *Journal of the Commons House of Assembly for 1702* (Columbia: South Carolina Department of Archives and History, 1932), 6, 18, 19, 21–22, 97, 99; Chapman J. Milling, *Red Carolinians* (Chapel Hill: University of North Carolina Press, 1940), 105–106, 110.

19. Memorials, RG 30, series 2, p. 262, item 2, S.C. Archives; Land Grants, RG 2, series 5, box 38, no. 587, May 10, 1705, S.C. Archives; Converse R. Clowse, *Economic Beginnings in Colonial South Carolina, 1670–1732* (Columbia: University of South Carolina Press, 1971), incorrectly lists only one land grant for Granville County in 1705 (see table 2, p. 255). Crane, *Southern Frontier,* p. 163, shows numerous grants in Granville.

20. Crane, *Southern Frontier,* 163–64; Sanders, "Beaufort," 58–59.

21. W. L. McDowell, ed., *Journal of the Commissioners of the Indian Trade, September 20, 1710–August 29, 1718* (Columbia: South Carolina Department of Archives and History, 1955), 11, 16–17.

22. Parish boundaries defined political units beginning in 1712. St. Helena's encompassed all of Granville County.

23. Captain John Palmer became a South Carolina hero during the Yamassee War; Barnaby Bull was related to William Bull, who became governor of the colony. Bellinger, whose first name was not given in the record, might have been Edward, who became the largest landowner in the southern region. Captain John Cochran was also listed in the same complaint by the Indians for having sold a free Indian man into slavery. The Cochrans were yet another leading family of the community.

24. For the Yamassee War, see Sanders, "Beaufort," 57–70; Sirmans, *Colonial South Carolina,* 111–14; Crane, *Southern Frontier,* 162–86; Milling, *Red Carolinians,* 135–64; David Duncan Wallace, *The History of South*

Carolina, 2 vols. (New York: American Historical Association, 1934), 1:204–14; Gary B. Nash, *Red, White, and Black: The Peoples of Early America* (Englewood Cliffs, N.J.: Prentice-Hall, 1974): 149–53.

25. Records in the British Public Record Office Relating to South Carolina (hereafter cited as BPRO), microfilm, roll 2, vol. 7, pp. 235–40, S.C. Archives.

26. Sanders, "Beaufort," 60, 69–70, 139–46; Crane, *Southern Frontier,* 162–86, 247–48, 264; Wallace, *History of South Carolina,* 1:202–14, 217–20; Tobias Fitch, "Journal of Captain Tobias Fitch's Mission from Charleston to the Creeks, 1726," in *Travels in the American Colonies,* 175–212; Tepaske, *Governorship of Spanish Florida,* 130–32, 198–99.

27. Crane, *Southern Frontier,* 169–71; Wallace, *South Carolina,* 1:207–9.

28. Sanders, "Beaufort," 141.

29. As soon as the land office opened, the former Indian traders turned in completed surveys of the tracts they desired; they wasted no time establishing their claims. This speed illustrates both their desire and their thorough familiarity with the land they coveted.

30. Bryan Genealogy, by Daniel Elliot Huger Smith, 1902, file 36, Smith to Captain Screven, RG 30, p. 21, South Carolina Historical Society, Charleston.

31. Memorials, RG 30, series 2, vol. 3, p. 40, S.C. Archives.

32. Purchases of land recorded in Conveyances, RG 7, series 1, vol. HO, p. 285, S.C. Archives; ibid., vol. GO, p. 241; ibid., vol. 10, p. 346 (hereafter all Conveyances from S.C. Archives are from RG 7, series 1).

33. Sirmans, *Colonial South Carolina,* 170; Robert K. Ackerman, *South Carolina Colonial Land Policies* (Columbia: University of South Carolina Press, 1977).

34. Harvey H. Jackson, "The Carolina Connection: Jonathan Bryan, His Brothers, and the Founding of Georgia, 1733–1752," *Georgia Historical Quarterly* 68 (Summer 1984): 149–50; Allen D. Candler, ed., *The Colonial Records of the State of Georgia,* 26 vols. (Atlanta: Franklin-Turner, 1904–16; Kenneth Coleman and Milton Ready, eds., *The Colonial Records of the State of Georgia,* vols. 27–39, Atlanta: University of Georgia Press, 1975–). 35:36. (hereafter cited as *CRG*). Transcript copies of vols. 27–39 are at the Georgia Department of Archives and History, Atlanta.

35. Noble Jones to James Oglethorpe, July 3–7, 1735, in Mills Lane, ed., *General Oglethorpe's Georgia: Colonial Letters, 1733–1743,* 2 vols. (Savannah: Beehive Press, 1975), 208–209; Jackson, "Carolina Connection," 155; Candler, *CRG,* 20:429, 35:36; for the carving of piraguas, see Larry Ivers, *British Drums on the Southern Frontier: The Military Colonization of Georgia, 1733–1749* (Chapel Hill: University of North Carolina Press, 1974), 53–58.

36. From 1732 to 1738 exportation of rice increased from 37,000 to 67,000 barrels per year (Sirmans, *Colonial South Carolina,* 167); Weir, *South*

Carolina, 145, 165–66; Peter A. Coclanis, "Rice Prices in the 1720s and the Evolution of the South Carolina Economy," *Journal of Southern History* 48 (Nov. 1982): 531–44. John J. McCusker and Russell R. Menard recently questioned the impact of this legislation on long-term rice production. They found that ports south of Cape Finistere took about 9 percent of colonial rice exports between 1712 and 1717. This "figured doubled in the 1730s, but afterward . . . [these] countries took a declining share of the Lower South's rice crop" (*The Economy of British America 1607–1789* [Chapel Hill: University of North Carolina Press, 1985]). Nevertheless, South Carolina's planters gained new confidence from this legislation, as evidenced by the doubling of acreage devoted to rice.

37. For the division of land and the dates of plats and land grants, see John R. Todd and Francis Hutson, *Prince William's Parish and Plantations* (Richmond: Garnett and Massie, 1935), map, 30–31.

38. Colonial Plats, series 3, box 1, item 1, S.C. Archives; Land Grants, RG 2, series 5, vol. 43, p. 8, item 2, S.C. Archives.

39. The land rush did not please everyone. Squabbling arose after conflicting claims were pressed by various interest groups. Speculators and a group of yeomanry who had recently arrived in the colony combined their interests against the longtime inhabitants of Port Royal. Hugh Bryan, as deputy surveyor of the county, became enmeshed in a widening land dispute. The land for which the Port Royalites had fought the Yamassees—and then had to wait fifteen years for the land office to open—appeared to be slipping from their grasp. But a fortuitous turn of events saved the land for the Port Royalites. The colony's chief justice intervened on the side of the speculators and farmers, which transformed the dispute into a political battle over jurisdiction between the court and the Commons House. South Carolina's powerful Commons House, in defense of their constitutional prerogative, was led to support the claims of the Port Royalites. The Bryans and their neighbors were thus able to claim the Indian land for themselves (Sirmans, *Colonial South Carolina,* 173–74, 177–82; Wallace, *South Carolina,* 325–33; Weir, *South Carolina,* 111–15; Sanders, "Beaufort," 131–34; Records of the States of the United States of America, microfilmed by the Library of Congress, 1949, South Carolina, A16, reel 4, pp. 915–16, 923–25).

40. Examples of these plats are printed in Todd and Hutson, *Prince William's Plantations.* The originals are located in the S.C. Archives.

41. The patrons included Edmund Bellinger, William Bull, Thomas Waring, Barnaby Bull, Thomas Drayton, William Hazzard, Stephen Bull, Paul Jenys, John Bull, Richard Bland, James St. John. Arthur Middleton, and Isaac Mazyck.

42. See BPRO, microfilm, roll 2, vol. 7, p. 187, Apr. 21, 1719.

43. Inventories of Estates, book R, pp. 153–56, S.C. Archives; Samuel

Urlsperger, ed. *Americanisches Ackerwerck Gottes* (Halle, 1755), 242–43. I am indebted to Harvey H. Jackson and George Fenwick Jones for this reference; Candler, *CRG*, 7:154–55.

44. Jonathan Bryan to John Wesley, printed in *Methodist Magazine* 5 (1785); reprinted in Redding, *Life and Times of Jonathan Bryan*, 44–45.

45. Hugh surveyed for Governor Robert Johnson an 8,000-acre tract of land in Purrysburg. This important political connection may have helped him receive government contracts. Examples of Bryan's work for the government can be found in Easterby et al., *Colonial Records*, 1:432, 434, 443, 454, 479–80, 485–86, 634, 659; 2:58, 106, 150, 210–11, 230, 503.

46. Ibid., 1:432, 434, 543, 577, 631; 9:444, 452.

47. A. S. Salley, *Minutes and Vestry of St. Helena's Parish, South Carolina, 1726–1812* (Columbia, 1919).

48. See, for instance, Russell R. Menard's review of Thomas Doerflinger, *A Vigorous Spirit of Enterprise: Philadelphia Merchants, 1730–1790*, in *Reviews in American History* 15 (June 1987): 232–38, quotation on 237.

49. South Carolina worked very hard to create enmity between blacks and Indians and to forestall contacts that could lead to cooperation. Indian traders, for instance, were forbidden by legislative act in 1731 from employing blacks. Indians often were hired to capture runaways, and South Carolina made treaties with several Indian nations to provide for the return of escaped blacks. Wood, *Black Majority*, 116, 260–63; William S. Willis, "Divide and Rule: Red, White, and Black in the Southeast," *Journal of Negro History* 48 (July 1963): 157–76.

50. Weir, *Colonial South Carolina*, 121–22; Walter L. Dorn, *Competition for Empire, 1740–1763* (New York: Harper and Brothers, 1940), 164–73. For South Carolina's constant requests for help, see BPRO, rolls 5 and 6.

51. Bolton and Ross, *The Debatable Land;* John Tate Lanning, *The Diplomatic History of Georgia: A Study in the Epoch of Jenkins' Ear* (Chapel Hill: University of North Carolina Press, 1936).

52. Robert L. Merriwether, *The Expansion of South Carolina, 1729–1765* (Kingsport, Tenn.: Southern Publishers, 1940), 17–30; Crane, *Southern Frontier*, 292–95; Ivers, *British Drums on the Southern Frontier*, 6–7, 23–29; Larry Ivers, *Colonial Forts of South Carolina, 1670–1775* (Columbia: University of South Carolina Press, 1970), 8–15, 24–36; Richard P. Sherman, *Robert Johnson: Proprietary and Royal Governor of South Carolina* (Columbia: University of South Carolina Press, 1966), 107–17.

53. Merriwether, *Expansion of South Carolina*, 34; Henry A. M. Smith, "Purrysburg," *South Carolina Historical Magazine* 10 (Oct. 1909): 187–219; Wallace, *History of South Carolina*, 1:333–335; Kenneth Coleman, *Colonial Georgia: A History* (New York: Scribner's, 1976), 9.

54. Arlin Charles Migliazzo, "Ethnic Diversity on the Southern Frontier: A

Social History of Purrysburg, South Carolina, 1732–1792" (Ph.D. diss., Washington State University, 1982), 187–90.

55. Merriwether, *Expansion of South Carolina*, 134–36. When Purrysburg was firmly established at mid-decade the miserly Commons House withdrew its support of the nearby garrison at Pallachicola.

56. The map is reproduced in Smith, "Purrysburg," facing 187. Hugh's expert drawings and surveys were used in the later regional maps produced by the famed cartographer William Gerard De Brahm. See, for instance, De Brahm's *A Map of South Carolina and a Part of Georgia,* Map Room, Library of Congress, Washington, D.C. The map was published in several editions and reprinted in France in French. Hugh received credit for his contributions to the map.

57. The disputed title of Purrysburg waterfront land haunted Bryan for thirty years. See *Lessee of Loyer vs. Jonathan Bryan,* Charleston Judgment Rolls, box 68A, no. 337A, S.C. Archives; Anne King Gregorie, ed., *Records of the Court of Chancery of South Carolina, 1671–1779* (Washington, D.C.: American Historical Association, 1950), 588–89; *Georgia Gazette,* May 16, Aug. 1, Sept. 19, 1765.

58. Jackson, "Carolina Connection," 148–49. In addition to works already mentioned, for Georgia under the trustees see Harvey H. Jackson and Phinizy Spalding, eds., *Forty Years of Diversity: Essays on Colonial Georgia* (Athens: University of Georgia Press, 1984); Amos Aschbach Ettinger, *James Edward Oglethorpe: Imperial Idealist* (Oxford: Clarendon Press, 1936); Webb Garrison, *Oglethorpe's Folly: The Birth of Georgia* (Lakemont, Ga.: Copple House Books, 1982); Albert Saye, "Was Georgia a Debtor Colony?" *Georgia Historical Quarterly* 24 (Dec. 1940): 323–41; Phinizy Spalding, *Oglethorpe in America* (Chicago: University of Chicago Press, 1977); Paul S. Taylor, *Georgia Plan: 1732–1752* (Berkeley: University of California Press, 1972); Betty Wood, *Slavery in Colonial Georgia, 1730–1775* (Athens: University of Georgia Press, 1984).

59. Easterby et al., *Colonial Records,* 1:153, 156.

60. George Fenwick Jones, ed., *Detailed Reports on the Salzburger Emigrants Who Settled in America . . . Edited by Samuel Urlsperger,* 8 vols. to date (Athens: University of Georgia Press, 1968–), 1:97, 100, 101, 157, 188; E. Merton Coulter, ed., *The Journal of William Stephens, 1741–1743,* 2 vols. (Athens: University of Georgia Press, 1958), 2:202; Candler, CRG, 2:121, 150, 168, 4:56; Thomas Gapen to the Trustees, June 13, 1735, in Lane, *General Oglethorpe's Georgia,* 188.

61. James Oglethorpe to the Trustees, June 9, 1733, in Lane, *General Oglethorpe's Georgia,* 18. Three years later Oglethorpe remarked favorably about Bryan to Thomas Broughton: "Mr. Jonathan Bryan and [his brother-in-law] Mr. [Nathanial] Barnwell have been with me to the frontiers and behaved

very handsomely." Together they visited the southern reaches of the colony where they inspected fortifications and conferred with Creek Indians. (ibid., March 28, 1733, p. 259); the generosity of Jonathan Bryan and William Bull in providing their slaves was especially valued by Oglethorpe because "we were some time before we could get any other assistance from Carolina, the people refusing to hire out their Negroes, though we offered security for them" (James Oglethorpe to the Trustees, Dec. 1733 [ibid., 27]). And: "Colonel Bull and Mr. Bryan came up again in the midst of the sickness to assist us with twenty slaves whose labor they gave us as a free gift to the colony" (ibid., 28); see also Thomas Causton to James Oglethorpe, July 7, 1735 (ibid., 215); Thomas Christie to James Oglethorpe, Dec. 14, 1734 (ibid., 69); E. Merton Coulter, ed., *The Journal of Peter Gordon, 1732–1735* (Athens: University of Georgia Press, 1963), 43–44.

62. Jackson, "The Carolina Connection," 151–52, 156. Under orders of Oglethorpe, Noble Jones diligently prevented "any depredations being committed in any part of the province, particularly, the cutting down cypress and live oak trees." Jonathan Bryan appears to have been the only individual allowed to cut the trees, the former of which were used for building canoes and piraguas. Jones wrote Oglethorpe: "I knowing Your Honour did give [Bryan] five trees formerly and he being a person that you respected, I did not dispute it" (July 3–6, 1735; Lane, *General Oglethorpe's Georgia*, 208–209).

63. Jackson, "Carolina Connection," 156–57; the Bryans knew the Indians around Pallachicola well enough to recommend the Indian Jack Smallwood to William Stephens as a guide and hunter in 1736 (Coulter, *Journal of William Stephens,* vol. 1, pp. 239–40); Harvey H. Jackson has concluded that Oglethorpe's presence at the ceremonies elevated Jonathan's status among Georgians. I agree with Jackson and would add that while Oglethorpe lent prestige to Bryan among white Georgians, Bryan's presence conferred status to Oglethorpe among the Indians.

64. Jackson, "Carolina Connection," 155–58.

65. For the published pamphlets of the "malcontents," see *The Clamorous Malcontents, Criticisms and Defenses of the Colony of Georgia, 1741–1743,* with an introduction by Trevor R. Reese (Savannah: Beehive Press, 1973).

66. Jackson, "Carolina Connection," 165–66; David R. Chestnutt, "South Carolina's Expansion into Colonial Georgia, 1720–1765" (Ph.D. diss., University of Georgia, 1973).

67. Jones, *Detailed Reports on the Salzburgers,* 8:363–64, 377–78; see also 8:483, 488, 491.

68. In 1735 he wrote the Associates of Thomas Bray to thank the philanthropic society for the Bibles, primers, spelling books, testaments, psalters, and hornbooks they had sent for the conversion of his bondspeople (Hugh Bryan to the Rev. Samuel Smith, Mar. 4, 1735, discussed in John C. Van

Horne, ed., *Religious Philanthropy and Slavery: The American Correspondence of the Associates of Dr. Bray, 1717–1777* [Urbana: University of Illinois Press, 1985], 71).

69. For an account of the events leading to hostilities, see Lanning, *Diplomatic History of Georgia;* Richard Pares, *Colonial Blockade and Neutral Rights, 1739–1763* (Oxford: Clarendon Press, 1939), and *War and Trade in the West Indies, 1739–1763* (Oxford: Clarendon Press, 1936); Harold William Vazeille Temperley, "The Causes of the War of Jenkins' Ear, 1739," *Transactions of the Royal Historical Society,* 3d series, 3 (1909), 197–236.

70. The best account of the Stono Rebellion is Wood, *Black Majority,* 313–20.

71. BPRO, microfilm, roll 6, vol. 20, pp. 251–53; Weir, *South Carolina,* 113; Ettinger, *Oglethorpe,* 234.

72. "Deposition of Captain Richard Wright," Easterby et al., *Colonial Records,* 3:202–205. The invasion force included a mixture of men and motivations. One group of participants were the Indian allies of the English who had their own reasons for joining the expedition to Florida: they were paid; they welcomed the opportunity to plunder; they sought to further their own private disputes with Indian allies of the Spanish. Indian intertribal wars of vengeance were often continued over several generations, much like European intertribal wars. These vendettas were sometimes conducted as conquests but more often as rites of passage and of habit. Young Indians earned *their* laurels by bringing home scalps and by disturbing their enemies' camp and returning with plunder. To many Indians, the white man's wars were secondary to their own grievances with one another.

Another group of participants in the invasion force was composed of British regulars. Their motivation was directly related to the individual circumstances of their enlistment. There were as many different reasons for enlisting in the army as there were men who enlisted. Regulars chose neither the cause nor the location of where they fought, though both of these factors certainly affected the quality of their performance. They were paid to perform a task, wherever, however, and whenever their leaders ordered them to do so.

A third contingent of the invasion force was composed of Georgians. They believed the invasion necessary to protect their homes and to secure the province. Oglethorpe and the magistrates ceaselessly reminded them of the Spanish threat to the colony's welfare. The Georgians rewarded Oglethorpe with loyalty for his leadership and the attention he paid to Georgia's fighting men. Whereas the regulars had once mutinied against Oglethorpe, Georgia's own sons could be counted on to perform their duties to the best of their ability.

73. For Barnwell, see Crane, *Southern Frontier,* 81, 158–60, 163; Weir, *South Carolina,* 29, 83–84. For Palmer, see Crane, *Southern Frontier,* 249–

51; Ivers, *British Drums,* 9, 114–15; Sirmans, *Colonial South Carolina,* 157. For Moore, see Weir, *South Carolina,* 80–82; Sirmans, *Colonial South Carolina,* 84–87; Crane, *Southern Frontier,* 75–80. For Cochran, see Crane, *Southern Frontier,* 264 n. 26.

74. The size of the force fluctuated as reinforcements from South Carolina and sundry Indian nations continued to arrive and depart. Ivers, *British Drums,* 103, 112, asserts there were about fifteen hundred men in the British force by mid-June.

75. Ibid., 105–107.

76. Ibid., 108–109.

77. "Deposition of Lieutenant Jonathan Bryan," in Easterby et al., *Colonial Records,* 3:188–91.

78. Ibid.

79. Ibid.; Ivers, *British Drums,* 108–109.

80. "Deposition of Lieutenant Bryan."

81. Ibid.; "Deposition of Captain Wright," in Easterby et al., *Colonial Records,* 202–205.

82. "Deposition of Captain Wright," 202–205.

83. The fort was difficult to defend, and it lacked a front gate. Oglethorpe failed to man the fort with a force sufficient to accomplish the designated task of preventing a Spanish escape. Added to this, the general fostered insecurity and confusion among his men by establishing no clear order of command in the fort, so that Colonel Palmer, a South Carolina volunteer, and Captain Hugh Mckay, Jr., of the Georgia Rangers, were left to dispute who was in charge, which they did in front of the men. It was not a situation conducive to successful offensive or defensive action. And it was a situation which Oglethorpe had created.

84. Weir, *South Carolina,* 145–46.

85. This may be seen in the governor's correspondence and the numerous petitions of the South Carolina Commons House to the king, in BPRO, microfilm, roll 6, vols. 21 and 22.

86. John T. Lanning, "American Participation in the War of Jenkins' Ear," *Georgia Historical Quarterly* 2 (Sept. 1927): 191–204; Spalding, *Oglethorpe,* 128.

87. Bryan had to wait more than thirty-five years to attempt to prove his theory correct. During the American Revolution he became the leading advocate of a patriot invasion of St. Augustine (which would be commanded by his son-in-law John Houstoun). The zealousness with which Bryan entreated the patriots to undertake a new conquest of St. Augustine reveals the extent to which the failure of 1740 haunted him: perhaps he expected success in 1777 to vindicate him in his dispute with the general.

88. "Deposition of Lieutenant Bryan." Oglethorpe's ignorance of Indians

was a particular point of irritation to Bryan. The general insulted the Indians by turning away in disgust when they offered him some scalps they had taken. Also, his refusal to take the offensive disappointed them. They had traveled hundreds of miles expecting to fight. Bryan sympathized with the Indians and may have felt partially responsible for their disappointment: his brother Hugh had transported many of the Indians to Florida by boat.

89. Oglethorpe and Bryan shared a sincere interest in Georgia's impoverished immigrants; they both treated Indians with respect; and as Oglethorpe once championed debtor rights in Parliament, Bryan would do so in South Carolina.

90. "Deposition of Captain Wright," italics added.

CHAPTER 2: IMPASSIONED DISCIPLES: THE GREAT
AWAKENING, GEORGE WHITEFIELD, AND THE REFORM OF
SLAVERY

1. Alan Heimert, *Religion and the American Mind from the Great Awakening to the Revolution* (Cambridge: Harvard University Press, 1966); Gary B. Nash, *The Urban Crucible: Social Change, Political Consciousness, and the Origins of the American Revolution* (Cambridge: Harvard University Press, 1979); Rhys Isaac, *The Transformation of Virginia, 1740–1790* (Chapel Hill: University of North Carolina Press, 1982); William G. McLoughlin, *Revivals, Awakenings, and Reform: An Esssay on Religion and Social Change in America, 1607–1977* (Chicago: University of Chicago Press, 1978); Patricia U. Bonomi, *Under the Cope of Heaven: Religion, Society, and Politics in Colonial America* (New York: Oxford University Press, 1986); Robert Wearmouth, *Methodism and the Common People of the Eighteenth Century* (London: Epworth Press, 1945); Elie Halévy, *The Birth of Methodism in England* (Chicago: University of Chicago Press, 1976); Umphrey Lee, *The Historical Background of Early Methodist Enthusiasm* (New York: Columbia University Press, 1931); Edwin Scott Gaustead, *The Great Awakening in New England* (New York: Columbia University Press, 1957); Susan O'Brien, "A Transatlantic Community of Saints: The Great Awakening as the First Evangelical Network, 1735–1755," *American Historical Review* 91 (Oct. 1986): 811–32.

2. Benjamin Franklin, *The Autobiography with Sayings of Poor Richard, Hoaxes, Bagatelles, Essays, and Letters,* selected and arranged by Carl Van Doren (New York: Pocket Books, 1940), 119–124; quotations from Ronald Knox, *Enthusiasm: A Chapter in the History of Religion* (New York: Oxford University Press, 1961), 486, 491.

3. Sirmans, *Colonial South Carolina,* chap. 5; Ver Steeg, "Internal Politics in Proprietary Carolina"; Weir, *Colonial South Carolina,* 72.

4. The records of the bishop of London relating to the American colonies have been transcribed and are available as part of the Fulham Palace collection, Manuscript Division, Library of Congress, Washington, D.C. The correspondence and journals of the Society for the Propagation of the Gospel are also at the Manuscript Division, Library of Congress. Important secondary works dealing with the role of religion in colonial South Carolina include Frank Klingberg, *An Appraisal of the Negro in Colonial South Carolina: A Study in Americanization* (Washington, D.C.: Associated Publishers, 1941); Charles Bolton, *Southern Anglicanism: The Church of England In Colonial South Carolina* (Westport: Greenwood, 1982); Frederick Dalcho, *An Historical Account of the Protestant Episcopal Church in South-Carolina* (Charleston: E. Thayer, 1820); George Howe, *History of the Presbyterian Church in South Carolina*, 2 vols. (Columbia: Duffie and Chapman, 1870); Sirmans, *Colonial South Carolina*, 79, 81, 99.

5. Bolton, *Southern Anglicanism*, 102–107; Sirmans, *Colonial South Carolina*, 99; Carson I. A. Ritchie, *Frontier Parish* (Rutherford: Farleigh Dickinson University Press, 1976), 80–87.

6. Bolton, *Southern Anglicanism*, 108–120; Klingberg, *Appraisal of the Negro*, 122.

7. Lewis Jones to Bishop Gibson, June 21, 1730, Lambeth Palace, Bishop of London Papers (hereafter cited as Lambeth Palace Papers), 9:250, Manuscript Division, Library of Congress, Washington, D.C. (hereafter cited as Library of Congress); Lewis Jones to Dr. Humphreys, Nov. 3, 1732, SPG Papers, B4, 2, 253.

8. Act passed May 29, 1736, see Todd and Hutson, *Prince William's Parish*, 71.

9. De Brahm, *Map of South Carolina and a Part of Georgia*. Records of the church have since been destroyed, making it difficult to fathom the exact nature of its usage, but the chapel was certainly used on Sundays. *An Abstract of the Procedings of the SPG* (London, 1736), 50, cited in Klingberg, *Appraisal of the Negro*, 167.

10. Lewis Jones to Dr. Humphreys, July 14, 1738, SPG Papers, B7, 231.

11. Hugh Bryan and Mrs. Mary Hutson, *Living Christianity, delineated in the diaries and letters of two eminently pious persons, lately deceased . . .* (London: J. Buckland, 1760), 8–19, quotations on 19, 8, 18, 10.

12. *Ibid.*, first and third quotations on 23, 11; George Whitefield, *Journals, 1737–1741, to which is prefixed his "Short Account" (1746) and "Further Account" (1747)* (London, 1756; repr., Gainesville, Fla.: Scholars Facsimiles and Reprints, 1969), second quotation, 437.

13. Bryan and Hutson, *Living Christianity,* 11–14.

14. In another instance, when George Whitefield visited Charlestown in January 1740 he preached at the Presbyterian Meeting House to an unrespon-

sive audience. The following day he preached at the Huguenot church and witnessed a "glorious alteration in the audience" where "many were melted into tears." His success was so great that though he was to depart that night, the determination of Charlestownians persuaded him to delay his trip and preach once more at the Presbyterian Meeting House (Whitefield, *Journals,* 431, 444–47, quotation on 447).

15. Ibid., 447–49, quotation on 448.

16. Ibid., 451.

17. Anthony Armstrong Willis, *The Church of England, the Methodists and Society, 1700–1850* (London: University of London Press, 1973); Bolton, *Southern Anglicanism;* Elie Halévy, *England in 1815* (London: E. Benn, 1949), 391–92, 403, 550; W. R. Ward, *Religion and Society in England, 1790–1850* (New York: Schocken Books, 1972), 1; William Lecky, *A History of England in the Eighteenth Century,* 8 vols, (New York: Appleton, 1892–93), 2:581–89.

18. Whitefield, *Journals,* 397–98; Arnold A. Dallimore, *George Whitefield: The Life and Times of the Great Evangelist of the Eighteenth-Century Revival,* 2 vols. (London: Banner of Truth Trust, 1970–79), 1:515; David T. Morgan, "The Great Awakening in South Carolina, 1740–1775," *South Atlantic Quarterly* 70 (Autumn 1971): 595–606; David T. Morgan, Jr., "The Consequences of George Whitefield's Ministry in the Carolinas and Georgia, 1739–1740," *Georgia Historical Quarterly* 55 (Spring 1971): 62–81; William Howland Kenny III, "Alexander Garden and George Whitefield: The Significance of Re- vivialism in South Carolina, 1738–1741," *South Carolina Historical Maga- zine* 71 (June 1970): 1–16.

19. Nash, *Urban Crucible;* Isaac, *Transformation of Virginia.*

20. George Whitefield, *The Works of the Reverend George Whitefield,* 6 vols. (London: Edward and Charles Dilly, 1772), 4:35–41, first quotation on 41; Whitefield, *Journals,* 382); George Fenwick Jones, trans., "John Martin Boltzius' Trip to Charleston, October 1742," *South Carolina Historical Maga- zine* 82 (Jan. 1981), 101–102.

21. Whitefield, *Works,* 4:35–41, quotations on 38.

22. Ibid.

23. Ibid., 38–39.

24. Ibid., 39–40. Also see Whitefield's "A Prayer for a poor Negroe," ibid., 473–75.

25. Bryan and Hutson, *Living Christianity,* 33; Jones often disagreed with Whitefield but allowed him the pulpit, entertained him at his home, and visited him in Georgia. Despite his inability to achieve the mystical experience of grace, which Evangelicals deemed necessary for achieving salvation, Jones re- tained the respect of his parishioners, like Hugh Bryan, who denounced an unregenerate clergy but wrote approvingly of Jones's ministry. Lewis Jones had

become an integral part of the Beaufort community, and he never left for his newly assigned parish at Goose Creek (Whitefield, *Journals,* 383, 437–38; Bryan and Hutson, *Living Christianity,* 32–33).

26. Jon Butler, "Enthusiasm Described and Decried: The Great Awakening as Interpretive Fiction," *Journal of American History* 69 (Sept. 1982): 311–12.

27. On Wesley and religious structures see Wearmouth, *Methodism and the Common People,* esp. 136.

28. Whitefield, *Works.* The first three volumes are correspondence. Vol. 1 has been reprinted as *Letters of George Whitefield for the Period 1734–1742* (Carlisle, Pa.: Banner of Truth Trust, 1976).

29. When the Bryan family was recruited into the ranks of active supporters, Whitefield wrote of them to several correspondents. He complimented one follower on the effect of her book upon his recent converts and suggested to another that they begin a correspondence with the Bryans. See Whitefield to Mrs. A. D., Jan. 20, 1741, in Whitefield, *Works,* 1: 250; Whitefield to Mrs. D., July 17, 1741, ibid. 1:277.

30. "Much Work must be done upon my heart, before I arrive at any Tolerable share of it [grace]. But I will not, I dare not despair, God had already done much for me. . . . My heart wants words to express its gratitude to you my dear Friend & kindest Companion. That I love you is saying too little, because I find my affections for you, would make me think nothing too good, or dear to part with for your sake, not even my life" (James Habersham to Hugh Bryan, Nov. 26, 1739, folder 56, box 5, Jones Family Papers, Georgia Historical Society, Savannah); "Herewith you will receive what sermons I have got of Mr. Whitefield's. God has made them instrumental to the conversion of thousands, & I pray that these may do as such to all that read them. Indeed dear Sir the interest of religion is very much strengthened in England and xtians begin to be less ashamed of the Gospel of Jesus Christ, that great restorer of poor fallen man—O that we . . . may awaken" (Habersham to Bryan, Nov. 30, 1739, ibid.); "I was much rejoiced to hear glad tidings of Mr. Tennents success in his ministry at Boston. The Lord gives us great hopes that he intends great things in New England" (Habersham to Bryan, undated, folder 3, Joseph Vallence Bevan Papers, Georgia Historical Society, Savannah); "Believing as I do, that our work is of God, I am not surprised to find Satan and his emissaries rage. . . . It was a saying of Luther, that he never understood the New Testament till he was persecuted, not David's psalms till he had experienced spiritual conflicts" (Habersham to Bryan, 1741, folder 3, Bevan Papers).

31. Whitefield to Jonathan Bryan, Feb. 1, 1753, in Whitefield, *Works,* 3:3; Jan. 19, 1753, 2:478.

32. Butler, "Enthusiasm Described and Decried," 319.

33. For the Whitefield-Bryan correspondence on the Bethesda Orphanage and on Providence Plantation, which they established for its support, see

Whitefield to Mr. P——, Sept. 19, 1740, in Whitefield, *Works*, 1:207; White-field to J[onathan] B[ryan], Feb. 16, 1741, ibid., 1:240; Whitefield to Mr. [James] H[abersham], Sept. 24, 1742, ibid., 1:439; Whitefield to Mr. [James] H[abersham], May 21, 1743, ibid., 2:24; Whitefield to Trustees, Dec. 6, 1748, ibid., 2:208–209; Whitefield to Mr. [Johann] B[oltzius], Mar. 22, 1751, ibid., 2:404–405; Whitefield to Mr. J[ames] H[abersham], May 26, 1752, ibid., 2:429–30; Whitefield to Mr. T——, June 4, 1752, ibid., 2:430; Whitefield to Mr. H[ugh] B[ryan], Jan. 7, 1753, ibid., 2:471–72; Whitefield to Mr. J[onathan] B[ryan], Feb. 1, 1753, ibid., 3:3–4; James Habersham to White-field, Oct. 2, 1741, ibid., 3:445; Habersham to Whitefield, July 14, 1742, ibid., 3:453–54; Habersham to Whitefield, July 11, 1742, ibid., 3:454– 57; Habersham to Whitefield, Aug. 19, 1742, ibid., 3:459–60. See also Jonathan Bryan to Whitefield, Apr. 9, 1753, no. 20, vol. 2; Jonathan Bryan to White-field, July 4, 1753, no. 36, vol. 1; William Brisbane to Whitefield, Sept. 10, 1753, no. 23, vol. 2; Hugh Bryan to Whitefield, May 4, 1753, no. 22, vol. 2, all in George Whitefield Papers, Manuscript Division, Library of Congress; Whitefield to Hugh Bryan, Dec. 16, 1745, in John W. Christie, ed., "Newly Discovered Letters of George Whitefield, 1745–1746," *Journal of Presbyterian History* 32 (June 1954): 74–76.

34. E. Merton Coulter, ed., *The Journal of William Stephens, 1741–1743*, 2 vols. (Athens: University of Georgia Press, 1958), 1:29–31, 33–34, 36–37; William Stephens, *A Journal of the Proceedings in Georgia . . .* , 2 vols. (London: J. Meadows, 1740), 1:307–309, 314–15, 329–30, 2:111–12, 172–74, 307–308; Harold E. Davis, *The Fledgling Province: Social and Cultural Life in Colonial Georgia, 1733–1776* (Chapel Hill: University of North Carolina Press, 1976), 217–18, 220–21; Candler, *CRG*, 4 (Supplement): 73.

35. James Habersham to George Whitefield, July 14, July 11, Aug. 19, 1742, in Whitefield, *Works*, 3:453–57, 459–60.

36. Joseph Bryan and wife to George Whitefield, Lease and Release of 640 acres, Dec. 21, 1747, Conveyances, book D-D, 52, S.C. Archives.

37. Whitefield to James Habersham, May 26, 1752, in Whitefield, *Works*, 2:430; Whitefield to Mr. T——, June 4, 1752, ibid., 2:430; Whitefield to Jonathan Bryan, Feb. 1, 1753, ibid., 3:3–4; Jonathan Bryan to Whitefield, Apr. 2, 1753, vol. 2, no. 20; and William Brisbane to Whitefield, Oct. 10, 1753, no. 23, vol. 2, Whitefield Papers.

38. Whitefield to Hugh Bryan, Jan. 7, 1753, in Whitefield, *Works*, 2:471; Whitefield, *Journals*, 438, 445–49, 451, 504–506; Jones, *Detailed Reports on the Salzburger Emigrants*, 8:488.

39. Klingberg, *Appraisal of the Negro*, 13, 58, 110–18, 136; for the Anglican church and slave conversions, see Bolton, *Southern Anglicanism*, 116–19. Bolton is correct in his assessment that later Anglican attempts at slave reform were a direct response to the Evangelical program.

40. Klingberg, *Appraisal of the Negro,* 6–7; Wood, *Black Majority,* 138–39.

41. Van Horne, *Religious Philanthropy and Slavery,* 71.

42. Bryan and Hutson, *Living Christianity,* 36, 33, 40–41 and 44, 39.

43. *South Carolina Gazette,* Jan 1–7, 1741. The letter, however, is dated Nov. 20, 1740.

44. Bolton, *Southern Anglicanism,* 55. Harvey H. Jackson provides an excellent analysis of this episode in "Hugh Bryan and the Evangelical Movement in Colonial South Carolina," *William and Mary Quarterly,* 3d ser., 43 (Oct. 1986): 600–603.

45. Bryan and Hutson, *Living Christianity,* 38.

46. Whitefield, *Journals,* 504–505.

47. *South Carolina Gazette,* Jan. 1–7, 1741.

48. Whitefield, *Journals,* 506–507; George Whitefield to the Rev. Mr. C, Jan. 12, 1741, in Whitefield, *Works,* 1:231.

49. Letter printed in *South Carolina Gazette,* June 18–25, 1741.

50. George Howe, *History of the Presbyterian Church in South Carolina* 1:243–44; Dallimore, *George Whitefield,* 1:586; Bolton, *Southern Anglicanism,* 56; Morgan, "The Great Awakening in South Carolina," 601; Edward McCrady, *The History of South Carolina under the Royal Government, 1719–1776* (New York: Macmillan, 1899), 238–41; Tracy, *Great Awakening* (Boston: Lewis Tappan, 1842), 113.

51. Whitefield to H[ugh] B[ryan], Feb. 16, 1741, in Whitefield, *Works,* 1:238–39. The biblical references are from Gen. 3:13–15.

52. Whitefield to Jonathan Bryan, Feb. 16, 1741, in Whitefield, *Works,* 1:239–40.

53. Charges against the Bryans appear to have been dropped. The South Carolina Commons House of Assembly was preparing for its investigation of the failed invasion of St. Augustine when the libel occurred. The Commons House committee responsible for the investigation had required Jonathan's attendance before them on Aug. 12, 1740. Bryan failed to appear on the scheduled date as he was with Whitefield in Georgia tending to the health of his soul. Bryan was to be a major witness for the prosecution in the house attempt to blame the defeat of the expedition upon Gen. James Oglethorpe. Not a few on the house committee must have grown anxious at Bryan's statement. At the time of their arrest the Bryans were owed a stately sum of money. Hugh was owed and had petitioned for £438 for miscellaneous services provided before and after the St. Augustine expedition. In addition, at the outbreak of the war with Spain, because the assembly had not been in session, he, Jonathan, and five others had taken it upon themselves to hire a scout boat to cruise "along shoar to the Southward." They were denied reimbursement of £177 17s. 6d. because "it did not appear to this House . . . that the Petitioners had any Direction from his Honour the Lieutenant Governor to hire such Scout Boat and

Men, or had ever made any Application to his Honour for that Purpose." Then a strange turn of events occurred in Feb. 1741. Only a few weeks after their arrest the Bryans' financial fortunes changed dramatically. Hugh's personal petition for reimbursement was fortuitously accepted. The resubmitted group petition was also accepted, the lieutenant governor peculiarly changing his testimony by affirming that he *had* provided orders "to fit out a Scout Boat" after all. One week later Jonathan Bryan signed an affidavit of his experiences with Oglethorpe at St. Augustine. Thus in a matter of weeks the charges against the Bryans were dropped and a formerly rejected petition was accepted. Hugh Bryan was reimbursed in full for money recently expended for the colony's defense, and Jonathan Bryan provided testimony that would be used to strengthen the colony's case against the military competency of James Oglethorpe. This freed the Bryans from charges of libel and left them in an excellent financial position vis-à-vis the government (Easterby et al., *Colonial Records*, 2:210–11, 373, 482, 492, 495, 502–504, 531, 533, 541, and 3:97, 188–91; Hugh Bryan's account, Jan. 26, 1740–1 [1741], voucher no. 34, Bills to the Public, 1740, South Carolina Historical Society, Charleston).

54. Whitefield, *Journals*, first quotation on 451; Easterby et al., *Colonial Records*, 3:380, 381.

55. Ibid., 380, 388, 405–407; Todd and Hutson, *Prince William's Parish*, map, 30–31, displays the layout of the Bull and Bryan plantations.

56. Lewis Jones to Dr. Bearcroft, Dec. 12, 1743, B11 26, SPG.

57. Easterby et al., *Colonial Records*, 3:461–62; Elise Pinckney, ed., *The Letterbook of Eliza Lucas Pinckney, 1739–1762* (Chapel Hill: University of North Carolina Press, 1972), 30. Secondary sources include Tracy, *The Great Awakening*, 113; McCrady, *The History of South Carolina*, 240–42; Morgan, "Consequences of George Whitefield's Ministry," 72; Jackson, "Hugh Bryan and the Evangelical Movement," 607–10.

58. Jackson, "Hugh Bryan and the Evangelical Movement," 607–10.

59. *South Carolina Gazette*, Mar. 20–27, 1742.

60. Jones, "Boltzius' Trip to Charleston," 102.

61. *South Carolina Gazette*, Apr. 10–17 and 17–24, 1742.

62. John W. Davis, "George Liele and Andrew Bryan, Pioneer Negro Baptist Preachers," *Journal of Negro History* 3 (Apr. 1918): 119–27; William Jay, *The Works of the Rev. William Jay of Argyle Chapel, Bath . . .* , 3 vols. (New York: Harper and Brothers, 1858), 3:30; *Georgia Gazette*, Oct. 23, 1788.

63. Among the churches that were captured by the Evangelicals were the Independent meeting houses in Charlestown and Dorchester, several Presbyterian chapels in St. Helena Parish, and the Baptist congregation at Ashley Ferry. The Independent meeting in St. Helena Parish was established in 1743 by former Anglicans who split from their parish church. The Independent Presbyterian church in Savannah was also started by the followers of Whitefield.

64. Jones, "Boltzius' Trip to Charleston," 106–107.

65. Boltzius's colleagues told him that on a visit to South Carolina they "heard a Moorish slave woman on a plantation [presumably the Bryans'] singing a spiritual at the water's edge. After they had come to her master, they learned that, a few days ago, this heathen woman attained a certain assurance of the forgiveness of sins and the mercy of God in Christ and that she, along with others who love Christ, was shouting and jubilating because of this treasure. Her masters themselves fear God heartily and endeavor by word and example to further the kingdom of Christ in the hearts of men, also in the hearts of their and other peoples' Moorish slaves, who gather from the vicinity at this plantation for sake of spiritual exercises and edification" (Jones, *Detailed Reports on the Salzburger Emigrants*, 8:512, entry of Dec. 3, 1741). This gathering of slaves from different plantations took place before charges were brought against the Bryans by the government.

66. Jones, "Boltzius' Trip to Charleston," 107.

67. "Register Kept by the Rev. Wm. Hutson, of Stoney Creek Independent Congregational Church and (Circular) Congregational Church in Charles Town S.C., 1743–1760," contributed by Mrs. R. W. Hutson, *South Carolina Historical and Genealogical Magazine* 38 (Oct. 1937): 21–36; Todd and Hutson, *Prince William's Parish*, 86; Lewis Jones to SPG, Aug. 11, 1743, SPG Papers, B11 225.

68. For the South Carolina Anglican church and slave conversions, see Bolton, *Southern Anglicanism*, 116–19; and Klingberg, *Appraisal of the Negro*, 110–18, 136.

69. "Register of Stoney Creek Church," 21–22. For Hutson's role in the education of slaves and the Evangelical movement, see Howe, *Presbyterian Church*, 1:248–50, 264–65, 310. Hutson was an actor whom Whitefield had converted in New York.

70. Henry Laurens to Jonathan Bryan, Sept. 4, 1767, in Philip M. Hamer, George C. Rogers, Jr., and David R. Chestnutt, eds., *The Papers of Henry Laurens*, 10 vols. (Columbia: University of South Carolina Press, 1968–1985), 5:288–91, quotation on 289 (hereafter cited as *Laurens Papers*).

71. Benjamin Quarles, *The Negro in the American Revolution* (Chapel Hill: University of North Carolina Press, 1961), 60–64.

72. *Methodist Magazine* 5 (1785); repr. in Redding, *Life and Times of Jonathan Bryan*, 44–45.

73. George Whitefield to Mr. [William] Hutson, Dec. 16, 1745, in Christie, "Newly Discovered Letters of George Whitefield," 76–77.

74. George Whitefield to a generous benefactor, Mar. 15, 1747, in Whitefield, *Works*, 2:90. Purchase of the plantation is recorded in Conveyances, Book D-D, p. 52, Joseph Bryan and wife to George Whitefield, Lease and Release of 640 acres, S.C. Archives. Documents concerning the subsequent

return of the plantation to the Bryan family may be found in the Special Collections of the College of Charleston, Charleston, S.C.

75. George Whitefield to the Trustees of Georgia, Dec. 4, 1748, in Whitefield, *Works*, 2:208–209; George Whitefield to Mr. Johann Martin B[oltzius], Mar. 22, 1751, ibid., 404–405.

76. George Whitefield to the Trustees of Georgia, Dec. 4, 1748, ibid., 2:208–209.

77. George Whitefield to Mr. Johann Martin B[oltzius], Mar. 22, 1751, ibid., 404–405.

78. Ibid.

79. Ibid.

80. "Letter From Mr. John Martin Boltzius to the Revd. Mr. Whitefield," Dec. 24, 1745, Candler, *CRG*, 24:434–44.

81. Bryan and Hutson, *Living Christianity*, first and third quotations on 91, 92; second quotation on 70, fourth quotation on 92; 101–102, 111.

82. Eugene D. Genovese, *Roll, Jordan, Roll: The World the Slaves Made* (New York: Random House, 1974), 132–33; Herbert G. Gutman, *The Black Family in Slavery and Freedom, 1750–1925* (New York: Vintage Books, 1976), 312–17.

83. David Benedict, *A General History of the Baptist Denomination in America, and Other Parts of the World*, 2 vols. (Boston, 1813; repr., Freeport: Books for Libraries Press, 1971), 2:190–91.

84. *Georgia Gazette*, Oct. 23, 1788.

85. "Letters Showing the Rise and Progress of Early Negro Churches of Georgia and the West Indies," *Journal of Negro History* 1 (Jan. 1916), 86. The slaves Bryan owned were family members. He implied in a letter that he had to keep them enslaved. We see here a difference between the public face of slavery and the private one. To the white population, Bryan was a slaveowner, but in the private capacity there can be little doubt that he treated his bondsmen as family.

The church still exists. For an early history of the church, see Rev. James M. Simms, *The First Colored Baptist Church in North America* (Philadelphia: J. B. Lippincott, 1888; repr., New York: Negro Universities Press, 1969).

86. Benedict, *History of the Baptist Denomination*, 2:192–93; Albert J. Raboteau, *Slave Religion: The "Invisible Institution" in the Antebellum South* (New York: Oxford University Press, 1978), 141–42, 189–94.

CHAPTER 3: FROM ONE FRONTIER TO ANOTHER: THE ASSUMPTION OF POLITICAL POWER

1. Weir, *Colonial South Carolina*, 121–22; Dorn, *Competition for Empire*, 164–73.

2. The government actively petitioned for the relief of Port Royal. See BPRO, microfilm, role 6, vol. 21, pp. 11–13, 14, 17–22, 37–46. Governor James Glen wrote to the board of trade outlining both the need for defense of Beaufort at Port Royal and the manner by which he sought to appease the southerners. "My principle concern is to express to your Lordships how sensibly that loss [of HMS *Loo*] affects this Province. The long neglected Town of Beaufort, upon the arrival of this Ship, and the Assurances given that another would be sent over, began to revive and many good Houses were built and many Grants for Town Lots were applied for, so that I am persuaded that Town and the adjacent Country would soon have been well settled, and consequently our Southern Frontier, where we are most Vulnerable, would have been strengthened, but now I receive Letters and Petitions dayly from the best people in those parts, representing their Fears and the dangers to which they are exposed, and everything is at a stand, tho' I have stationed one of our Galleys (a very fine small vessel) there . . . what chiefly has quieted them, is the hopes that I have given them that some large ships would soon be sent to Port Royal" (ibid., 245–46). Town lots were granted in Beaufort as early as 1717, but it was not until 1743 that most of them were taken. For the dispersal of town lots in Beaufort, see Henry A. M. Smith, "Beaufort—the Original Plan and the Earliest Settlers," *South Carolina Historical Magazine* 9 (1908):141–60. Jonathan Bryan received his lot on July 28, 1744.

3. For the refortification of Fort Frederick, see Easterby et al., *Colonial Records,* 4:347, 350–52; 7:172, 374. For the supplying of cannon see BPRO, microfilm, roll 6, vol. 20, pp. 653–55. It took the South Carolina government several years to install the cannon, however; they were conspicuously left on Charlestown beach but unmounted (BPRO, roll 6, 21:237).

4. The parish was created May 25, 1745.

5. Sanders, "Eighteenth Century Beaufort," 172–74.

6. Easterby et al., *Colonial Records,* 7:5.

7. Ibid., 7:9, 19, 21, 24, 25.

8. Ibid., 7:38, 44, 58, 86, 87.

9. The Antipaedobaptists complained that the "General Baptists" denied them burial in the meeting house yard and their "Rt of having Divine Service performed by a Minister of their own Persuasion, whom they approve of" (Ibid., 7:94).

10. Ibid., 7:152, bill 16.

11. Ibid., 7:93, 98. Just a few years later the people of Prince William objected to supporting the pilot, in light of the refusal by the people of St. Helena to help them with the building and maintenance of their roads.

12. Ibid., vol. 8, bill 18; Smith, "Beaufort—The Original Plan," 147.

13. Easterby et al., *Colonial Records,* 7:196.

14. Ibid., 7:74, 77.

15. Ibid., 7:63–68, 81. Craven County was not a southern parish, it was

located on the North Carolina border. Relatively undeveloped, it shared economic interest for government aid with the southern parishes.

16. Ibid., 7:85. For debt-reduction legislation, see bills 4 and 24. Legislation lowering the interest rate would not be passed until 1748, when it was reduced from 10 to 8 percent. Bill 6, to "prevent exportation of slaves from this province to His Majesty's enemies," was rejected by the upper house (ibid., 7:260). The indebted had hoped this legislation would deter creditors from seizing their slaves for the payment of debt, whereby sales were made to the Spanish who possessed cash. See also ibid., vol. 7, bill 7. The debtor-relief bill was modeled after Oglethorpe's Insolvent Debtors Relief Act of 1729. See ibid., vol. 7, bill 8.

17. Ibid., 7:165, 395.

18. For Hugh's debts see the following in Judgment Rolls, S.C. Archives: *Estate of Payne vs. Estate of Hugh Bryan,* box 41b, no. 41a; *Estate of Dr. Reeve vs. Estate of Hugh Bryan,* box 37a, no. 19a; *Estate of Joseph Blake vs. Estate of Hugh Bryan,* box 39b, no. 33a; *Estate of Burnaby Bull vs. Estate of Hugh Bryan,* box 41b, no. 36a; *John Matthews vs. Estate of Hugh Bryan,* box 43b, no. 1a; *James Kinloch vs. Estate of Hugh Bryan,* box 41b, no. 4a; *Estate of Benjamin Savage vs. Hugh Bryan,* box 32b, no. 7a.

19. Two percent of the seats were left vacant in 1745–46, 5 percent in 1746–47, and 11 percent in 1747–48. In addition to the vacancies mentioned in the text, St. George Dorchester and St. James Santee both failed to return a full contingent of representatives. These two parishes were akin to the southern parishes, as they did not develop economically until after the 1720s. The parishes which developed first in South Carolina were those that surrounded Charlestown. They were: St. Paul, St. Andrew, St. James Goose Creek, St. Philip Charlestown, St. John Berkeley, St. Thomas and St. Dennis (the last two named were a single parish). These parishes had a majority of the seats in the Commons House.

20. Chestnutt, "South Carolina's Expansion into Georgia," 125.

21. Ibid., 125–26; W. W. Abbot, *The Royal Governors of Georgia, 1754–1775* (Chapel Hill: University of North Carolina Press, 1959), 21–22; Wood, *Slavery in Colonial Georgia,* 91–93; Jackson, "Carolina Connection," 165–72.

22. This may have been due to the "great expense," that is, legal costs, he incurred by evangelizing slaves. Hugh Bryan to Thomas Jenys, Conveyances, vol. VO, pp. 438–43, S.C. Archives; debt contracted Oct. 22, 1742, from James Kinloch; see *Kinloch vs. Estate of Hugh Bryan,* Judgment Rolls, box 41b no. 4a, S.C. Archives.

23. Miscellaneous Records, 1729–1825, vol. FF, 315–19, S.C. Archives.

24. The ratio of South Carolina currency to British sterling was slightly over seven to one. See Wallace, *History of South Carolina,* 1:315.

25. Bryan and Hutson, *Living Christianity,* 4; Hugh Bryan to George

Whitefield, May 4, 1753, Whitefield Papers, vol. 2, no. 22, Library of Congress.

26. Hugh's slaves were valued at more than £14,000 local currency. His livestock were appraised at £3,000, his personal effects at £2,500. It is difficult to measure the value of his real estate, but I have estimated it to have amounted to £20,000. This figure is based upon the sale of land to cover his debts and upon the estimated value of the estate inherited free and clear by his widow. The appraisal of Hugh's estate may be found in Inventories of Estates, Book R, 153–56, S.C. Archives.

27. Mary's estate after Hugh's death was listed in her marriage settlement with William Hutson, Miscellaneous Records, 1729–1825, Book LL, 264–71, S.C. Archives. Hugh's Cedar Grove Plantation, which included his home, passed into the Hutson family after Mary's death (Todd and Hutson, *Prince William's Parish,* 232).

28. Easterby, et al., *Colonial Records,* vol. 1, bill 48; vol. 9, act 37.

29. Coulter, *Journal of William Stephens,* 2:202; Jackson, "Carolina Connection," 165–66. Hugh had enough income to pay the interest charges on some of his debts, see *Estate of Benjamin Savage vs. Hugh Bryan,* Judgment Rolls, box 32b, no. 7a, S.C. Archives.

30. Samuel Urlsperger, ed., *Americanishes Ackerwerck Gottes* (Halle, 1755), 242–43.

31. It is possible that Jonathan could have invested in the purchase and outfitting of the *Elizabeth and Mary.*

32. For the purchase of slaves, see Chestnutt, "South Carolina's Expansion into Georgia," 147; Bryan's purchase of 1059 3/4 acres from Ann and William Palmer is recorded in Conveyances, Book S-S, 115, S.C. Archives. Money lent in the years 1749–50 led to three court cases in 1751: see *Jonathan Bryan vs. William Palmer,* Judgment Rolls, box 31b, no. 31a, S.C. Archives; *Jonathan Bryan vs. James Hendrick,* ibid., box 31a, no. 58a; *Jonathan Bryan vs. William Holman,* ibid., box 31a, no. 61a.

33. Bryan plantations raised corn and cattle besides rice: the family would not have had to purchase food items for their labor force. On indigo, see Sanders, "Beaufort," 146–47.

34. The sale of more than 5,000 acres had not been enough for Hugh to withstand the sharp economic downturn. From Hugh's estate, 2,000 acres in Prince William and almost 5,000 acres of varying quality in St. Peter's had to be sold to pay a single debt of £3,848. See the following in Conveyances, S.C. Archives: Book R-R, 44 and 492, and Book S-S, 100.

35. For the cost of establishing a plantation, see the survey done by Johann Martin Boltzius in John M. Boltzius and Israel Christian Gronau, "John Martin Bolzius Answers a Questionaire on Carolina and Georgia," trans. and ed. Klaus G. Loewald, Beverly Starika, and Paul S. Taylor, *William and Mary Quarterly,* 3d ser., 14 (Apr. 1957): 218–61, and 15 (Apr. 1958): 228–52. See

also Louis De Vorsey, Jr., ed., *De Brahm's Report of the General Survey in the Southern District of North America* (Columbia: University of South Carolina Press, 1971), 161–63. Analyses of these estimates are provided in chapter 4. The estimate provided for the cost of male slaves (in South Carolina currency) is taken from the Inventories of Estates, S.C. Archives.

36. Wood, *Slavery in Colonial Georgia,* 111–13, 204–205. Carolinians may have played a key role in the Trustees' allowance of slavery in Georgia. Moreover, the colony would continue to influence her neighbor in substantial ways over the next century and a half. Kenneth Coleman asserts the often-repeated dictum that had there been no revolutionary movement in South Carolina there would have been none in Georgia (Kenneth Coleman, *The American Revolution in Georgia, 1763–1789* [Athens: University of Georgia Press, 1958], 75); see also Abbot, *Royal Governors of Georgia,* 182.

37. Attention is again directed to Todd and Hutson, *Prince William's Parish* and to De Brahm's maps of South Carolina in the Library of Congress. They identify the large planters of the region. The number of slaves each of these planters possessed can be found in the probates of their estates in the S.C. Archives.

38. Jackson, "Carolina Connection," 171–72.

39. Chestnutt, "South Carolina's Expansion into Georgia," 125–26.

40. Bryan gathered information on Georgia's political situation from his many visits there and through the offices of his good friend and fellow Evangelical, James Habersham, who was one of the Trustees' assistants in Savannah and was soon to be appointed a member of the colony's council.

41. Before 1765, 330 Carolinians applied for land in Georgia. It would be impossible to determine exactly how many people this represented, but we can make an estimate. Each Carolinian who claimed land does not represent a single family. Some, like Jonathan Bryan, claimed land in their children's names. If we estimate the number of claims made in this manner at 10 percent and subtract that amount from the sum total, we are left with 297. Multiplying this number by the average family size of five we come up with 1,485. Using the same calculation, we find that 956 Carolinians migrated to Georgia in the ten-year period 1751–60. This would have approximated 2 to 3 percent of the total white population in a given year. This figure is the high end. It is much more likely that less than 1 percent of the white Carolinians moved to Georgia in the 1750s. Thus, we can see that the migration southward was significant, but by no means was it an avalanche. (The estimate of five people per Carolina family and the population estimates for South Carolina were taken from Wallace, *History of South Carolina,* 1:379. The number of Carolinians migrating to Georgia was calculated from a compilation provided in the appendix to Chestnutt, "South Carolina's Expansion into Georgia," 216–30).

42. The sea coast, where the white pioneers had settled, was only sparsely populated by Indians, at least since the Yamassee War. For the most part, it

appears that Indians had deserted the region, although a small band of Yamacraws inhabited land around modern-day Savannah. Georgians were perfectly willing to displace the aboriginal population from their lands (though the Trustees frowned upon such measures) but were unable to do so until the 1770s, as the neighboring Indians were more powerful than the British colony.

43. Jackson, "Carolina Connection," 167–71; Candler, *CRG,* 6:333–34.

44. Purchase of the plantation is recorded in Joseph Bryan and wife to George Whitefield, in Conveyances, Book D-D, 52, S.C. Archives.

45. George Whitefield to Jonathan Bryan, Feb. 1, 1753, in Whitefield, *Works,* 3:3–4.

46. Jonathan Bryan to George Whitefield, Apr. 2, 1753, Whitefield Papers, vol. 2, no. 20.

47. William Brisbane to George Whitefield, Oct. 10, 1753, ibid., vol. 2, no. 23.

48. For examples of Whitefield's instructions to reduce the number of orphans at Bethesda, see George Whitefield to Mrs. C., Oct. 30, 1756; Feb. 5, 1757; and Nov. 29, 1758, in Whitefield, *Works,* 3:191–92, 199–200, 248–49.

49. Hugh Bryan's will, Wills, Book 1752–56, 152–156, S.C. Archives.

50. Hugh's widow, Mary, bought 856 acres; his executor, who was his niece's husband, and quite likely his best friend, John Smith, purchased almost 5,000 acres; and fellow Evangelical William Brisbane purchased 1,100 acres. Charles Lowndes, who auctioned the land, purchased 450 acres for himself. Jonathan brought the land back into the Bryan family by purchasing it from him in Dec. 1763. See the following in Conveyances, S.C. Archives: Book R-R, 441, 492; Book S-S, 100; Book x-3, 213–23.

51. Mary Bryan and John Smith, executors of *Hugh Bryan vs. Jonathan Bryan, Administrator of Joseph Bryan,* Judgment Rolls, box 41b, nos. 6a and 11a, S.C. Archives; *Estate of Burnaby Bull vs. Estate of Hugh Bryan,* Judgment Rolls, box 41a, no. 36a, S.C. Archives.

52. "The Final Account of Joseph Bryan's Estate by Administrator Jonathan Bryan," Miscellaneous—Bonds, Book R, 173–75, Georgia Department of Archives and History, Atlanta (hereafter cited as Georgia Archives).

53. Jonathan fathered thirteen children: Hugh, 1738; Jonathan, 1740; John, 1741; Joseph, 1743; Mary, 1744; Josiah, 1746; William, 1748; John, 1750; James, 1752; Elizabeth, 1755; Hannah, 1759; Ann, 1763; Sarah Janet Cochran, 1769. The first John died in 1749, before the move to Georgia.

54. Candler, *CRG,* 7:468. He may have retained as many if not more slaves in South Carolina.

55. A descendant of the Bryans, who was also a noted genealogist, speculated in 1901 that Bryan might first have married seventeen-year-old Mary Price, an orphan, in 1727. She died of childbirth within a year. The child might

have been raised by Jonathan's brother Hugh and his wife, Mary. See Frank
Screven to D. E. Huger Smith, May 31, 1901, in Huger Collection, file 30–4,
Bryan folder, South Carolina Historical Society.

56. Redding, *Life and Times of Jonathan Bryan,* 81–84.

57. Jonathan Bryan to George Whitefield, July 4, 1753, Whitefield Papers,
vol. 1, no. 36.

58. Candler, *CRG,* 6:333–34. In 1752 the president and assistants of Georgia granted him five hundred acres of land for his son Jonathan, because the
elder Bryan had proven himself in cultivating the previous five hundred acres
(ibid., 6:369).

59. Candler, *CRG,* 7:45–48; Coleman and Ready, *CRG,* 27:114–15.

60. Candler, *CRG,* 7:47, 591. The General Court tried noncriminal cases in
which the suit was over forty shillings. Oyer and Terminer tried criminal cases.

61. Ibid., 7:175, 177, 181, 261, 335. Bryan gave up these positions, ostensibly because he was displeased with the governor but also because they were of
little benefit to him.

62. The power of the council and the weakness of the lower house resulted
partly from the colony's reliance upon the mother country in matters of defense. The lower house had less control over money bills than in other colonies
because the large appropriations for defense and Indian diplomacy originated
from Parliament and were placed in the hands of Georgia's executive (Jack P.
Greene, *The Quest for Power: The Lower Houses of Assembly in the Southern
Royal Colonies, 1689–1776* [Chapel Hill: University of North Carolina Press,
1963], 325).

63. Ibid., 46–47; R. C. Simmons, *The American Colonies: From Settlement
to Independence* (New York: Norton, 1976), 250, 345. The Proceedings of the
Council of Georgia are located in Candler, *CRG,* vols. 7–12.

64. Ibid., 27:103–106, 111–16; Abbot, *Royal Governors of Georgia,* 55–
56. Georgians were concerned with defense but they were more interested in
protecting their property and promoting the colonial economy. This was reflected by the spate of bills passed at the first legislative session in the winter of
1755. An impost on shipping was enacted for the benefit of a lighthouse. Interest rates were regulated and a public market established in Savannah. After
passage of a preliminary slave code, laws were passed to prevent fraudulencies
in deeds, trusts, and mortgages, which protected property acquired through
inheritance, gift, or sale. The speed with which legislation was enacted exhibited the warm support of Georgia slaveholders for the new government. At last
they would have a legislative body through which necessary laws could be
passed—and the power of the Crown fully behind them in matters of defense.

65. Candler, *CRG,* 7:650–51, 702; Book C-1, 133–34, Georgia Archives.

66. Jonathan Bryan to the Earl of Halifax, Apr. 6, 1756, in Candler, *CRG,*
27:114–15.

67. Ibid., 7:22–23, 24; 16:46; 13:61.

68. Ibid., 7:70, 72–73.

69. Ibid., 16:76; 13:50, 58. There was but a single display of opposition to the new government. Edmund Gray, a backcountry Quaker from Virginia was disaffected with the new government for reasons that remain unknown. When his followers failed to attain seats in the lower house, Gray threatened a march on Savannah. The governor called out the militia, and Gray and his followers fled southward. The manner by which the opposition was quickly and efficiently dismissed by the new governor elevated his prestige among the men of property in the houses of assembly. All was in place for Reynolds to pursue his political ends with the expectation of warm support in the Georgia legislature (ibid., 7:26–27, 134; 16:17; 13:33–34, 35, 39; Abbot, *Royal Governors of Georgia,* 38–43; Coleman, *Colonial Georgia,* 181).

70. The council believed Little a "Designing, Evil-Minded Man" and accused him of misappropriating the Indian presents and of absconding with public funds in his other political offices. Their charges were cavalierly dismissed by the governor, who acknowledged Little's malfeasance but allowed him to continue his service in six of the seven offices he held in the colony. The council blamed Little for the dispute between them and Reynolds. They found unfathomable Reynolds's easy toleration of his friend's use of public funds and were so angered with Little's unconstitutional withholding from the governor of acts of legislation which had passed both houses of assembly that they refused to conduct any business until the situation was rectified. But Little's "Principal" crime was "to destroy the harmony which used to subsist between your Excellency and the Council." The crux of the dispute was the council's insistence upon its right to participate in the administration of Georgia. The councillors berated the governor for Little's selection as personal secretary and determined that his elevation to chief adviser was a usurpation of their own proper role and duties. They complained that "of the Eight Proclamations You have been pleas[e]d to issue, Four appear to have [been] issued without the Advice and Consent of your Council." They "humbly insist[ed], that the Council are commanded by those unerring Rules [the king's Instructions] to Cooperate with your Excellency." Therefore, the council claimed, it had "just Pretensions to a decent Freedom of Speech and Debate in delivering That Advice." and also a right to dissent from the governor's decisions. Candler, *CRG,* 7:270–72. According to Albert B. Saye, *A Constitutional History of Georgia, 1739–1945* (Athens: University of Georgia Press, 1948), 57, the governor could not act without the advice and consent of the council in certain specific areas: summoning the assembly, appointment of inferior officers, issuing money from the treasury, creating courts, and establishing martial law. In other matters he was permitted to act without the advice and consent of council but he was to seek their support in the executive decision-making process.

71. Abbot, *Royal Governors of Georgia,* 45–54, contains an excellent sum-

mary of the Little case. But see also, Coleman, *Colonial Georgia*, 181–85. The account that follows examines the episode from a somewhat different perspective, as a showdown by which the council consciously asserted its right to active participation in the executive decision-making process.

72. Jonathan Bryan to the Earl of Halifax, Apr. 6, 1756, in Candler, *CRG*, 27:114–15.

73. Board of Trade to Henry Fox with Enclosures to His Majesty on Georgia, July 29, 1756, CO, 5/672, pp. 193–212; Candler, *CRG*, 7:270–72, 368–69, 450.

74. Candler, *CRG*, 13:56; Greene, *Quest for Power*, 68–71.

75. Candler, *CRG*, 18:464–72.

76. Georgia's constitution of 1777 limited the vote to Protestants. See Elisha P. Douglass, *Rebels and Democrats: The Struggle for Equal Political Rights and Majority Rule during the American Revolution* (Chapel Hill: University of North Carolina Press, 1955), 340–47. Voices of opposition from backwoods farmers (already known as "crackers") and from small slaveholders are muted before 1765 in the historical record. In the 1760s, migration southward from Virginia along the Piedmont added to the number of complainants. Their grievances provided impetus in the challenge that erupted between the mother country and her colonies: notably, the formation of an opposition to the Crown and to low-country Whig rule. The political victories of the backwoods farmers were many, and included the establishment of one of the most radical state constitutions in the revolutionary period. But in the late 1750s, discontented backwoodsmen and farmers were not factors of influence within the Georgia government. Abbot, *Royal Governors of Georgia*, 19–21; Coleman, *American Revolution in Georgia*, 279, and *Colonial Georgia*, 223–44.

77. Abbot, *Royal Governors of Georgia*, 140; Greene, *Quest for Power*, 9, 47, 324–25; Jackson T. Main, *The Upper House in Revolutionary America, 1763–1788* (Madison: University of Wisconsin Press, 1967), 8. Lower-house control over money bills in Georgia was less substantive than in other colonies because the large appropriations for defense and Indian diplomacy originated from the Crown and were in the hands of the executive.

78. The early statutes of the "Royal Legislature" are located in ibid., 18:7–144. In the first three months after the creation of the houses of assembly, the following subjects were legislated: militia, paper money, the supremacy of the new government's laws, the fencing of property, an impost to raise money for the lighthouse, regulation of transference of property, the public market, interest rate on loaned money, public roads, and a slave code.

79. *A Pair of Odes Commemorating the Departure of the Royal Governor of the Colony of Georgia for England, and the welcoming of his successor, February the sixteenth of the year 1757 By an Unknown hand. From the Origi-*

nals in the Special Collections Division of the University of Georgia Libraries
(Darien, Ga.: Ashantilly Press, 1960).

80. The best summary of Ellis's career in Georgia is Abbot, *Royal Governors of Georgia,* 58–59. But also see the excellent essay on Ellis, "The Spectrum of Imperial Possibilities: Henry Ellis and Thomas Pownall, 1763–1775," in John Shy, *A People Numerous and Armed: Reflections on the Struggle for American Independence* (London: Oxford University Press, 1975), 35–72.

81. Georgia had a reputation in England as a most inhospitable place.

82. In an excellent assessment of Georgia's colonial governors, William W. Abbot wrote of Ellis's character and tenure, that he was a "gifted dilettante [who] was faced with a situation which demanded the full play of his powers. As a result, a really first-rate talent for politics and diplomacy bloomed briefly in Georgia" (*Royal Governors of Georgia,* 57, 62).

83. See appendix 1.

84. Candler, *CRG,* 7:485, 491, 566–69, 590, 626–27.

85. Bryan also headed the upper-house investigation of Edmund Atkin, the king's superintendent of Indian Affairs. Atkin had tried to preempt Georgia's influence with the Creeks (Candler, *CRG,* 8:5–8; 16:393, 394, 399, 401, 402, 403, 407, 408). This coincided with the consideration of major legislation to regulate Georgia relations with the Creeks; the preventing of "private Persons from purchasing Lands from the Indians" and from "trading with them without Licence." The final bill can be found in ibid., 18:359–61. Ironically, although Bryan worked for this legislation in 1759, in the 1770s he was utilizing loopholes to avoid its strictures and that of the Crown's successor legislation, the Proclamation Act of 1763. For further discussion, see chapter 6. It is unclear whether Bryan actually filled his appointment, for Joseph Wright, who was fluent in the Creek language, was also enlisted to invite the Creeks. But Bryan was given presents by the council to induce the Creeks to attend (ibid., 18:589–99, 643).

86. Ibid., 7:615, 665–68.

87. Ibid., 7:644.

88. Ibid., 7:644–45.

89. Ibid., 7:665–67.

90. For the effect of the French and Indian War and the Cherokee War upon the Deep South, see John Richard Alden, *John Stuart and the Southern Colonial Frontier: A Study of Indian Relations, War, Trade, and Land Problems in the Southern Wilderness, 1754–1775* (1944; repr., New York: Gordion Press, 1966); John Shy, *Toward Lexington: The Role of the British Army in the Coming of the American Revolution* (Princeton: Princeton University Press, 1965); Merriwether, *Expansion of South Carolina,* 213–40.

91. See appendix 1. Bryan refrained from all political activity from May 2, 1764, to Apr. 24, 1765. During this time he was building his villa at Brampton

Plantation. Excluding this prolonged absence Bryan attended all council meetings in 1764 and 44 percent of them in 1765. Including the absence, in our calculations he attended 30 percent and 32 percent, respectively, a higher rate than he enjoyed in 1756.

92. Francis Harris's attendance from 1758 to 1762: 45 percent, 74 percent, 46 percent, 53 percent, 56 percent. Patrick Houstoun, from 1758 to 1760: 70 percent, 55 percent, 46 percent. James Habersham, from 1758 to 1762: 79 percent, 45 percent, 57 percent, 69 percent, and 86 percent. A few councillors, such as James McKay and William Grover, rarely attended council meetings. Others, such as William Knox, William Clifton, and James Edward Powell, ordinarily attended council meetings with greater frequency than their counterparts. See n. 93.

93. Clifton's attendance, 1758–62: 55 percent, 26 percent, 100 percent, 93 percent, 97 percent. (Clifton attended 61 meetings without fail in 1760, 42 of 45 in 1761, and 35 of 36 in 1762.) William Knox's attendance was 94 percent, 69 percent, 95 percent, 62 percent, and 11 percent for the same period. Powell's attendance rate was 91 percent, 71 percent, 71 percent, 53 percent, and 44 percent.

94. Knox, like Clifton, arrived in Georgia with an appointment to the council in hand, the former to serve in addition as provost marshal, the latter as attorney general.

95. James Habersham, who was secretary of the council, had diverse economic interests yet attended the mundane business of the council with frequency, though still less often than the "professionals." Habersham was a clerk before he was a rich merchant-planter and may have enjoyed performing "clerk's" duties for the council. Noble Jones attended the council intermittently. Some years he rarely showed up for meetings, while in others he attended with great regularity. Jones was not quite as rich as the other long-term councillors, but his medical duties may have kept him busy for extensive periods of time.

96. Candler, *CRG*, 7:500–501, 505, 692–93; 16:381; 18:351.

97. Commissions, Apr. 2, 1757, Book B, 57, Georgia Archives.

98. Candler, *CRG*, 18:205, 300–303, 408–17, 472–78, 570; 16:513.

99. Ibid., 18:80–86, 570.

100. Ibid., 18:276–82; Davis, *Fledgling Province*, 97–98, believed these laws to have been ineffective; Richard Walsh, *Charleston's Sons of Liberty: A Study of the Artisans 1763–1789* (Columbia: University of South Carolina Press, 1959), 24–25, 57–58, 109–10.

101. For the Union Society, see Davis, *Fledgling Province*, 169–70. This episode will be discussed in detail in chapter 5.

102. See appendix 1.

103. Candler, *CRG*, 16:76, 177.

104. Ibid., 16:12, 223, 233, 250, 276–77, 280, 381, 392, 436–38, 513; 18:88, 180–88, 300, 351, 413, 475; 7:214–16, 500–501, 505, 692–93; 13:216, 230, 284, 289.

105. Bryan was a justice of the peace during most of his life in Georgia, as were all the leading men of the colony. But he never became involved in legislation regulating the behavior of Georgia citizens within the colony except for a bill for "keeping holy the Lord's day."

106. Candler, *CRG*, 13:75.

107. Ibid., 13:126. When Reynolds signed the bill he already knew of his recall. He may have approved it for the sake of appearances, to show he was getting along with the houses of assembly.

108. Ibid., 13:95, 111, 117; 18:157–59. The bill was disallowed in 1759 by the Privy Council because Dissenters in Great Britain were not permitted the privilege of refusing oaths (Reba Strickland, *Religion and the State in Georgia in the Eighteenth Century* [New York: Columbia University Press, 1939], 122).

109. There were approximately one hundred Jews in Savannah before the American Revolution. The number of Catholics and Dissenters is unknown. Prohibitions against the former may have deterred members of the faith from settling in Georgia. It is difficult to enumerate the number of adherents to the different faiths because there were so few organized congregations, ministers, and surviving records. Anglican rectors could be found only in Savannah and Augusta. There were Congregational chapels at Midway and Sunbury; the Independent Presbyterians were in Savannah, the Methodist-Anglicans at Bethesda, and the Lutherans at New Ebenezer. In addition, there were scattered settlements of Baptists and Quakers through the colony. The institutional weakness of religion should not necessarily be interpreted as insouciance on the part of the populace. For instance, Presbyterian settlements at Queensborough and Wrightsborough probably used lay ministers when ordained clergymen could not be found. Quakers and Jews, in fact, held regular worship services without the presence of a ministry or specially constructed buildings for meetings. Until such time as further research is made into the religious life of the populace—specifically, in terms of identifying religious affiliation quantitatively and qualitatively—all conclusions must remain tenuous at best.

110. Candler, *CRG*, 14:181; 8:46–47; 7:183; 16:642, 653; 18:508–515.

111. Charles Colcock Jones, Jr., *The Dead Towns of Georgia* (Savannah: Morning News Steam Printing House, 1878), 178.

112. For the effect of the establishment on Dissenters, see Strickland, *Religion in Georgia,* 100–28; a more cohesive discussion, though, can be found in Coleman, *Colonial Georgia,* 231–36. Both agree that establishment had little effect on the religious and political life of Dissenters. Georgia did put political restrictions on Jews and Catholics well into the revolutionary period, but it is often argued that these were of little consequence.

113. Candler, *CRG*, 16:310.

114. Ibid., 18:786–89.

115. Ibid., 18:335–37; 16:335; Easterby, et al., *Colonial Records,* vol. 7, bills 4 and 24; vol. 8, bill 16.

116. In Duke University's Special Collections can be found the Ledger of Edward Telfair, 1773–93. Telfair was one of Georgia's leading merchants. In the years 1773–75 there were twenty-four entries under the name of Jonathan Bryan. Five of the entries were for petty cash borrowed by Jonathan from the store, in amounts from six shillings to five pounds. There were also eleven purchases from the store, only two of which were over ten pounds—unfortunately, we do not know exactly what these purchases were, but they were considered "sundries." The store also paid out cash to men whom Jonathan Bryan owed money, including £91 to James Hume in 1775. The only other large transaction was the £195 Telfair paid in 1774 to or for the ship *Mary.* This could have been for purchases Bryan made from abroad, but Bryan may have been buying out someone's share of a ship in which he was co-owner. (The name of the vessel was the same as his wife's, and he had owned several vessels.) The total amount of credit allotted by Telfair to Bryan in the three-year period was £250 Georgia currency. This was a large amount of money to most Georgians, but for Bryan it was barely significant. Although Bryan and Telfair had disputed a bond for £280 in 1769, it does not seem to have had any effect on Bryan's credit with the firm. The bond is dated July 30, 1769 (Edward Telfair Papers, Special Collections, Duke University, Durham, N.C.; repository hereafter cited as Duke University).

117. The only example I found in which Bryan paid on terms is Jonathan Bryan to Thomas Vincent for accounts due Jan. 1, 1765, and Aug. 8, 1765, Miscellaneous—Bonds, Book O, 380, Georgia Archives.

118. Judgment Rolls, box 31b, no. 31a, S.C. Archives; ibid., box 31a, nos. 58a and 64a; Miscellaneous—Bonds, Book R, 3–4, and Book J, 261, Georgia Archives; Bond of John Martin and Jonathan Bryan to the King, Jan. 3, 1769, Georgia Miscellaneous Papers, Duke University.

119. Loans Bryan made in South Carolina were recorded in the official records of the colony only when legal action was taken for nonpayment. Bryan sued four men for defaulting on loans he made between 1749 and 1753. We may presume that the percentage of defaulters was small and that Bryan made considerably more loans than were recorded. Likewise, in Georgia, loans were rarely recorded in the official records. A few of the bonds Bryan cosigned for others have been found in private papers, but the original number may have been very high considering the destruction and loss of papers from the colonial period in Georgia.

120. The importance of the patron-client relationship as a "bond" between men has been insightfully explored in Stephen Innes, *Labor in a New Land: Economy and Society in Seventeenth-Century Springfield* (Princeton: Prince-

ton University Press, 1983). Innes pointed out that the "patron" is "never an autonomous figure" in the relationship. The "client," whether a tenant, debtor, or underling, could establish a relationship elsewhere. Innes (39–40) cites Sydel F. Silverman, "Patronage and Community-Nation Relationships in Central Italy," *Ethnology* 4 (1965): 176, for a definition of the ties between the two parties as an "informal contractual relationship between persons of unequal status and power, which imposes reciprocal obligations of a different kind on each of the parties." Innes's observations of John Pynchon can be similarly applied to Jonathan Bryan. As a "patron," he "exchanged the fruits of his status, power, influence, and authority for the loyalty and political support of the client." Bryan lent money, provided jobs (for both public works projects [see next section] and on his plantations), and he sponsored settlers who desired land grants (see chapter 4). For instance, he hired James Whitefield, ostensibly to serve as a secretary, and then probably was influential in gaining for him a position as secretary of the house. Although we have no documentation on what Bryan received in return—besides Whitefield's loyal service—we may presume that during the Revolutionary War, when Bryan was a member of the executive council and Whitefield was secretary of state, their earlier patron-client relationship contributed to a good working relationship between them. As long as a demand on Bryan's time and resources was light (to him), he could paternalistically bestow favors on the less fortunate and not expect to receive an immediate return. In fact, he may not have desired that the favor be repaid right away. He was more likely to receive a favor from a man who was indebted to him than one who was not: there was always the possibility that Bryan could demand repayment.

121. David McCord Wright, comp., "Petitioners to the Crown against the Proprietors, 1716–1717," *South Carolina Historical Magazine* 62 (1961): 88–89; BPRO, microfilm, roll 5, vol. 11, pp. 225–26; M. Eugene Sirmans found the issue of paper money to have been a major factor of division in Carolina between those who supported the proprietors of that colony and those who were against them. The supporters of paper money comprised the opposition and were known as the "Landed Men" and the "Country Gentlemen." The poorer parishes on the northern and southern frontiers were the strongholds of the paper-money faction (Sirmans, *Colonial South Carolina,* 116, 145–46).

122. Sirmans, *Colonial South Carolina,* 145. An excellent discussion of the relationship between agriculture, debt, and paper money can be found in Daniel P. Szatmary, *Shay's Rebellion: The Making of an Agrarian Insurrection* (Amherst: University of Massachusetts Press, 1980), 19–36.

123. Wood, *Slavery in Colonial Georgia,* 96–98, 228 n. 25; De Vorsey, *De Brahm's Report,* 162–63.

124. Candler, *CRG,* 16:12, 250; 18:272–77.

125. Bryan and Powell proposed the bill in 1759. It was not fully accepted until 1767 (ibid., 16:392, 18:352–59, 802–10). Bryan's support of the yeomanry would continue into the era of the American Revolution: as a member of the Commons House in the 1770s he would support legislation benefiting the backcountry farmers' right to hunt at night, a practice frowned upon by most members of the gentry. See discussion in chapter 5.

126. Henry Laurens to Jonathan Bryan, Sept. 4, 1767, quoted in Hamer et al., *Laurens Papers,* 5:288.

127. *Georgia Gazette,* Mar. 13, 1788.

128. Henry Laurens to Jonathan Bryan, Sept. 4, 1767, quoted in Hamer et al., *Laurens Papers,* 5:289.

CHAPTER 4: LAND AND POLITICS

1. Candler, *CRG,* 6:333–34; 7:284–85; Coleman and Ready, *CRG,* 27:84, 135.

2. Redding, *Life and Times of Jonathan Bryan,* 33–34.

3. Conveyances, Book R-R, 62, 92; Book S-S, 120; Book V-V, 1, S.C. Archives.

4. Candler, *CRG,* 6:434; Coleman and Ready, *CRG,* 27:84, 135.

5. Georgia's first two governors promoted moving the capital there (Candler, *CRG,* 6:434; 7:103; Coleman and Ready, *CRG,* 27:135, 142); Jones, *Dead Towns of Georgia,* 224–32.

6. Candler, *CRG,* 7:229–30.

7. Conveyances, Book C, 184–90, 989–90, Georgia Archives; Candler, *CRG,* 10:370–71.

8. De Vorsey, *De Brahm's Report,* 148.

9. Candler, *CRG,* 7:229–30, 512, 609–10, 650–51, 698, 702, 746; Conveyances, Book S-S, 120, S.C. Archives.

10. All money is expressed in Georgia currency. Although Georgia currency was close to par with that of England, the exchange into English currency entailed additional costs of about 7 percent. Many of the original notations state that the sum is sterling, but as John J. McCusker has shown, this is a misnomer (*Money and Exchange in Europe and America, 1600–1775: A Handbook* [Chapel Hill: University of North Carolina Press, 1978], 120–21, 227–29).

11. *Georgia Gazette,* Feb. 10, 1768; Chatham County Wills, no. 14, Georgia Archives.

12. Proclamations, Book H, 488–89, Georgia Archives.

13. Ibid.; John Rutledge to Jonathan Bryan, Aug. 19, 1777, John Rutledge, Jr., Papers, Duke University.

14. Conveyances, Book B-3, 33; Book D-3, 479; Book X-3, 213–23, S.C. Archives. Miscellaneous—Bonds, Book O, 341–43; Proclamations, Book H, 488–89; Chatham County Wills, no. 14, Georgia Archives. *Georgia Gazette,* Feb. 10, 1768. Unfortunately, many of these transactions were unrecorded, though we know that Bryan possessed the land because he later willed or sold it. Dispute over the ownership of one tract brought him several lawsuits and an argument with Adrian Loyer in the press. *Williams vs. Loyer and Others,* Oct. 4, 1771, in Anne King Gregorie, ed., *Records of the Court of Chancery, 1671–1779* (Washington, D.C.: American Historical Association, 1950), 588–89; *Lessee of Loyer vs. Jonathan Bryan,* Sept. 9, 1766, Judgment Rolls, box 68A, no. 337, S.C. Archives; *Georgia Gazette,* May 16 and Aug. 1, 1765.

15. Habersham, who bought Dean Forrest from Bryan, did not mind locating his operations on the Little Ogeechee River. His position as the colony's leading merchant enabled him easily to direct oceangoing vessels to his plantations.

16. Candler, *CRG,* 7:702, 776–77, 791; 8:108; Coleman and Ready, *CRG,* 28 (part 1): 238, 321. Conveyances, Book C, 989–90; Book X-1, 493; Book CC-1, 156–59, Georgia Archives.

17. Candler, *CRG,* 8:439.

18. Ibid., 10:400–401, 975; Conveyances, Book X-1, 493; Book DD, 114–15; Book S, 367, 374, Georgia Archives. Henry Laurens to Jonathan Bryan, Sept. 4, 1767, in Hamer, et al., *Laurens Papers,* 5:288–91.

19. *Georgia Gazette,* July 21, 1763; Candler, *CRG,* 10:400–401, 975. Conveyances, Book X-1, 493; Book S, 365–71, Georgia Archives.

20. Candler, *CRG,* 7:229–30, 512, 698, 746; 8:550–51, 719.

21. Conveyances, Book C, 184, 989, Georgia Archives; Candler, *CRG,* 7:809; 8:67, 125; 10:983.

22. Candler, *CRG,* 8:155, 318, 719; Coleman and Ready, *CRG,* 28 (part 1): 432.

23. Candler, *CRG,* 18:723.

24. This map, of unknown authorship, is entitled *Savannah & Ogeechee River.* It may be seen at the geography and Map Room, Library of Congress. The map's call number is G3922. S3 178- .S3 Vault (Force 214).

25. Colonists first began referring to the cowpen when describing their grants in March 1761. Elizabeth Didcott requested 500 acres "within three Miles of Jonathan Bryan's Cowpen" (Candler, *CRG,* 11:414); Christopher Ring requested 250 acres "within four Miles of Mr. Bryan's Cowpen," and Micajah Plumer wanted 150 acres "near a Place called the Flat ford joining the Upper Line below the Ford about Ten Miles above Bryans Cowpen" (ibid., 9:290). For other examples see ibid., 8:652, 654; 9:495; 10:447, 464, 467, 825, 826, 890, 961, 962.

26. Ibid., 19 (part 2): 61–66.

27. Ibid., 7:702; Conveyances, Book C, 807–12, Georgia Archives.

28. Candler, *CRG*, 8:67; Coleman and Ready, *CRG*, 28 (part 1): 432. Conveyances, Book C, 1045–49; Book X-2, 865, Georgia Archives. See also Savannah Unit, Georgia Writers Project, Works Project Administration in Georgia, "Brampton Plantation," *Georgia Historical Quarterly* 27 (Mar. 1943): 28–55.

29. Bryan was expert in the Indian art of carving piraguas from cypress and cedar trees. See E. Merton Coulter, *Wormsloe: Two Centuries of a Georgia Family* (Atlanta: University of Georgia Press, 1955), 44–45; Egmont Manuscripts, in Phillips Collection, series no. 14201, pp. 61–63, University of Georgia, Athens; Coleman and Ready, *CRG*, 20:429.

30. Julia Floyd Smith, *Slavery and Rice Culture in Low Country Georgia, 1750–1860* (Knoxville: University of Tennessee Press, 1985), 4–5, 10–11, 20–21, 24. On the origins of rice cultivation in the Deep South, see Wood, *Black Majority*, 35–37, 55–63, and Daniel C. Littlefield, *Rice and Slaves: Ethnicity and the Slave Trade in Colonial South Carolina* (Baton Rouge: Louisiana State University Press, 1981).

31. In addition to the discussion of maps below and those mentioned in n. 58 below, see Archibald Campbell's *Sketch of the Northern Frontiers of Georgia, Extending from the Mouth of the River Savannah to the Town of Augusta*, engraved by William Faden, 1780. A copy of the map has been inserted in Joseph Clay *Letters of Joseph Clay, Merchant of Savannah, 1776–1793 . . .* , Collections of the Georgia Historical Society, vol. 8 (Savannah: Georgia Historical Society, 1913), facing p. 32.

Milton Sydney Heath estimated that 5 percent of the Georgia landowners possessed 20 percent of the colony's land. This figure seems to suggest a more equitable division of land than in other southern colonies. But Heath correctly noted that this 20 percent "constituted the bulk of the best quality and most favorably situated lands" (*Constructive Liberalism: The Role of the State in Economic Development in Georgia to 1860* [Cambridge: Harvard University Press, 1954], 64–65). Heath also estimated that the top 5 percent of the landowners owned over half of Georgia's slaves. For the division of land in other colonies, see Jackson Turner Main, *The Social Structure of Revolutionary America* (Princeton: Princeton University Press, 1965).

32. Female heads of household were entitled to grants of land in royal Georgia. See Lee Ann Caldwell, "Women Landholders of Colonial Georgia," in Jackson and Spalding, *Forty Years of Diversity*, 183–97.

33. Land day was established on Feb. 25, 1755 (Candler, *CRG*, 7:127). Petitions were heard on other days than land days because of an overflow of requests or for the convenience of the board or the petitioner, but throughout the colonial period the first Tuesday was the traditional day for adjudging claims.

34. The council's responses to petitions are located in its journals. See Candler, *CRG*, vols. 7–12.

35. The number of petitions per year: 1755, 357; 1756, 177; 1757, 287; 1758, 303; 1759, 430; 1760, 231; 1761, 187; 1762, 197; 1763, 117; 1764, 284; 1765, 376; 1766, 536; 1767, 697; 1768, 579; 1769, 629. These figures were compiled by counting the petitions given in Candler, *CRG*, vols. 6–10. The increase beginning in 1764 was a result of the end of the Seven Years' War and of the migration of Virginians and North and South Carolinians into the Georgia backcountry.

36. Candler, *CRG*, 6:369; 7:204, 229–30, 284–85, 650–51, 702; 8:439, 760; 9:23; 10:160, 400–401, 975; Coleman and Ready, *CRG*, 27:87.

37. Candler, *CRG*, 10:438, 463, 604.

38. In *Colonial Georgia*, 126, 207, Coleman breaks down the number of acres granted as follows: before 1752: 245,948; 1752–63: 390,645; 1763–73: 771,940. The council began granting land in 1755. The peak year was 1769, when 129,971 acres were claimed. There followed a great decline until 1772, when only 46,585 acres were granted.

39. One reason for the high rate of acceptance was that most of the land sought was considered undesirable by low-country planters; the petitions came from backcountry settlers for land distant from the routes of transportation.

40. Computations are based upon petitions for land in Candler, *CRG*, vols. 7–12. Requests for land, 1755–69, totaled 5,387. See appendix 2.

41. There is no record of a petition by Noble in Candler, *CRG*. One may have been submitted and not recorded, but that is unlikely. Laurens was in South Carolina at the time, so he probably had heard of Noble's intent to petition. For Laurens's letters to Georgians on the subject, see Laurens to Lachlan McIntosh, May 10, 1769, and Laurens to John Polson, Sept. 3, 1769, Hamer et al., *Laurens Papers*, 6:444–45, 7:130–31.

42. See appendix 2.

43. See ibid. Claims that were accepted in part, where the amount of acreage requested by the claimant was trimmed, have been counted as accepted petitions.

44. Candler, *CRG*, 10:189–90, 208.

45. Bryan's attendance on land days was as follows: 1755, 86%; 1757, 75%; 1758, 91%; 1759, 92%; 1760, 58%; 1761, 89%; 1762, 75%; 1763, 91%; 1764, 100%. Computation for 1756 is excluded because land day was infrequently held. Computation for 1764 excludes meetings after May 2, 1764, when Bryan was completely absent from the council.

46. For a full list of these petitions see appendix 3.

47. Two petitions were "postponed untill the Expiration of the Term limited by Act of Assembly and given to absentee Claimants of Land in this Province to come in & claim the same." Many people who received grants during the

Trustee period never made good their claims by settling the tracts. The above-mentioned legislation provided a final grace period for them to claim their tracts, but Bryan and other Georgians were impatient (Candler, *CRG*, 7:837; 8:181, 184).

48. Ibid., 10:238. The council attempted to limit purchases to 300 acres but made exceptions in several cases.

49. Ibid., 8:439.

50. Ibid., 10:189.

51. From Oct. 10 to Oct. 25, 1767, Bryan made five purchases totaling over 4,000 acres. In 1768 he bought 2,000 acres and in 1769 an additional 1,500 (Conveyances, Book S, 357, 360, 363, 366–67, Georgia Archives).

52. Records of transactions for over 14,500 acres have survived. See appendix 4. For three tracts of about 7,000 acres on the South Carolina side of the Savannah River there is no record of purchase.

53. Renunciation of dower rights was still required for land obtained by freehold but not by purchase.

54. James Habersham to John Ellis, Oct. 18, 1770, in James Habersham, *The Letters of the Hon. James Habersham, 1756–1775*, Collections of the Georgia Historical Society, vol. 6 (Savannah: Georgia Historical Society, 1904), 91–93. Habersham suggested that Ellis correspond with Bryan, John Mullryne, and James Jackson for the purpose of experimenting with plants in the Georgia environment. Each of the three Georgians lived in a different environment, "which must produce very different Plants of all Kinds"—Mullryne on a saltwater river, Bryan on fresh water, and Jackson "far up in the country." Habersham was "persuaded, whatever you send them by the Way of Experiment, they will carefully attend to, and whatever you may hint may be acceptable from hence, they will endeavor to furnish you with" (p. 93).

55. Francis Harper, ed., *The Travels of William Bartram* (New Haven: Yale University Press, 1958), 297–99, 418.

56. Benjamin Franklin to John Bartram, Oct. 17, 1772; Franklin to Noble W. Jones, Oct. 7, 1772; Noble Wimberly Jones to Franklin, Jan. 13, 1773, in Leonard W. Labaree et al., eds., *The Papers of Benjamin Franklin* (New Haven: Yale University Press, 1963), 19:316–17, 324, and n.8; 20:24. Malcolm Bell III, *Some Notes and Reflections upon a Letter from Benjamin Franklin to Noble Wimberly Jones, October 7, 1772* (Darien, Ga.: Ashantilly Press, 1966).

57. In 1767 Bryan had his good friend James Habersham claim 1,100 acres on Little Cumberland Island, which he then bought for £50. To expedite the transaction Bryan traveled to the distant island and surveyed the tract (Conveyances, Book S, 366, Georgia Archives).

58. Unfortunately, most of Hugh's maps have not survived. There is an extant copy of a map he made of Purrysburg. A map of Beaufort may be his: the

town lots belonging to the Bryan family are labeled, while most of the others are not. Otherwise, we have only De Brahm's generous gratitude expressed in the titles of his maps of South Carolina and Georgia. Bryan's Purrysburg map is in *South Carolina Historical Magazine* 10 (Oct. 1909), 187. The Beaufort map is in ibid., 9 (July 1908), foldout. Surveys made by Hugh Bryan exist in plenty, and some are quite artistic. These may be found at the S.C. Archives, in repositories throughout the South, and in published form in Todd and Hutson, *Prince William's Parish.* Copies of De Brahm's maps are widely scattered. An excellent collection is housed in the Map Room at the Library of Congress. See John R. Sellers and Patricia Molen Van Ee, comps., *Maps and Charts of North America and the West Indies, 1750–1789: A Guide to the Collections in the Library of Congress* (Washington, D.C.: Government Printing Office, 1981). For a discussion of De Brahm and his Carolina predecessors, see William P. Cumming, *The Southeast in Early Maps, with an Annotated Check List of Printed and Manuscript Regional and Local Maps of Southeastern North America during the Colonial Period* (Chapel Hill: University of North Carolina Press, 1962), 54–55, 227–28.

59. De Vorsey, *De Brahm's Report,* 9; George Whitefield to Jonathan Bryan, Feb. 1 and Jan. 19, 1753, in Whitefield, *Works,* 3:3, 2:478; Jonathan Bryan to George Whitefield, July 4, 1753, Whitefield Papers, 1:36, Library of Congress.

60. Sold in the colonies and England, the map went through several editions and included markings not only of roads, rivers, and landmarks of the two colonies but major plantations with a key to the landowners. We may be sure that Bryan was proud of the depiction of his family's many holdings. *A Map of South Carolina and a Part of Georgia; containing the Whole Sea-Coast; All the Islands, Inlets, Rivers, Creeks, Parishes, Townships, Boroughs, Roads, and Bridges: As Also, Several Plantations, with Their Proper Boundary-Lines, Their Names and the Names of Their Proprietors. Composed from Surveys Taken by the Hon. William Bull, Esq. Lieutenant Governor, Captain Gascoign, Hugh Bryan, Esq; and the Author William De Brahm, Surveyor General to the Province of South Carolina, One of the Surveyors of Georgia, and Late Captain Engineer under His Imperial Majesty Charles VII . . .* formed the basis of many later maps, including Cook, 1773; Mouzon, 1775; and Stuart, 1780. De Brahm's map was published in several editions and reprinted in France in French. Many editions of the map, including the first edition, can be found in the Map Room, Library of Congress. For information on these maps, see Cumming, *Southeast in Early Maps,* 227–28.

61. Francis Moore, "A Voyage to Georgia Begun in the Year 1735," in *Our First Visit in America: Early Reports from the Colony of Georgia, 1732–1740,* ed. Trevor R. Reese (Savannah: Beehive Press, 1974), 133.

62. Jackson, "Carolina Connection," 157–58.

63. Candler, *CRG,* 6:334.

64. Ibid., 18:88, 723.

65. *South Carolina Gazette,* June and July 1770; Conveyances, Book V, 351, 502, and Book X-2, 856, Georgia Archives.

66. The stamina he displayed, in what should have been his declining years, was considered remarkable by contemporaries. When Henry Laurens heard that Bryan intended to settle land on the Altamaha River, he welcomed "the acquisition of so good a Neighbour" but wondered whether Bryan possessed the physical capabilities for so wearisome a task at his age. He wrote Bryan, "I could not forbear expressing my feelings [to Lachlan McIntosh] upon your own Account, from an apprehension that all the vexations attendant upon the establishment of new Plantations, must expose you to a great deal of troubles." But McIntosh had reassured Laurens "that in point of bodily health & constitution" Bryan was "a Young Man, & that he feared no ill consequences . . . from your removal" (Sept. 4, 1767, in Hamer et al., *Laurens Papers,* 5:289).

67. Miscellaneous—Bonds, Book R, 83, and Conveyances, Book S, 12–13, Georgia Archives.

68. Ten years after its purchase, Josiah's widow considered selling 450 acres of the Wilmington tract. Her advertisement described the land as "supposed to be as good as any land upon the island for corn and indigo, with a proportion of valuable pine land fit for sawing; this land is so well known that it needs no farther recommendation" (*Georgia Gazette,* May 17, 1775).

69. Conveyances, Book C, 807–12; Book S, 365–71; Book V, 351, 502; Book X-1, 493; Book X-2, 856, 374, Georgia Archives.

70. Candler, *CRG,* 7:154–55, 8:318, 9:23.

71. Wood, *Slavery in Colonial Georgia,* 97–105; Weir, *Colonial South Carolina,* 147, 155–56, 175–76; Smith, *Slavery and Rice Culture,* 93–97.

72. Miscellaneous—Bonds, Book J, 289; Book Y-2, 471–75; Book HH, 24–25; Chatham County Deeds, 1785–1910, Book D, 75–77, Georgia Archives. The precise makeup of Bryan's slave labor force, whether creole, African, or West Indian, is unknown.

73. De Vorsey, *De Brahm's Report,* 162–63.

74. Wood, *Slavery in Colonial Georgia,* 107–108.

75. Conveyances, Book X-2, 853–56, Georgia Archives; Davis, *Fledgling Province,* 141.

76. Conveyances, Book X-2, 865, Georgia Archives.

77. Bryan originally learned of the land from his brother, who owned it but apparently did not develop it. The land passed through other hands before Jonathan Bryan brought it back into the family (Conveyances, Book X-3, 213–23, S.C. Archives).

78. The revised figure is based upon the price Bryan received for both developed and undeveloped low-country rice land in the late 1760s. See ibid.; Conveyances, Book V, 502, and Book X-2, 853, 856, 865, Georgia Archives.

79. Chatham County Wills, no. 14, Georgia Archives.

80. Jones, "Boltzius' Trip to Charleston," 106–107; George Whitefield to Jonathan Bryan, Oct. 26, 1757, in Whitefield, *Letters,* 3:217; Winter's observations were reprinted in Jay, *Works of the Rev. William Jay,* 3:30. Two other members of the Georgia council, James Habersham and William Knox, followed Bryan's example and allowed their slaves Christianity. Perhaps this contributed to their success as well.

81. Bryan sold his excess lumber. See *Georgia Gazette,* Mar. 22 and Nov. 29, 1775. His will provided that the labor of his carpenters and sawyers should be used for four years to pay off any of his estate's debts. This would have prevented his estate from being divested of land and laborers.

82. Henry Laurens forwarded a packet from Devonshire, Reeve, & Lloyd to Jonathan Bryan in 1765. Lloyd operated out of Bristol. The Lloyds were a merchant family of New York and England. Bryan remained in correspondence with Lloyd in the 1770s. I have not been able to locate the merchant records of the English branch of this family.

Bryan referred to himself as a planter. Some of the British during the war believed him to be a merchant, but there is nothing to substantiate their belief. Bryan may have helped others transport their goods to market or used his credit to purchase goods for others, but he was not a merchant.

83. See appendix 1.

84. Because Bryan had two sons named John and one named Jonathan, confusion has arisen over the date of death of the two Johns. It is possible that neither of the Johns died in 1762 and that one died in 1749 and the other in 1767. Nevertheless, it is clear that Jonathan, Jr., died in 1761 and Joseph in 1762.

85. Conveyances, Book C, 807–812, Georgia Archives; *Georgia Gazette,* July 21, 1763.

86. Bryan made no transaction between May 25, 1764, and April 20, 1765.

87. For a superb discussion of the gentry's use of their houses as a statement of social standing, see Isaac, *Transformation of Virginia,* 35–42, 354.

88. Figures derived from the tabulations found in Davis, *Fledgling Province,* 32; Edward J. Cashin, "Sowing the Wind: Governor Wright and the Georgia Backcountry on the Eve of the Revolution," in Jackson and Spalding, *Forty Years of Diversity,* 236.

89. The experience of the refugees from North and South Carolina with the Regulator movement was an important factor in the Georgia backcountry's political success against the low country during and after the American Revolution.

90. Coleman, *Colonial Georgia,* 207; De Vorsey, *Indian Boundary,* 149–57; Alden, *John Stuart,* 181–86; W. Stitt Robinson, *The Southern Colonial Frontier, 1607–1763* (Albuquerque: University of New Mexico Press, 1979), 224–25.

91. See appendix 2.

92. Except for the one-year period when he was completely absent from council, Bryan's attendance on land day never wavered, though his overall attendance at council meetings declined significantly in the 1760s.

93. Coleman, *Colonial Georgia*, 297.

94. See appendix 3.

95. Wallace, *History of South Carolina*, 2:47; Abbot, *Royal Governors of Georgia*, 100–102.

96. Wright wrote to the board of trade on Sept. 25, 1766, relative to the Altamaha: "This matter Remaining in the State it is, is a Manifest Injury to the Province. . . . neither the People who have the Grants, nor I, can tell how to Proceed, and of Course the Lands will Lye waste & Unimproved" (Coleman & Ready, *CRG*, 28 [part 2]: 160). Georgia's problems with the Altamaha can best be followed in Wright's extensive correspondence with the earl of Hillsborough. See ibid., 28 (part 1): 400–14, 428–29; 28 (part 2): 38–39, 71, 78–79, 159–60, 178, 233–35, 255–56. Georgia's act to amend the situation passed Mar. 26, 1765. Its rejection was not learned in Georgia until 1768. See Candler, *CRG*, 18:627–36; 9:39, 40–43; 10:460.

97. Coleman and Ready, *CRG*, 28 (part 1): 409, 455, 461; Candler, *CRG*, 9:341.

98. Wallace, *History of South Carolina*, 2:47.

99. Candler, *CRG*, 9:441; 10:60, 160; Coleman and Ready, *CRG*, 28 (part 2): 268.

100. *Georgia Gazette*, Feb. 10, 1768.

101. Candler, *CRG*, 10:189–90.

102. On his next request for land along the Altamaha, Bryan was careful to show that the land he desired was not for speculation, for it was located "contiguous to Land already ordered him there and which he was then settling" (ibid., 10:400).

103. Conveyances, Book S, 363, Georgia Archives.

104. Ibid., 357, 360, 366.

105. Ibid., 365–71, 374.

106. Ibid., Book V, 502.

107. Ibid., Book X-1, 493.

108. Bryan's letter to Laurens recommending the project has disappeared. Laurens's reply can be found in Hamer et al., *Laurens Papers*, 5:288–91, Sept. 4, 1767.

109. For Laurens, see Hamer et al., *Laurens Papers;* David Duncan Wallace, *The Life of Henry Laurens, with a Sketch of the Life of Lieutenant-Colonel John Laurens* (New York: Putnam's, 1915).

110. Candler, *CRG*, 18:627–36, 10:460.

111. The congregation in South Carolina was the Stoney Creek Independent Presbyterian Church, the one in Savannah was the Independent Pres-

byterian Church. It is not entirely clear why these churches opted to call themselves Presbyterian. For instance, John J. Zubly, the Swiss pastor of the Savannah congregation was not a Presbyterian. Zubly's congregation almost split over the qualifications for membership; the pastor apparently wished to allow anyone to join who professed the Westminster Confession. The Independent churches ostensibly attracted Calvinists who adopted the Congregationalist style of Independent congregations but the Presbyterian mode for determining church membership. If Zubly's experience is indicative, then the Independent churches also adopted the Presbyterian emphasis upon the preeminence of the clergy within the church. On Savannah's Independent Presbyterian Church, see Davis, *Fledgling Province,* 202–204.

112. *Georgia Gazette,* Mar. 13, 1788; also see his work "for the ease of Persons who have Scruples about the form of taking Oaths" (Candler *CRG,* 13:75, 95, 111, 117, 126; 18:157–59).

113. *Georgia Gazette,* Mar. 14, 1770; *South Carolina Gazette,* Apr. 4, 1770.

114. Richard Walsh found land "the most popular investment" of Charlestown mechanics, "not alone for reasons of investment, but also as a means of entering the planting class" (*Charleston's Sons of Liberty,* 17–18).

115. Land speculation in the 1770s is discussed at great length in Bernard Bailyn, *Voyagers to the West: A Passage in the Peopling of America on the Eve of the Revolution* (New York: Knopf, 1986).

116. Henry Laurens to Jonathan Bryan, Sept. 4, 1767, Hamer et al., *Laurens Papers,* 5:289.

117. Candler, *CRG,* 10:438, 463, 604.

118. Miscellaneous—Bonds, Book Y-2, pp. 467–75, Georgia Archives.

119. Candler, *CRG,* 10:911. The marriage took place in Feb. 1767, and Morel was elected to the first of many terms in the house in 1769. He had been a resident of Georgia for at least fifteen years when elected.

CHAPTER 5: POLITICS, 1761–1773

1. On the reorganization of the empire, see Bernard Knollenberg, *Origins of the American Revolution, 1759–1766* (New York: Macmillan, 1960); John C. Miller, *Origins of the American Revolution* (Boston: Little, Brown, 1943), 1–78; Simmons, *The American Colonies,* 287–307; Alden, *South in the Revolution,* 51–63. For colonial smuggling, see Arthur M. Schlesinger, *The Colonial Merchants and the American Revolution* (1917; repr., New York: Atheneum, 1968), 39–49, 52.

2. Coleman and Ready, *CRG,* 28 (part 2): 256; Greene, *Quest for Power,* 390–96; Joseph Ernst, *Money and Politics in America, 1755–1775* (Chapel Hill: University of North Carolina Press, 1973), 169–72.

3. Coleman, *American Revolution in Georgia,* 27; Alden, *South in the Revolution,* 55.

4. Alden, *John Stuart,* 139–55.

5. Ibid., 17–18, 95, 254 n. 57.

6. Nash, *Urban Crucible;* Patricia U. Bonomi, *A Factious People: Politics and Society in Colonial New York* (New York: Columbia University Press, 1971), 281; Douglass, *Rebels and Democrats,* 68–70; Gordon Wood, *The Creation of the American Republic, 1776–1787* (Chapel Hill: University of North Carolina Press, 1969), 24–28, 164, 184, 546–47, 596–600; Bernard Bailyn, *The Ideological Origins of the American Revolution* (Cambridge: Harvard University Press, Belknap Press, 1967), 161–75.

7. Bonomi, *Factious People,* 261–67, 279–80.

8. When the new states created constitutions during the American Revolution, in almost every instance the chief executive was extremely limited in powers. The delimiting of executive power was not solely a reaction of the people to the perceived tyrannies of King George III (who mostly earned the wrath of Americans after 1775) but the outcome of years of hostility against colonial governors who served a distant master rather than followed the wishes of provincials.

9. Coleman, *American Revolution in Georgia,* 18–19.

10. The best work on the Stamp Act is Edmund S. Morgan and Helen Morgan, *The Stamp Act Crisis: Prologue to Revolution,* rev. ed. (New York: Collier Books, 1962). But also see Miller, *Origins of the American Revolution,* 134–47; Esmond Wright, *Fabric of Freedom 1763–1800,* rev. ed. (New York: Hill and Wang, 1978), 51–52; Schlesinger, *Colonial Merchants,* 71–73.

11. Legal affairs came to a halt in some colonies as government officials awaited further directions from London. In a few colonies business was carried on as usual. In South Carolina, for instance, ships were cleared from port by permission of Lieutenant Governor Bull.

12. Abbot, *Royal Governors of Georgia,* 114; Coleman, *American Revolution in Georgia,* 21.

13. Morgan and Morgan, *Stamp Act,* 139, 202–203, 213; Candler, *CRG* 28 (part 2): 129–38; Coleman, *American Revolution in Georgia,* 17–24.

14. Candler, *CRG,* 9:459, Dec. 18, 1765.

15. His only appearance was on Feb. 3, 1766 (Candler, *CRG,* 9:470).

16. Ibid., 540–41.

17. Support for Wright among the populace was scarce during the Stamp Act crisis. The governor found only ten civilians who were willing covertly to help him and the soldiers save the stamps. His constant plea for deference to himself, his office, the Crown, and Parliament, won few supporters. His iron will to enforce the Stamp Act was unmatched in other colonies, and his success earned Georgians the wrath of patriots everywhere. Georgians were the only ones who had succumbed to using the stamps, an embarrassment publicized

through the North American continent. Rebel Carolinians threatened with death anyone who traded with Georgia. The latter's citizenry did not have far to turn to place the blame for this unhappy state of affairs: it was Wright who had protected the stamps and prompted their sale. Wright was hardened by the experience and strengthened his resolve to defend the prerogative of the Crown and Parliament to legislate for the colonies.

18. Greene, *Quest for Power,* 212–19.

19. Cashin, "Sowing the Wind," 233–50; Edward J. Cashin, "'But Brothers, It Is Our Land We Are Talking About': Winners and Losers in the Georgia Backcountry," in *An Uncivil War: The Southern Backcountry during the American Revolution,* ed. Ronald Hoffman, Thad W. Tate, and Peter J. Albert (Charlottesville: University Press of Virginia, 1985), 240–75; Harvey H. Jackson, "The Rise of the Western Members: Revolutionary Politics and the Georgia Backcountry," in Hoffman et al., *An Uncivil War,* 276–320. Compare Georgia's experience with that of South Carolina in Rachel N. Klein, "Frontier Planters and the American Revolution: The South Carolina Backcountry, 1775–1782," in Hoffman et al., *An Uncivil War,* 37–69, and "Ordering the Backcountry: The South Carolina Regulation," *William and Mary Quarterly,* 3d ser., 38 (Oct. 1981): 661–80.

20. Cashin, "Sowing the Wind," 245; Harvey H. Jackson, "Georgia Whiggery: The Origins and Effects of a Many-Faceted Movement," in Jackson and Spalding, *Forty Years of Diversity,* 259–60.

21. Candler, *CRG,* 10:433, and 17:364–71; Coleman, *American Revolution in Georgia,* 25–26; Ella Lonn, *The Colonial Agents of the Southern Colonies* (Chapel Hill: University of North Carolina Press, 1945), 105–108; Greene, *Quest for Power,* 425–27.

22. Candler, *CRG,* 17:372–75.

23. Americans not only argued "no taxation without representation" but also rejected as early as 1768 the alternative of colonial representation in Parliament. The colonies and the mother country, it was argued in the Massachusetts circular letter, were "separated by an Ocean of a thousand Leagues," and were in possession of their own representative houses formed by "His Majesty['s] Royal Predecessors." The circular is dated Feb. 11, 1768, and reprinted in the journals of the Georgia Commons House of Assembly, in Candler, *CRG,* 14:646–51.

24. Ibid., 17:455.

25. Ibid., 17:455–57.

26. The other two members on the upper-house committee were strong supporters of the governor and, given the chance, would undoubtedly have steered the upper house into making a clear expression of support for the governor. Therefore, it must have been Bryan who persuaded the others to keep the upper house on an independent course. The other two members of the committee

were James Edward Powell and James Read. Powell, an original councillor, was known for his "zeal for his Majestys Service" (Coleman and Ready, *CRG,* 28 [part 1]: 183). Read had been nominated by the board of trade to join the council in 1759, but Governor Ellis rejected his appointment, asking "whether I am to impute this nomination to the powerful solicitation of . . . friends at London" (ibid., 28 [part 1]: 180). Wright earned Read's loyalty by recommending the latter for a position on the council for four years, finally achieving his appointment in 1765 (ibid., 28 [part 1]: 304, 406; 9:302).

27. Candler, *CRG,* 14:644–659.

28. James Wright to Earl of Hillsborough, Aug. 15, 1769, reprinted in Charles Colcock Jones, Jr., *The History of Georgia,* 2 vols. (Boston: Houghton Mifflin, 1883), 2:109–12.

29. *Georgia Gazette,* Sept. 20, 1769; Jones, *History of Georgia,* 2:112–13.

30. *Georgia Gazette,* Sept. 20, 1769; Schlesinger, *Colonial Merchants,* 147. The resolves are reprinted in Jones, *History of Georgia,* 2:113–15. The moving force behind these meetings is unknown, but resolutions encouraging manufacturing and opposed to the importation of slaves would indicate that Savannah's white artisans had a decisive say in creating the agenda. They believed that both slaves and imports took work away from them. Also, the Union Society, a society of artisans and mechanics, rewarded Bryan for his patriot activities shortly after this meeting. See discussion later in text.

31. The slave code of 1767 had been rejected by the king, though it was a few years before the colony learned the reason for its disallowance. It appears that the Crown disapproved of bondsmen being referred to as chattels instead of real estate. The Georgians, however, persuaded the board of trade to allow their definition of slaves to stand and a new code was drawn in 1770. The new code, according to Betty Wood, had two main differences from the previous code made in 1765. It classified rape and attempted rape of a white woman and the destruction or entry into a private dwelling as capital crimes. And it removed a clause from the previous code that was designed to "attract" free blacks to the colony (Wood, *Slavery in Colonial Georgia,* 125–27).

32. Candler, *CRG,* 17:486.

33. Ibid., 17:491–93.

34. Allen D. Candler, ed. "The Colonial Records of the State of Georgia," typescript, vol. 37, p. 421, Georgia Archives.

35. Resentment of the council by the populace festered on the eve of the American Revolution. This resulted from the power it held over the lives of Georgians, the fact that it was an appointive body, and its close association with the governor. The council's strong support of royal government is often overlooked as a factor in the peculiar shaping of Georgia's first state constitution in 1777. This revolutionary document did away with the upper house, considerably weakened the chief executive, and made the executive council

appointive by the assembly. Albert B. Saye, the leading authority on Georgia's constitutional history, believed the changes to have been an outgrowth of the patriot movement's "democratic temper," and that the precedent for a unicameral legislature could be found in the colony's revolutionary Provincial Congress. One might add that twenty years of domination by the executive council and unabashed support for British imperial policies prepared the way for the radical changes engendered (Saye, *A Constitutional History of Georgia, 1739–1945* [Athens: University of Georgia Press, 1948]).

36. *Georgia Gazette,* Mar. 14, 1770. For the Union Society, see Davis, *Fledgling Province,* 170. Artisans and mechanics dominated the society, but professionals were accepted as members. The latter might have been allowed membership during the era of the American Revolution when the society became oriented toward support of American rights. The two men who signed the announcement were Joseph Parker, a silversmith, and William Young, a lawyer.

37. *Georgia Gazette,* Mar. 21, 1770.

38. *South Carolina Gazette,* Apr. 4, 1770. It is interesting to note that news of Bryan immediately preceded a report on the now famous "freedom of the press" trial of Alexander McDougal, then taking place in New York.

39. Candler, *CRG,* 15:164–67, and 19:54–59; *Georgia Gazette,* Apr. 4, 1770. There is no conclusive evidence to show that Bryan expected patriotic politics to lead to the building of the road to his cowpen. Nevertheless, the manner in which the assembly directed the road to be built to his property, almost immediately after he had been rebuked by the king, certainly gives the appearance that the former councillor was being rewarded for his patriotic activities.

40. *South Carolina Gazette,* June 28, 1770.

41. Ibid. The forty-five toasts referred to John Wilkes's publication of the *North Briton Number 45,* for which he was arrested in 1763. Wilkes fled England but returned and became a cause célèbre in the American colonies. His imprisonment in 1768 for *Number 45* and his *Essay on Women* clinched his popularity in the colonies, where he was viewed as the foremost British exponent of Whig ideology; Pauline Maier notes that "'Wilkes and Liberty' were toasted from New England to South Carolina" (*From Resistance to Revolution: Colonial Radicals and the Development of American Opposition to Britain, 1765–1776* [New York: Knopf, 1974], 163–67).

42. For the relationship between the Townshend duties and the rise of opposition movements, see John C. Miller, *Sam Adams, Pioneer in Propaganda* (Boston: Little, Brown, 1936), 193–275; Alden, *South in the American Revolution,* 111–17; Dirk Hoerder, "Boston Leaders and Boston Crowds, 1765–1776," in *The American Revolution: Explorations in the History of American*

Radicalism, ed. Alfred Young (De Kalb: Northern Illinois University Press, 1976), 252–60; Walsh, *Charleston's Sons of Liberty,* 45–55. Bryan's elections to the assembly can be found in Candler, *CRG,* 15:228, 304, 320, 335.

43. Candler, *CRG,* 15:300, 305, 311–12, 322–23, 330–34, 337, 338. Secondary accounts of the dispute over the speakership can be found in Abbot, *Royal Governors of Georgia,* 154–58; Greene, *Quest for Power,* 433–36; Coleman, *American Revolution in Georgia,* 34–36.

44. James Habersham to James Wright, Nov. 30, 1771, in Habersham, *Letters,* 154–58.

45. Candler, *CRG,* 15:330–34.

46. Habersham was mildly rebuked by the earl of Hillsborough for dissolving the assembly. The acting governor had displayed good intentions in defending the king, but "it does not appear, however, from the minutes of . . . [the House] that they did in direct terms so draw into question His Majesty's right to put a negative upon their choice of a Speaker . . . [for] you to come to that extremity" of prorogation (Earl of Hillsborough to James Habersham, Aug. 7, 1772, in K. G. Davies, ed., *Documents of the American Revolution, 1770–1783,* Colonial Office Series, vol. 5, Transcripts 1772 [Dublin: Irish University Press, 1974], 162–63).

47. James Habersham to James Wright, June 3, 1772, in Habersham, *Letters,* 183–84.

48. Candler, *CRG* 15:345.

49. See appendix 6, votes 4, 5, and 7.

50. Ibid., vote 3.

51. Ibid., votes 2 and 6.

52. Ibid., vote 1.

53. Candler, *CRG,* 19 (part 1): 288–90.

54. Cattle had free rein to roam in colonial Georgia. Crops rather than livestock had to be enclosed in fences. The owners of pigs and cattle were not liable for damage done to farmers' crops if the latters' land was not fenced to the precise specifications of statute regulations. See the insightful discussion of the evolution of fencing legislation and common rights in Steven Hahn, *The Roots of Southern Populism: Yeoman Farmers and the Transformation of the Georgia Upcountry, 1850–1889* (New York: Oxford University Press, 1983), 58–63, 240, 243, 246, 251–55.

55. See appendix 6.

56. Treutlen became governor; Clay, paymaster general of the Continental army; Houstoun, surgeon for the Continental army. See, George Fenwick Jones, "John Adam Treutlen's Origin and Rise to Prominence," in Jackson and Spalding, *Forty Years of Diversity,* 217–28; Clay, *Letters;* Edith Duncan Johnston, *The Houstouns of Georgia* (Athens: University of Georgia Press, 1950).

57. All these men were declared enemies of the state by the revolutionary government and/or filed claims in Great Britain after the war as Loyalists.

58. Coleman, *American Revolution in Georgia*, 66, 176; Bailyn, *Ideological Origins of the American Revolution*.

59. See appendix 6, vote 8.

60. Alexander Hamilton, *A Full Vindication of the Measures of the Congress, from the Calumnies of their Enemies; . . .* (New York, 1774), repr. in Harold C. Syrett, ed., *The Papers of Alexander Hamilton*, 10 vols. (New York: Columbia University Press, 1961), 1:56.

CHAPTER 6: DREAMS OF EMPIRE: JONATHAN BRYAN AND THE CREEK INDIANS

1. W. W. Abbot, "Lowcountry, Backcountry: A View of Georgia in the American Revolution," in Hoffman et al., *An Uncivil War*, 321–32.

2. Henry Laurens to Jonathan Bryan, May 29, 1771, in Hamer et al., *Laurens Papers*, 7:504–506.

3. Bryan was not the only one with dreams of exploiting vast reaches of territory in Florida. Many high-ranking officers of empire in London schemed to settle this frontier. See E. P. Panagopoulous, *New Smyrna: An Eighteenth-Century Greek Odyssey* (Gainesville: University Presses of Florida, 1966); Bailyn, *Voyagers to the West*; Denys Rolle, *The Humble Petition of Denys Rolle, Esq; setting forth the Hardships, Inconveniences, and Grievances, which have attended him in his Attempts to make a Settlement in East Florida, humbly praying such Relief as in their Lordships Wisdom shall seem meet*, A facsimile reproduction of the 1765 edition (Gainesville: University Presses of Florida, 1977).

4. See appendix 6, vote 9.

5. Crane, *The Southern Frontier*, 185. A brief summary of Creek diplomacy in the eighteenth century can be found in Nash, *Red, White, and Black*, 273–75. A fuller treatment can be found in David H. Corkran, *The Creek Frontier, 1540–1783* (Norman: University of Oklahoma Press, 1967) and in Crane's seminal work, noted above. Crane discusses Creek diplomacy in the context of competition between France and Britain for control of the Southeast. Additional works that explore Georgia's relations with the Creeks include Coleman, *Colonial Georgia;* Abbot, *Royal Governors of Georgia;* John Pitts Corry, *Indian Affairs in Georgia, 1732–1756* (Philadelphia: George S. Ferguson, 1936).

6. Historians have argued that factionalism within the Creek Confederacy precluded their alliance with either the French or the British. There is no doubt that factionalism existed, but it in no way compared with the severe divisions

within the confederacy during and after the American Revolution. Before that war the Creeks were able to present a united diplomatic front through the National Council. The decision-making process of the Creek Nation, as I argue later, created strength. The Creeks' difficult diplomatic position during the Revolution, and the alteration in the balance of power after the war, laid the groundwork for the disintegration of national unity. For discussion of Creek factionalism after 1776, see Michael D. Green, *The Politics of Indian Removal: Creek Government and Society in Crisis* (Lincoln: University of Nebraska Press, 1982); J. Leitch Wright, Jr., *Creeks and Seminoles: Destruction and Regeneration of the Muscogulge People* (Lincoln: University of Nebraska Press, 1987); Martha Condray Searcy, *The Georgia-Florida Contest in the American Revolution, 1776–1778* (Tuscaloosa: University of Alabama Press, 1985).

7. Secondary sources which discuss the New Purchase cession include De Vorsey, *Indian Boundary*, 162–72; Coleman, *American Revolution in Georgia*, 7–8; Alden, *John Stuart*, 300–305; Cashin, "'But Brothers, It Is Our Land We Are Talking About,'" 245.

8. James Wright to the Secretary of State for the Colonies, Dec. 12, 1771, in Coleman and Ready, *CRG*, 28 (part 2): 353; Lieutenant Governor John Moultrie to the Earl of Dartmouth, Feb. 21, 1774, in Davies, *Documents of the American Revolution*, 54–55, italics added.

9. James Wright to the Creek Indians, Apr. 14, 1774, in Davies, *Documents of the American Revolution*, 9:90–95.

10. Candler, *CRG*, 12:407–409.

11. John Stuart to Earl of Dartmouth, May 6, 1774, in Davies, *Documents of the American Revolution*, 9:110.

12. For example, see Alden, *John Stuart*, 300–305; J. Leitch Wright, Jr., *Florida in the American Revolution* (Gainesville: University of Florida Press, 1975), 24–25.

13. *Georgia Gazette*, Nov. 2, 1774.

14. Ibid.

15. Ibid., Nov. 16, 1774. Allegedly, the Indians tore their seals from the lease and the governor kept the document.

16. Ibid., Nov. 23, 1774.

17. Quotation from ibid., Nov. 2, 1774, Testimony of Jacob Moniac and Samuel Thomas. See also Affidavit of Thomas Grey, taken by John Forbes, Oct. 10, 1775, enclosed with Patrick Tonyn to Earl of Dartmouth, Oct. 25, 1775, CO, 5/555, p. 242, Library of Congress. It is evident that the offer of trade goods was the reason for the lease of land by the Creeks. The leases did not mention this factor, but the Indians told British officials in Savannah that this had been Bryan's offer, the Indian interpreters claimed that the Indians said this was the reason for the lease, and Bryan said as much in his letter to Cowkeeper,

the most important leader of the Seminole branch of the Creek Nation. He told Cowkeeper that he wanted "to bring with me people to make a settlement . . . in some place which you approve of where I can have the advantage of Planting in good lands and good navigation [to] carry on a trade for the mutual advantage of both Indians and White people" (Jonathan Bryan to Cowkeeper, June 15, 1775, enclosed with Patrick Tonyn to Lord George Germain, Mar. 7, 1777, CO, 5/556, p. 210).

18. John Stuart to Earl of Dartmouth, Jan. 3, 1775, CO 5/76, p. 30; reprinted in Davies, *Documents of the American Revolution*, 9:23–24.

19. David Taitt to John Stuart, Dec. 17, 1774, enclosed in John Stuart to Earl of Dartmouth, CO, 5/76, pp. 37–38. An identical copy can be found enclosed with John Stuart to General Gage, Jan. 18, 1775, Thomas Gage Papers, William L. Clements Library, University of Michigan, Ann Arbor.

20. John Stuart to Earl of Dartmouth, Jan. 3, 1775, Davies, *Documents of the American Revolution*, 9:23–24; Stuart to Gage, Jan. 18, 1775, Gage Papers.

21. Samuel Thomas to David Taitt, Dec. 10, 1774, enclosed with John Stuart to Earl of Dartmouth, Jan. 3, 1775, CO, 5/76, pp. 33–34. A different rendering of the same letter can be found in Samuel Thomas to David Taitt, Dec. 10, 1774, enclosed with John Stuart to General Gage, Jan. 18, 1775, Gage Papers. Alden, *John Stuart*, 312; the author concluded from this letter that Bryan had "waylaid" the Creeks.

22. John Stuart to General Gage, Jan. 18, 1775, and its enclosure, Abstract of a letter from Governor Wright to John Stuart, Jan. 12, 1775, Gage Papers.

23. Samuel Thomas to David Taitt, Dec. 10, 1774, enclosed with John Stuart to Earl of Dartmouth, Jan. 3, 1775, CO, 5/76, pp. 33–34.

24. Abstract of a letter from Governor Wright to John Stuart, Jan. 12, 1775, enclosed with John Stuart to General Gage, Jan. 18, 1775, Gage Papers.

25. *Proceedings and Minutes of the Governor and Council of Georgia, October 4, 1774, through November 7, 1775, and September 6, 1779, through September 20, 1780*, ed. Lilla M. Hawes, Collections of the Georgia Historical Society, vol. 10 (Savannah: Georgia Historical Society, 1952), 6; De Vorsey, *Indian Boundary*, 171, 176–77.

26. Governor Tonyn's reply to Drayton's defense, undated, enclosed in Patrick Tonyn to Lord George Germain, Mar. 7, 1776, CO, 5/556, pp. 165–67; John Forbes to James Grant, Dec. 28, 1774, Letters of James Grant, Ballindalloch Castle Muniments, Ballindalloch Estates, Banffshire, Scotland (hereafter cited as Grant Letters).

27. Governor Tonyn's reply to Drayton's defense, ibid., 165–67; Patrick Tonyn to Earl of Dartmouth, Dec. 14, 1774, CO, 5/555, pp. 7–8. Drayton and Tonyn, among others, believed that if the lease were confirmed by the Creeks, half of Georgia would follow Bryan to Florida.

28. Patrick Tonyn to Earl of Dartmouth, Dec. 18, 1774, CO, 5/556, pp. 171–72. Governor Wright recognized the Indians' rights to their land, though he spoke of them in the same terms as Tonyn: they were "savages, strange, treacherous, faithless wretches and no man can answer for them" (James Wright to Earl of Dartmouth, Apr. 24, 1775, CO, 5/664, p. 86; repr. in Davies, *Documents of the American Revolution,* 9:106–107). The term "savages" was used by Englishmen to dehumanize the Indians, in order to rationalize cruelty and to justify the stealing of land. By creating the "savage," the English were then able to define Indians as wild beasts of the forests who possessed no claim to the land. In reality, the Indians were agricultural peoples, possessed of their own government, culture, and religion. See Francis Jennings's insightful discussion of the etymology and use of the word "savage" by the English in *Invasion of America,* 58–84.

29. An excellent discussion of the relative holdings of the Creeks and British in Florida can be found in De Vorsey, *Indian Boundary,* 181–203, and map, 232.

30. Abstract of a letter from Patrick Tonyn to John Stuart, Dec. 18, 1774, enclosed in John Stuart to General Gage, Jan. 18, 1774, Gage Papers; Patrick Tonyn to Earl of Dartmouth, Dec. 18, 1774, enclosed in Patrick Tonyn to Lord George Germain, Mar. 7, 1776, CO, 5/556, pp. 171–72.

31. The Proclamation Act did not provide penalties for noncompliance with its measures. Earl of Dartmouth to Patrick Tonyn, May 3, 1775, CO, 5/555, pp. 62–63; Earl of Dartmouth to John Stuart, Mar. 3, 1775, CO, 5/76, pp. 59–60; Earl of Dartmouth to James Wright, Feb. 1, 1775, CO, 5/664, pp. 33–34.

32. Charles Loch Mowat, *East Florida as a British Province, 1763–1784* (Gainesville: University Presses of Florida, 1964), chap. 6, and "The Enigma of William Drayton," *Florida Historical Quarterly* 12 (July 1943): 3–33.

33. Patrick Tonyn to Earl of Dartmouth, Oct. 25, 1775, CO, 5/555, pp. 238–39.

34. John Moultrie to James Grant, Dec. 23, 1774, Grant Letters; John Forbes to James Grant, Dec. 28, 1774, ibid.; Frederick George Mulcaster to James Grant, July 19, 1775, ibid; John Stuart to General Gage, Jan. 18, 1775, and enclosure, Abstract of Patrick Tonyn to John Stuart, Dec. 18, 1774, Gage Papers.

35. William Drayton to John Stuart, July 14, 1775, enclosed in John Stuart to Earl of Dartmouth, July 27, 1775, CO, 5/76, pp. 133–38; Patrick Tonyn to Earl of Dartmouth, Dec. 30, 1774, CO, 5/555, pp. 29–32.

36. Jonathan Bryan to William Drayton, Nov. 23, 1774, CO, 5/76, pp. 138–39.

37. David Taitt to John Stuart, Dec. 17, 1774, enclosed in John Stuart to Earl of Dartmouth, CO, 5/76, pp. 37–38. An identical copy can be found

enclosed with John Stuart to General Gage, Jan. 18, 1775, Gage Papers; Governor Tonyn's reply to William Drayton's defense, undated, enclosed in Patrick Tonyn to Lord George Germain, Mar. 7, 1776, CO, 5/556, pp. 167–68.

38. Thomas Brown to Patrick Tonyn, May 8, 1776, enclosed with Patrick Tonyn to Lord George Germain, June 10, 1776, CO, 5/556, p. 312.

39. Jonathan Bryan to William Drayton, Nov. 23, 1774, enclosed with John Stuart to Earl of Dartmouth, July 27, 1775, CO, 5/76, pp. 138–39.

40. Quotation from De Vorsey, *Indian Boundary,* 35–36.

41. Lease of land from the Creek Indians to Jonathan Bryan, Oct. 28, 1774, Jonathan Bryan Papers, file 98, item 1, Georgia Historical Society, Savannah.

42. Most of what we know about Adair comes from his work *The History of the American Indians, Particularly those Nations adjoining to the Mississippi East and West Florida, Georgia, South and North Carolina, and Virginia* (1775; repr., New York: Johnson Reprint, 1968). Also see the entry in *The Dictionary of American Biography,* 1:33–34. Adair arrived in Charlestown from Ireland in 1735 and proceeded to engage in the Indian trade. It is very likely that Bryan met him at this time.

43. Most, but not all, Creeks spoke dialects of the Muscogee language. They referred to themselves as Muscogees.

44. Affidavit of Thomas Grey, taken by John Forbes, Oct. 10, 1775, enclosed with Patrick Tonyn to Earl of Dartmouth, Oct. 25, 1775, CO, 5/555, pp. 242–44.

45. *Georgia Gazette,* Nov. 2, 1774, Testimony of the Georgia council.

46. For the internal politics of the Creeks, see John R. Swanton, "Social Organization and the Social Usages of the Indians of the Creek Confederacy," in *Forty-Second Annual Report of the Bureau of American Ethnology, 1924–1925* (Washington, D.C.: Government Printing Office, 1928), 279–325; Charles Hudson, *The Southeastern Indians* (Knoxville: University of Tennessee Press, 1976), 223–29, 235–36. On the use of Henihas and Yatikas, the Creek orators, see J. N. B. Hewitt, *Notes on the Creek Indians,* Bureau of American Ethnology Bulletin no. 123 (Washington, D.C.: Government Printing Office, 1939), 135–36; Swanton, "Social Organization," 295–97.

47. If Bryan had been merely speculating, then defrauding the Indians would have been an alternative. But populating land in an isolated section of Florida was out of the question if the Creeks were hostile.

48. Treaty between the Creek Nation and the colony of Georgia, Oct. 20, 1774, enclosed with James Wright and John Stuart to Earl of Dartmouth, Jan. 4, 1775, CO, 5/664, pp. 11–13. *Mecos* were Creek chiefs.

49. Beyond any doubt, several of the signees were considered their towns' emissaries by the English—and presumably by the Creeks—because they negotiated treaties with Governor Wright in this period.

Kaligy and Ockfuski were Upper Creek towns. Chehaw, Osoche, Hitchiti, Yuchi, Ocmulgee, and Oconee were Lower Creek towns. The Ocmulgee were a branch of the Hitchiti. Their leader, Taleeche, may have been the most influential leader from the Lower Creek towns. He had been a prominent leader since the 1740s, and his name frequently appears first among the signers of treaties between the British and the Creeks. He was a chief negotiator for the Creeks in the establishment of boundaries with both Georgia and East Florida.

50. For the importance of testanochies in Creek councils, see Swanton, "Social Organization," 297–98, and Hewitt, *Notes on Creek Indians,* 136, 138–39. Both of these sources use the spelling Tastanagi. Here I employ the spelling on the leases.

51. The author would like to thank Shirley Fields, Juanita Ray, and Marcella Giles, three members of the Creek Nation who were helpful in the interpretation and pronunciation of several of the Indian names on Jonathan Bryan's leases. On the emahtla, see Swanton, "Social Organization," 301, and Hewitt, *Notes on Creek Indians,* 136, 138.

52. The town of Telase Coosa increased in size and importance after a migration about the beginning of the nineteenth century to what is now Alabama. Its inhabitants were removed to Oklahoma in 1832, giving the city of Tulsa its name. They were an offshoot of the Coosa Upper Creek tribal group. Another Telase group may have settled in Florida, giving Tallahassee its name.

The Osoche and Chehaw mecos who signed the second lease appear to have been different from the mecos who signed the first lease. They each had towns along both the Flint and Chattahoochee rivers.

The towns and tribal groups of the Creek Indians are discussed extensively in John R. Swanton, *Early History of the Creek Indians and Their Neighbors,* Seventy-third Annual Report of the Bureau of American Ethnology (Washington, D.C.: Government Printing Office, 1922).

53. Ibid., 227–82.

54. The Coweta were probably represented among the signers whose tribal group cannot be identified.

55. Others also expected Bryan's colony to succeed. Two South Carolina merchants, Smith and McQueen, informed Tonyn that Bryan "was a very popular man and that half the settlers in Georgia would follow him into this Province." Drayton and Tonyn also believed that Bryan might succeed and attract a large number of Georgians to the province. See Governor Tonyn's reply to Drayton's defense, CO, 5/556, pp. 165–67; Patrick Tonyn to Earl of Dartmouth, Dec. 14, 1774, CO, 5/555, pp. 7–8.

56. James Wright to Earl of Dartmouth, Sept. 6, 1774, CO, 5/663, pp. 162–63.

57. Americans were infamous for their smuggling and were so adept at it that Great Britain made a concerted effort to stop them in the late 1760s and early 1770s. The concentration of Britain's antismuggling forces on Atlantic and West Indies ports left its naval power weak in Gulf waters. Nevertheless, even if forces could be spared, the innumerable coves of Florida's west coast

made smuggling easy for any determined party. The American colonists' propensity for smuggling is discussed in numerous works. Among these are Schlesinger, *Colonial Merchants;* Nash, *Urban Crucible;* Carl Bridenbaugh, *Cities in Revolt: Urban Life in America, 1743–1776,* rev. ed. (New York: Knopf, 1955).

58. Shy, *Toward Lexington,* 156–57, 284–87, 330, 419.

59. On the origins of the Seminoles, see Swanton, "Early History of the Creek Nation," 398–414; William C. Sturtevant, "Creek into Seminole," *North American Indians in Historical Perspective,* ed. Eleanor B. Leacock and Nancy O. Lurie (New York: Random House, 1971), 92–128; Wright, *Creeks and Seminoles.*

60. Affidavit of Thomas Grey, taken by John Forbes, Oct. 10, 1775, enclosed with Patrick Tonyn to Earl of Dartmouth, Oct. 25, 1775, CO, 5/555, pp. 244–45. St. Iago, also known as Santiago, signed the Creek treaty with Georgia in 1774.

61. Ibid.

62. Abstract of a letter from Patrick Tonyn to John Stuart, Dec. 18, 1774, enclosed with John Stuart to General Gage, Jan. 18, 1775, Gage Papers.

63. Governor Patrick Tonyn to Lord George Germain, Mar. 7, 1776, with enclosures of William Drayton's Defense and Governor Tonyn's reply to Drayton's Defense, CO, 5/556, pp. 141–70.

64. Ibid.

65. Ibid.

66. Ibid.; Jonathan Bryan to Messrs. Smith and Macquin [McQueen], undated, enclosed with ibid., CO, 5/556, p. 183.

67. Ibid.; Jonathan Bryan to William Drayton, Jan. 11, 1775, enclosed with ibid., 181.

68. Allen D. Candler, comp., *The Revolutionary Records of the State of Georgia,* 3 vols. (Atlanta: Franklin-Turner, 1908), 1:63–66.

69. James Wright to Earl of Dartmouth, Apr. 24, 1775, CO, 5/664, p. 84, and reprinted in Davies, *Documents of the American Revolution,* 9:106–107.

70. Jonathan Bryan to Cowkeeper, June 15, 1775, enclosed with Patrick Tonyn to Lord George Germain, Mar. 7, 1777, CO, 5/556, p. 210.

71. Candler, *Revolutionary Records of the State of Georgia,* 1:229–31. Jonathan's two sons-in-law, John Houstoun and John Morel, were also elected to the congress, as were his nephew Jonathan Cochrane and great-nephew, Seth John Cuthbert.

Bryan's son Hugh died in Dec. 1775, the result of a fall from a horse. It was one year minus one day after Josiah's death. He was thirty-seven years old and had spent much of his youth soldiering and had only recently settled down to the life of a planter. His political career had recently got under way with an appointment as commissioner of the roads. His election to the Provincial Congress pointed toward an increasingly active political career.

72. Patrick Tonyn to General Gage, Sept. 14, 1775, intercepted by the rebels, Papers of the Continental Congress, microfilm, M247, r65, 151, VI, pp. 83–85, National Archives, Washington, D.C.; Patrick Tonyn to Earl of Dartmouth, Sept. 20, 1775, CO, 5/555, p. 194.

73. Patrick Tonyn to General Gage, Sept. 14, 1775, Papers of the Continental Congress.

74. Patrick Tonyn to Earl of Dartmouth, Oct. 25, 1775, CO, 5/555, pp. 238–39.

75. Examination of Thomas Grey by William Drayton, Oct. 2, 1775, enclosed with ibid., 240–41.

76. Grey gave his confession, according to Tonyn, in exchange for land and sanctuary. He promised to return to Florida with his family. Affidavit of Thomas Grey, taken by John Forbes, Oct. 10, 1775, ibid., 242–44.

77. Grey testified that the Upper Creek headman, St. Iago, had left Bryan's party before it arrived at Latchaway, presumably because he was "not satisfied with the intended Bargaining with the Indians about Land." Tonyn did not see the inconsistencies in Grey's testimony, for he later stated that St. Iago had again only recently been employed by Bryan to visit the Seminoles, in order to induce them to sign his lease. Another statement Grey made to Forbes and Tonyn implied that Bryan had tricked the Indians. This concerned one of the signers of Bryan's lease. When Bryan produced his lease for Ohontholy, he named the many Creek headmen who had already signed the document. Among these was the Cuseeta king, who "the deponent has reason to believe that he really did not sign it or consent to it." In fact, however, the king and ten other Cuseetas had signed Bryan's second lease. Grey did not *lie* to Tonyn but only said that he had "reason to believe" that Bryan had lied to the Indians (ibid.).

78. Tonyn spent a great deal of time trying to prove Bryan had committed trespass, but it is doubtful that any court could have convicted on this charge, even if evidence had been brought forth that Bryan had attempted to take possession. Legally, the land was not the king's, and so Bryan could not have trespassed on his domain. On the other hand, he was subject to British law, and his taking possession could have been construed as a violation of the Proclamation Act. Of course, the author of that bill had not provided a penalty for violation.

79. [Second] Affidavit of Thomas Grey, taken by John Forbes, Dec. 30, 1775, enclosed with Patrick Tonyn to Earl of Dartmouth, Mar. 7, 1776, CO, 5/556, p. 206.

80. The rebels knew Tonyn believed that five hundred men were about to descend on Florida because they had intercepted his letter to General Gage. See n. 72 above.

81. [Second] Affidavit of Thomas Grey, taken by John Forbes, Dec. 30, 1775, enclosed with Patrick Tonyn to Earl of Dartmouth, Mar. 7, 1776, CO,

5/556, p. 206. Tonyn also considered Jospeph Penman to be a rebel, though in reality, he too, was a loyalist. See Searcy, *Georgia-Florida Contest,* 151. Drayton had to go twice to London to clear his name. After the war ended he retired to South Carolina, having lost most of his estate. In the Manuscript Division Library of Congress, is an "Inquiry" Drayton wrote but never published, defending himself against Tonyn's accusations. Turnbull also went to London and defended himself and also retired to South Carolina.

82. Stephen Bull to Henry Laurens, Mar. 13, 1776, in R. W. Gibbes, ed., *Documentary History of the American Revolution,* 2 vols. (New York: Appleton, 1855–57), 1:266–67. On July 14, 1777, the executive council of Georgia commissioned Thomas Grey as captain of a company of Indians to patrol the southern frontier. Searcy, *Georgia-Florida Contest,* 101.

83. Thomas Brown to Patrick Tonyn, May 8, 1776, CO, enclosed with Patrick Tonyn to Lord George Germain, June 10, 1776, CO, 5/556, p. 312. The son referred to in this letter is incorrectly identified as Marbury Bryan; Lilla M. Hawes, ed., "Collections of the Georgia Historical Society and Other Documents: Minutes of the Executive Council, May 7 through October 14, 1777," *Georgia Historical Quarterly* 33 (Dec. 1949): 330, minutes for June 6, 1777; Bryan also treated with the Cherokees. See Lachlan McIntosh, *The Papers of Lachlan McIntosh, 1774–1779,* Collections of the Georgia Historical Society, vol. 12, ed. Lilla M. Hawes (Savannah: Georgia Historical Society, 1957), 63.

84. James H. O'Donnell III, *Southern Indians in the American Revolution* (Knoxville: University of Tennessee Press, 1973), 21, 60; Searcy, *Georgia-Florida Contest,* 74–75, 109, 178; Homer Bast, "Creek Indian Affairs, 1775–1778," *Georgia Historical Quarterly* 33 (Mar. 1949): 1–25.

85. Jonathan Bryan to the Headmen of the Creek Nation, Sept. 1, 1776, enclosed with John Stuart to George Germain, Oct. 26, 1776, CO, 5/78, pp. 26–27.

86. "Collections of the Georgia Historical Society," 33:330 and 34:20, 28; *Proceedings of the Georgia Council of Safety, 1775–1777,* Collections of the Georgia Historical Society, vol. 5, part 1 (Savannah: Georgia Historical Society, 1901), 79; Searcy, *Georgia-Florida Contest,* 109.

CHAPTER 7: THE WAR AND AFTER, 1776–1788

1. For the Council of Safety, see *Proceedings of the Council of Safety,* 15–127; Candler, *Revolutionary Records of the State of Georgia,* 1:68–227. For the recruitment of troops, see Vice President Jonathan Bryan to General Washington, Feb. 24, 1777, George Washington Papers, Library of Congress; Washington to President [*sic*] Jonathan Bryan, Mar. 17, 1777, in John C. Fitz-

patrick, ed., *The Writings of George Washington from the Original Manuscript Sources, 1745–1799*, 39 vols. (Washington, D.C.: Government Printing Office, 1931–40), 7:298–99, and Washington to Bryan, June 2, 1777, 8:168–69. Bryan referred to himself as vice-president in his correspondence with Washington. Also see the permission he gave to the administrators of Michael Bener's estate, Georgia Miscellaneous Papers, William R. Perkins Library, Duke University.

2. *Proceedings of the Council of Safety*, 70–74; Peter Force, ed., *American Archives*, 5th series., 3 vols. (Washington, D.C.: M. M. St. Clair and Peter Force, 1848–53), 1:6–8; *The Lee Papers*, vol. 2: *1776–78*, Collections of the New-York Historical Society for the year 1872 (New York, 1873), 114–17; John Drayton, *Memoirs of the American Revolution*, 2 vols. (Charleston: A. E. Miller, 1821; repr., New York: Arno Press, 1969), 2:334–39; Archibald Bulloch to Charles Lee, July 26, 1776, Archibald Bulloch Papers, Georgia Historical Society, Savannah. Obviously, Bryan was willing to use the term "Savages" to describe the Indians when it was politically expedient for him to do so.

3. *Proceedings of the Council of Safety*, 92–94.

4. Ibid.

5. Ibid., 95.

6. Charles Lee to Archibald Bulloch, Aug. 23, 1776, *Lee Papers*, 2:238; Lee to General John Armstrong, Aug. 27, 1776, ibid., 2:246–47.

7. Searcy, *Georgia-Florida Contest*, 56–68; Jones, *History of Georgia*, 2:247–51.

8. Searcy, *Georgia-Florida Contest*, 61, 173–75.

9. Coleman, *American Revolution in Georgia*, 116–25.

10. Hyde Parker to Philip Stevens, Jan. 14, 1779, in B. F. Stevens, comp., *Facsimiles of Manuscripts in European Archives Relating to America, 1773–1783, with Descriptions, Editorial Notes, Collations, References and Translations*, 25 vols. (Wilmington: Mellifort Press, 1970), 12:1246: Military Service Record of _____ Bryan, microfilm, M881 and M1051, National Archives.

11. Hugh McCall, *The History of Georgia, Containing Brief Sketches of the Most Remarkable Events Up to the Present Day (1784)*, 2 vols. (Atlanta, 1811, 1816), 2:176.

12. Archibald Campbell to (?), Jan. 9, 1779, Prioleau Autograph Collection, file 11–329, South Carolina Historical Society, Charleston.

13. John Houstoun to Henry Laurens, Jan. 22, 1779, in Edmund C. Burnett, ed., *Letters of the Members of the Continental Congress*, 8 vols. (Gloucester, Mass.: Peter Smith, 1963), 4:321 n. 2. The complete letter can be found in the Letter-book of Henry Laurens, 1778–80, p. 146, South Carolina Historical Society, Charleston.

14. John Houstoun to Henry Laurens, June 5, 1779, in Burnett, *Letters of Continental Congress*, 4:321 n. 2; Letter-book of Laurens, 147, 335–37.

15. Henry Laurens to Benjamin Lincoln, July 17, 1779, in Burnett, *Letters of Continental Congress*, 4:322–23.

16. Jonathan Bryan to Henry Laurens, Feb. 7, 1779, Papers of the Continental Congress, microfilm, M247, r91, i78, v3, p. 283, National Archives.

17. Jonathan Bryan to John Houstoun, May 4, 1780, Massachusetts Historical Society, Boston.

18. Copies of these letters can be found in J. H. Redding, *Life and Times of Jonathan Bryan*, 81–84.

19. Hawes, *The Proceedings and Minutes of the Governor and Council of Georgia, October 4, 1774, through November 7, 1775, and September 6, 1779, through September 20, 1780*, Collections of the Georgia Historical Society, vol. 10 (Savannah: Georgia Historical Society, 1952), 69–70. While the confiscation and sale of Loyalist property after the Revolution has long been a subject of interest among historians, a similar operation by the British has generally been ignored. Yet rebels frequently were sued by Loyalist creditors, and the former were unable to defend themselves in court because they had been forced to flee, or like Bryan, they languished in prison. The pages of the *Georgia Gazette* from 1779 to 1782 are filled with auctions of rebel property and announcements of actions taken against rebel estates. For actions taken against Jonathan Bryan see *Georgia Gazette*, Jan. 24, Feb. 14, Feb. 22, May 17, and Aug. 16, 1781.

20. Petition of Jonathan Bryan to Sir Henry Clinton, June 24, 1780, Sir Henry Clinton Papers, William L. Clements Library, University of Michigan, Ann Arbor.

21. *Journals of the Continental Congress*, 34 vols. (Washington, D.C.: Government Printing Office, 1904–37), Nov. 7, 1780, vol. for 1780, p. 1031.

22. Jonathan Bryan to the delegates of South Carolina and Georgia, Nov. 12, 1780, Papers of the Continental Congress, microfilm, M247, r92, i78, v4, pp. 41–42.

23. Isaac Motte to Thomas Bee, Nov. 28, 1780, ibid., M247, r73, i59, v3, p. 37; *Journals of the Continental Congress*, Oct. 25, 1780, vol. for 1780, pp. 1092–95; ibid., Nov. 28, 1780, p. 1099.

24. Jonathan Bryan to Samuel Huntington, Feb. 26, 1781, Papers of the Continental Congress, microfilm, M247, r92, i78, v4, p. 117; Treasury Office to Congress, ibid., r147, i136, v5, p. 143; *Journals of the Continental Congress*, Feb. 27, 1781, vol. for 1781, p. 199; ibid., Mar. 5, 1781, p. 239.

25. Jonathan Bryan to Nathanial Greene, Aug. 16, 1781, Georgia Historical Society, copy of original in the University of South Carolina Library; Bryan to Greene, Aug. 27, 1781, William R. Perkins Library, Duke University.

26. Candler, *Revolutionary Records of the State of Georgia*, 2:255–399.

27. Cited from William J. Northen, ed., *Men of Mark in Georgia* (Spartanburg, S.C.: Reprint Company, 1974), 30.

28. *Georgia Gazette,* Apr. 15, 1784.

29. "Letters Showing the Rise and Progress of the Early Negro Churches," 77–80; Davis, "George Liele and Andrew Bryan," 119–27.

30. *Georgia Gazette,* Mar. 13, 1788.

31. On the Habershams see W. Calvin Smith, "The Habershams: The Merchant Experience in Georgia," in Jackson and Spalding, *Forty Years of Diversity,* 198–216.

32. *Methodist Magazine,* 1785, V; reprinted in Redding, *Life and Times of Jonathan Bryan,* 44–45.

33. Will, Inventory, and Appraisement of the Estate of Jonathan Bryan, Estate Records, Chatham County, 1777–1852, microfilm 175/4, Georgia Archives.

34. Johnston, *Houstouns of Georgia,* 286; Will of Josiah Bryan, Miscellaneous—Bonds, Book J, 19–20, Georgia Archives; Davis, *Fledgling Province; 79–80.*

35. On mediators see Innes, *Labor in a New Land,* 19–20, 172–74; Clifford Geertz, "The Javanese Kijaji: The Changing Role of a Cultural Broker," *Comparative Studies in Society and History* 2 (Jan. 1960), 228–49.

36. Lamplugh, *Politics on the Periphery.*

37. Bertram Wyatt-Brown, *Southern Honor: Ethics and Behavior in the Old South* (New York: Oxford University Press, 1982).

BIBLIOGRAPHY

MANUSCRIPT SOURCES

Archival Holdings

Georgia State Department of Archives and History, Atlanta

Office of the Surveyor General
Plat Books

Colonial Records

Wills—Ordinary's Office	Books A, AA
Commissions	Book B
Conveyances	Books C-1, C-2, S, U, V, X-1, X-2, CC-2, DD, BBB
Inventories—Ordinary's Office	Books F, FF, GG
Mortgages	Books E, P, Q, W, EE
Letters of Administration—Ordinary's Office	Books D, N, Z
Miscellaneous—Bonds, etc.	Books J, O, R, Y-1, Y-2, HH, JJ, KK-1, KK-2, CCC, DDD
Marks and Brands	Book K
Proclamations	Book H

National Archives, Washington, D.C.

Papers of the Continental Congress
Compiled Service Records of Soldiers who served in the American Army
    During the Revolutionary War

South Carolina Department of Archives and History, Columbia

Records of the Secretary of State
Conveyances, Books B-3, D-D, Q, R-R, S-S, T, VO, V-V, X-3
Inventories of Estates, 1736–76
Inventories of Estates, Copies, 1746–48
Land Grants, Record Group 2, Series 5
Memorials, Record Group 30, Series 2
Miscellaneous Records, 1729–1825, Books FF, LL

Mortgages, Charleston Series, 1736–1867
Wills, 1752–56

Office of the Surveyor General
Colonial Plats, Duplicates, 1731–75
Colonial Plats, Recorded Copies, 1731–73
Colonial Plats, Copies, 1731–75
List of Plats, transferred, 1731–45

Records of the South Carolina Court of Common Pleas
Judgment Rolls
Charleston Judgment Books
Renunciation of Dower, 1726–75

Records in the British Public Record Office Relating to South Carolina

Historical Societies

Georgia Historical Society, Savannah

Jonathan Bryan Papers
Joseph V. Bevan Papers
Archibald Bulloch Papers
Jones Family Papers
Tatnall-Jackson Papers
Wayne Papers

Massachusetts Historical Society, Boston

Letters of Jonathan Bryan

Presbyterian Historical Society, Montreat, N.C.

William Hutson's Stoney Creek Register

South Carolina Historical Society, Charleston

The Letter-book of Henry Laurens, 1778–80
Hugh Bryan's Account 1/26/40/41, Bills to the Public 1740, voucher No.
34
Prioleau Autograph collection
Bryan Genealogy, by Daniel Elliot Huger Smith

University and Library Collections

College of Charleston, Charleston, S.C.

Bryan-Whitefield Papers, 1747, 1752

William R. Perkins Library, Duke University, Durham, N.C.

John Rutledge, Jr. Papers
Georgia Miscellaneous Papers
Nathanial Greene Papers
Edward Telfair Papers
James Wright Papers

Manuscript Division, Library of Congress, Washington, D.C.

British Public Record Office, Colonial Office Papers, Series 5
William Drayton Papers
Peter Force Papers
Lambeth Palace, Bishop of London Papers
Society for the Propagation of the Gospel in Foreign Parts (SPG) Papers
George Washington Papers
George Whitefield Papers

William L. Clements Library, University of Michigan, Ann Arbor

Sir Henry Clinton Papers
Thomas Gage Papers

Other Collections

Ballindalloch Castle Muniments, Ballindalloch Estates, Banffshire, Scotland

Letters of James Grant

PUBLISHED PRIMARY WORKS

Adair, James. *The History of the American Indians, Particularly Those Nations Adjoining to the Mississippi, East and West Florida, Georgia, South and North Carolina, and Virginia.* 1775. Reprint. Introduction by Robert F. Berkhofer, Jr. New York: Johnson Reprint, 1968.
Bell, Malcolm, III. *Some Notes and Reflections upon a Letter from Benjamin Franklin to Noble Wimberly Jones, October 7, 1772.* Darien, Ga.: Ashantilly Press, 1966.
Benedict, David. *History of the Baptist Denomination in America, and Other Parts of the World.* Boston, 1813. Reprint. Freeport, N.Y.: Books for Libraries Press, 1971.
Boltzius, John M. "John Martin Bolzius Answers a Questionaire on Carolina

and Georgia." Translated and edited by Klaus G. Loewald, Beverly Starika, and Paul S. Taylor. *William and Mary Quarterly,* 3d ser. 14 (Apr. 1957): 218–61, and 15 (Apr. 1958): 228–52.

Boltzius, Johann M., and Gronau, Israel Christian. *Detailed Reports on the Salzburger Emigrants Who Settled in America . . . Edited by Samuel Urlsperger.* Edited by George Fenwick Jones. 12 vols. to date. Athens: University of Georgia Press, 1968–.

Bryan, Hugh, and Hutson, Mrs. Mary. *Living Christianity, delineated in the Diaries and Letters of two eminently pious persons, lately deceased.* London: J. Buckland, 1760.

Burnett, Edmund C., ed. *Letters of the Members of the Continental Congress.* 8 vols. Gloucester, Mass.: Peter Smith, 1963.

Candler, Allen D., ed. *The Colonial Records of the State of Georgia.* 26 vols. Atlanta: Franklin-Turner, 1904–16. Volumes 27–39 are in the process of being published by the University of Georgia Press, 1975–. Volumes 20, 27–31 have already appeared under the editorship of Kenneth Coleman and Milton Ready. Typescripts of all volumes are available at the Georgia Department of Archives and History.

————. *The Revolutionary Records of Georgia.* 3 vols. Atlanta: Franklin-Turner, 1908.

Christie, J. R., ed. "Newly Discovered Letters of George Whitefield." *Journal of Presbyterian History* 32 (June 1954): 69–90.

The Clamorous Malcontents, Criticisms and Defenses of the Colony of Georgia, 1741–1743. With an Introduction by Trevor R. Reese. Savannah: Beehive Press, 1973.

Clay, Joseph. *Letters of Joseph Clay, Merchant of Savannah, 1776–1793, and a List of Ships and Vessels Entered at the Port of Savannah for May 1765, 1766 and 1767.* Illustrated. Collections of the Georgia Historical Society, vol. 8. Savannah: Georgia Historical Society, 1913.

Coulter, E. Merton, ed. *The Journal of Peter Gordon 1732–1735.* Athens: University of Georgia Press, 1963.

————. *The Journal of William Stephens 1741–1743.* 2 vols. Athens: University of Georgia Press, 1958.

Davies, K. G., ed. *Documents of the American Revolution 1770–1783.* Colonial Office Series. 25 vols. Dublin: Irish University Press, 1974.

De Vorsey, Louis, Jr., ed. *De Brahm's Report of the General Survey in the Southern District of North America.* Columbia: University of South Carolina Press, 1971.

Easterby, J. H., R. Nicholas Oldsberg, and Terry Lipscomb, eds. *The Colonial Records of South Carolina: The Journal of the Commons House of Assembly.* 13 vols. Columbia: Historical Commission, 1951–86.

Fitch, Tobias. "Journal of Captain Tobias Fitch's Mission from Charleston to the Creeks, 1726." In *Travels in the American Colonies*. Edited by Newton D. Mereness. New York: Macmillan, 1916.

Fitzpatrick, John C., ed. *The Writings of George Washington from the Original Manuscript Sources, 1745–1799*. 39 vols. Washington, D.C.: Government Printing Office, 1931–40.

Force, Peter, ed. *American Archives*. 5th ser. 3 vols. Washington, D.C.: M. M. St. Clair and Peter Force, 1848–53.

Garden, Alexander. *Mr. Commissary Garden's Six Letters to the Reverend Mr. Whitefield. With Mr. Whitefield's Answer to the First Letter*. Boston: T. Fleet, 1740.

————. *Regeneration and the Testimony of the Spirit. Being the Substance of Two Sermons lately Preached in Parish Church St. Philip, Charlestown, In South Carolina. Occasioned by Some Erroneous Notions of certain Men Who Call Themselves Methodists*. Charlestown: Peter Timothy, 1740.

The *Georgia Gazette*, 1763–76.

Gibbes, R. W., ed. *Documentary History of the American Revolution*. 2 vols. New York: D. Appleton, 1855–57.

Gregorie, Anne King, ed. *Records of the Court of Chancery of South Carolina 1671–1779*. Introduction by J. Nelson Fierson. Washington, D.C.: American Historical Association, 1950.

Habersham, James. *The Letters of the Hon. James Habersham, 1756–1775*. Collections of the Georgia Historical Society, vol. 6. Savannah: Georgia Historical Society, 1904.

Hamer, Philip M.; George Rogers, Jr. and David R. Chestnutt, eds. *The Papers of Henry Laurens*. 10 vols. Columbia: University of South Carolina Press, 1968–85.

Harper, Francis, ed. *The Travels of William Bartram, Naturalist*. New Haven: Yale University Press, 1958.

Hawes, Lilla M., ed. "Collections of the Georgia Historical Society and Other Documents: Minutes of the Executive Council, May 7 through October 14, 1777." *Georgia Historical Quarterly* 33 (Dec. 1949): 318–30; 34 (Mar. 1950): 19–35; (June 1950): 106–25.

Jacobs, Wilbur R., ed. *The Appalachian Frontier: The Edmond Atkin Report and Plan of 1758*. Lincoln: University of Nebraska Press, 1967.

Jay, William. *The Works of the Rev. William Jay of Argyle Chapel, Bath. . . .* 3 vols. New York: Harper and Brothers, 1858.

Jones, George Fenwick, trans. "John Martin Boltzius' Trip to Charleston, 1742." *South Carolina Historical Magazine* 82 (Jan. 1981): 87–110.

Journals of the Continental Congress. 34 vols. Washington, D.C.: Government Printing Office, 1904–37.

Kingsbury, Susan Myra, ed. *The Records of the Virginia Company of London*. 4 vols. Washington, D.C.: Government Printing Office, 1906.

[Kirkpatrick, James.] *An Impartial Account of the Late Expedition Against St. Augustine under General Oglethorpe.* A facsimile reproduction of the 1742 edition. Introduction and indexes by Aileen Moore Topping. Gainesville: University Presses of Florida, 1978.

Labaree, Leonard, et al., eds. *The Papers of Benjamin Franklin.* 26 vols. New Haven: Yale University Press, 1963–87.

Lane, Mills, ed. *General Oglethorpe's Georgia: Colonial Letters 1733–1743.* 2 vols. Savannah: Beehive Press, 1975.

The Lee Papers. vol. 2: 1776–1778. Collections of the New-York Historical Society for the year 1872. New York, 1873.

"Letters Showing the Rise and Progress of the Early Negro Churches of Georgia and the West Indies." *Journal of Negro History* 1 (Jan. 1916): 69–92.

McDowell, W. L., ed. *Journal of the Commissioners of the Indian Trade, September 20, 1710–August, 29, 1718.* Columbia: South Carolina Department of Archives and History, 1955.

McIntosh, Lachlan. *The Papers of Lachlan McIntosh, 1774–1779.* Edited by Lillia M. Hawes. Collections of the Georgia Historical Society, vol. 12. Savannah: Georgia Historical Society, 1957.

McWilliams, Richebourg Gaillard, trans. and ed. *Fleur de Lys and Calumet: Being the Pénicaut Narrative of French Adventure in Louisiana.* Tuscaloosa: University of Alabama Press, 1953.

Montiano, Manuel de. *Letters of Montiano: Seige of St. Augustine.* Translated by C. de Witt Wilcox. Collections of the Georgia Historical Society, vol. 7, part 1. Savannah: Georgia Historical Society, 1909.

Moore, Francis. "A Voyage to Georgia Begun in the Year 1735." In *Our First Visit in America: Early Reports from the Colony of Georgia.* Edited by Trevor R. Reese. Savannah: Beehive Press, 1974.

Northen, William J., ed. *Men of Mark in Georgia.* Spartanburg, S.C.: Reprint Company, 1974.

A Pair of Odes Commemorating the Departure of the Royal Governor of the Colony of Georgia for England, and the Welcoming of His Successor, February the Sixteenth of the Year 1757 By an Unknown Hand. From the Originals in the Special Collections Division of the University of Georgia Libraries. Darien, Ga.: Ashantilly Press, 1960.

Pinckney, Elise, ed. *The Letterbook of Eliza Lucas Pinckney, 1739–1762.* Chapel Hill: University of North Carolina Press, 1972.

The Proceedings and Minutes of the Governor and Council of Georgia, October 4, 1774, through November 7, 1775, and September 6, 1779, through September 20, 1780. Edited by Lilla M. Hawes. Collections of the Georgia Historical Society, vol. 10. Savannah: Georgia Historical Society, 1952.

Proceedings of the First Provincial Congress of Georgia, 1775. Collections of the Georgia Historical Society, vol. 5, part 1. Savannah: Georgia Historical Society, 1901.

Proceedings of the Georgia Council of Safety, 1775–1777. Collections of the Georgia Historical Society, vol. 5, part 1. Savannah: Georgia Historical Society, 1901.

Records of the States of the United States, microfilmed by the Library of Congress, Washington, D.C., 1949.

Rolle, Denys. *The Humble Petition of Denys Rolle, Esq; setting forth the Hardships, Inconveniences, and Grievances, which have attended him in his Attempts to make a Settlement in East Florida, humbly praying such Relief as in their Lordships Wisdom shall seem meet.* A facsimile reproduction of the 1765 edition, with an introduction by Claude C. Sturgell. Gainesville: University Presses of Florida, 1977.

The *Royal Georgia Gazette,* 1779–82.

Salley, A. S., ed. *Journal of the Commons House of Assembly for 1702.* Columbia: South Carolina Department of Archives and History, 1932.

———. *Minutes and Vestry of St. Helena's Parish, South Carolina 1726–1812.* Columbia, 1919.

———. *Warants for Lands in South Carolina, 1672–1711.* Revised, with an Introduction by R. Nicholas Olsberg. Columbia: University of South Carolina Press, 1973.

Sellers, John R. and Patricia Molen Van Ee, comps. *Maps and Charts of North America and the West Indies, 1750–1789: A Guide to the Collections in the Library of Congress.* Washington, D.C.: Library of Congress, 1981.

"Ship Registers in the South Carolina Archives, 1734–1780." Introduction by R. Nicholas Olsberg. *South Carolina Historical Magazine* 74 (1973): 189–299.

The South Carolina Commons House of Assembly. *The St. Augustine Expedition of 1740: A Report of the South Carolina Assembly.* With an Introduction by John Tate Lanning. Columbia: South Carolina Department of Archives and History, 1954.

The *South Carolina Gazette,* 1732–75.

Stephens, Thomas. *The Castle-builder; or, The History of William Stephens.* London, 1759.

Stephens, William. *A Journal of the Proceedings in Georgia. . . .* 2 vols. London: J. Meadows, 1740.

Stevens, B. F., comp. *Facsimiles of Manuscripts in European Archives Relating to America, 1773–1783, with Descriptions, Editorial Notes, Collations, References and Translations.* 25 vols. Wilmington, Del.: Mellifort Press, 1970.

Taitt, David. "David Taitt's Journal of a Journey through the Creek Country, *1772*." In *Travels in the American Colonies*. Edited by Newton D. Mereness. New York: Macmillian, 1916.

Urlsperger, Samuel, ed. *Americanisches Ackerwerck Gottes*. Halle, 1755.

Van Horne, John C., ed. *Religious Philanthropy and Slavery: The American Correspondence of the Associates of Dr. Bray, 1717–1777*. Urbana: University of Illinois Press, 1985.

Walsh, Richard, ed. *The Writings of Christopher Gadsden*. Columbia: University of South Carolina Press, 1966.

Whitefield, George. *Journal, 1737–1741, to which is prefixed his "Short Account" (1746) and "Further Account" (1747)*. London, 1756. Reprint. Gainesville, Florida: Scholars Facsimiles and Reprints, 1969.

———. *Letters of George Whitefield*. 3 vols. Edinburgh: Edward and Charles Dilly, 1772. Vol. 1, covering the years 1734–1742, has been reprinted. Carlisle, Pa.: Banner of Truth Trust, 1976.

———. *Three Letters from the Rev. G. Whitefield*. Philadelphia: Benjamin Franklin, 1740.

———. *The Works of the Reverend George Whitefield. . . .* 6 vols. London: Edward and Charles Dilly, 1772.

Wright, David McCord, comp. "Petitioners to the Crown Against the Proprieters, 1716–1717." *South Carolina Historical Magazine* 62 (Apr. 1961): 88–95.

SECONDARY SOURCES

Abbot, William W. "Lowcountry, Backcountry: A View of Georgia in the American Revolution." In *An Uncivil War: The Southern Backcountry during the American Revolution*. Edited by Ronald Hoffman, Thad W. Tate, and Peter Albert, 321–34. Charlottesville: University Press of Virginia, 1985.

———.*The Royal Governors of Georgia, 1754–1775*. Chapel Hill: University of North Carolina Press, 1959.

———. "The Structure of Politics in Georgia: 1782–1789." *William and Mary Quarterly*, 3d ser., 14 (1957): 47–65.

Ackerman, Robert K. *South Carolina Land Policies*. Columbia: University of South Carolina Press, 1977.

Alden, John Richard. *John Stuart and the Southern Colonial Frontier: A Study of Indian Relations, War, Trade, and Land Problems in the Southern Wilderness, 1754–1775*. 1944. Reprint. New York: Gordion Press, 1966.

———. *The South in the American Revolution 1763–1789*. Baton Rouge: Louisiana State University Press, 1957.

Axtell, James. *The European and the Indian: Essays in the Ethnohistory of Colonial North America*. New York: Oxford University Press, 1981.

_____. *The Invasion Within: The Contest of Cultures in Colonial North America*. New York: Oxford University Press, 1985.

Bailyn, Bernard. *The Ideological Origins of the American Revolution*. Cambridge: Harvard University Press, Belknap Press, 1967.

_____. *Voyagers to the West: A Passage in the Peopling of America on the Eve of the Revolution*. New York: Knopf, 1986.

Bast, Homer. "Creek Indian Affairs, 1775–1778." *Georgia Historical Quarterly* 33 (Mar. 1949): 1–25.

Bellot, Leland J. *William Knox, The Life and Thought of an Eighteenth-Century Imperialist*. Austin: University of Texas Press, 1977.

Boles, John B. "Evangelical Protestantism in the Old South: From Religious Dissent to Cultural Dominance." In *Religion in the South*. Edited by Charles Reagan Wilson, 13–34. Jackson: University of Mississippi Press, 1985.

Bolton, Charles. *Southern Anglicanism: The Church of England in Colonial South Carolina*. Westport: Greenwood, 1982.

Bolton, Herbert E., and Mary Ross. *The Debatable land: A Sketch of the Anglo-Spanish Contest for the Georgia Country*. Berkeley: University of California Press, 1925.

Bonomi, Patricia U. *A Factious People: Politics and Society in Colonial New York*. New York: Columbia University Press, 1971.

_____. *Under the Cope of Heaven: Religion, Society, and Politics in Colonial America*. New York: Oxford University Press, 1986.

Bridenbaugh, Carl. *Cities in Revolt: Urban Life in America, 1743–1776,* Rev. ed. New York: Knopf, 1955.

Bryan, John Stewart. *Joseph Bryan, His Times, His Family, His Friends: A Memoir*. Richmond: Whittet and Shepperson, 1938.

Butler, Jon. "Enthusiasm Described and Decried: The Great Awakening as Interpretive Fiction." *Journal of American History* 69 (Sept. 1982): 305–25.

Caldwell, Lee Ann. "Women Landholders of Colonial Georgia." *Forty Years of Diversity: Essays on Colonial Georgia*. Edited by Harvey H. Jackson and Phinizy Spalding, 183–97. Athens: University of Georgia Press, 1984.

Cashin, Edward J. " 'But Brothers, It Is Our Land We Are Talking About,' Winners and Losers in the Georgia Backcountry." In *An Uncivil War: The Southern Backcountry during the American Revolution*. Edited by Ronald Hoffman, Thad W. Tate, and Peter J. Albert, 240–75. Charlottesville: University of Virginia Press, 1985.

_____. "Sowing the Wind: Governor Wright and the Georgia Backcountry on the Eve of the Revolution." In *Forty Years of Diversity: Essays on*

Colonial Georgia. Edited by Harvey H. Jackson and Phinizy Spalding, 233–50. Athens: University of Georgia Press, 1984.

Chestnutt, David R. "South Carolina's Expansion into Colonial Georgia, 1720–1765." Ph.D. diss., University of Georgia, 1973.

Clowse, Converse R. *Economic Beginnings in Colonial South Carolina, 1670–1732.* Columbia: University of South Carolina Press, 1971.

Coclanis, Peter A. "Rice Prices in the 1720s and the Evolution of the South Carolina Economy." *Journal of Southern History* 48 (Nov. 1982): 531–44.

Coleman, Kenneth. *The American Revolution in Georgia, 1763–1789.* Athens: University of Georgia Press, 1958.

————. *Colonial Georgia: A History.* New York: Scribner's, 1976.

Corkran, David H. *The Creek Frontier, 1540–1783.* Norman: University of Oklahoma Press, 1967.

Corry, John Pitts. *Indian Affairs in Georgia, 1732–1756.* Philadelphia: George S. Ferguson, 1936.

Coulter, E. Merton. *Wormsloe: Two Centuries of a Georgia Family.* Athens: University of Georgia Press, 1955.

Crane, Verner W. *The Southern Frontier, 1670–1732.* Ann Arbor: University of Michigan Press, 1929. Reprint. New York: Norton, 1981.

Cronon, William. *Changes in the Land: Indians, Colonists, and the Ecology of New England.* New York: Hill and Wang, 1983.

Cumming, William P. *The Southeast in Early Maps, with an Annotated Check List of Printed and Manuscript Regional and Local Maps of Southeastern North America during the Colonial Period.* Chapel Hill: University of North Carolina Press, 1962.

Dalcho, Frederick. *An Historical Account of the Protestant Episcopal Church in South-Carolina.* 2 vols. Charleston: E. Thayer, 1820.

Dallimore, Arnold A. *George Whitefield: The Life and Times of the Great Evangelist of the Eighteenth Century.* 2 vols. London: Banner of Truth Trust, 1970, 1979.

Davis, David Brion. *The Problem of Slavery in Western Culture.* Ithaca: Cornell University Press, 1966.

Davis, Harold E. *The Fledgling Province: Social and Cultural Life in Colonial Georgia, 1733–1776.* Chapel Hill: University of North Carolina Press, 1976.

Davis, John W. "George Liele and Andrew Bryan, Pioneer Negro Baptist Preachers." *Journal of Negro History* 3 (Apr. 1918): 119–27.

Deagan, Kathleen. *Spanish St. Augustine: The Archaeology of a Colonial Creole Community.* New York: Academic Press, 1983.

De Vorsey, Louis, Jr. *The Indian Boundary in the Southern Colonies, 1763–1775.* Chapel Hill: University of North Carolina Press, 1966.

Dimond, Sidney G. *The Psychology of the Methodist Revival.* London: Oxford University Press, 1926.

Dobyns, Henry F. *Their Numbers Become Thinned: Native American Population Dynamics in Eastern North America.* Knoxville: University of Tennessee Press, 1983.

Dorn, Walter L. *Competition for Empire, 1740–1763.* New York: Harper and Brothers, 1940.

Douglas, Elisha P. *Rebels and Democrats: The Struggle for Equal Political Rights and Majority Rule during the American Revolution.* Chapel Hill: University of North Carolina Press, 1955.

Drayton, John. *Memoirs of the American Revolution.* 2 vols. Charleston: A. E. Miller, 1821. Reprint. New York: Arno Press, 1969.

Dunn, Richard. *Sugar and Slaves: The Rise of the Planter Class in the English West Indies, 1624–1713.* Chapel Hill: University of North Carolina Press, 1972.

Ernst, Joseph. *Money and Politics in America, 1755–1775: A Study in the Currency Act of 1764 and the Political Economy of Revolution.* Chapel Hill: University of North Carolina Press, 1973.

Ettinger, Amos Aschbach. *James Edward Oglethorpe: Imperial Idealist.* Oxford: Clarendon Press, 1936.

Fairbanks, Charles H. *Florida Indians III: Ethnohistorical Report on the Florida Indians.* New York: Garland Publishing, 1974.

Galloway, Patricia K. "Choctaw Factionalism and Civil War, 1746–1750." In *The Choctaw before Removal.* Edited by Carolyn Keller Reeves, 120–56. Jackson: University of Mississippi Press, 1985.

Garrison, Webb. *Oglethorpe's Folly: The Birth of Georgia.* Lakemont, Ga.: Copple House Books, 1982.

Gaustead, Edwin Scott. *The Great Awakening in New England.* New York: Columbia University Press, 1957.

Geertz, Clifford. "The Javanese Kijaji: The Changing Role of a Cultural Broker." *Comparative Studies in Society and History* 9 (Jan. 1960): 228–49.

Genovese, Eugene D. *Roll, Jordan, Roll: The World the Slaves Made.* New York: Random House, 1974.

Georgia Writers Project, Savannah Unit, Works Project Administration in Georgia. "Brampton Plantation." *Georgia Historical Quarterly* 27 (Mar. 1943): 28–55.

Gewer, Wesley M. *The Great Awakening in Virginia, 1740–1790.* Durham, N.C.: Duke University Press, 1930.

Green, Michael D. *The Politics of Indian Removal: Creek Government and Society in Crisis.* Lincoln: University of Nebraska Press, 1982.

Gutman, Herbert G. *The Black Family in Slavery and Freedom, 1752–1925.* New York: Vintage Books, 1976.

Hahn, Steven. *The Roots of Southern Populism: Yeoman Farmers and the Transformation of the Georgia Upcountry, 1850–1889.* New York: Oxford University Press, 1983.

Halévy, Elie. *The Birth of Methodism in England.* Translated and edited by
    Bernard Semmel. Chicago: University of Chicago Press, 1976.
Hann, John H. *Apalachee: The Land between the Rivers.* Gainesville:
    University Presses of Florida, 1988.
Heath, Milton Sydney. *Constructive Liberalism: The Role of the State in
    Economic Development in Georgia to 1860.* Cambridge: Harvard
    University Press, 1954.
Heimert, Alan. *Religion and the American Mind from the Great Awakening
    to the Revolution.* Cambridge: Harvard University Press, 1966.
Hewitt, J. N. B. *Notes on the Creek Indians.* Bureau of American Ethnology
    Bulletin no. 123. Washington, D.C.: Government Printing Office, 1939.
Hoerder, Dirk. "Boston Leaders and Boston Crowds, 1765–1776." In *The
    American Revolution: Explorations in the History of American
    Radicalism.* Edited by Alfred Young, 233–71. De Kalb: Northern Illinois
    University Press, 1976.
Howe, George. *History of the Presbyterian Church in South Carolina.* 2 vols.
    Columbia: Duffie and Chapman, 1870.
Hudson, Charles. *The Southeastern Indians.* Knoxville: University of
    Tennessee Press, 1976.
Innes, Stephen. *Labor in a New Land: Economy and Society in Seventeenth-
    Century Springfield.* Princeton: Princeton University Press, 1983.
Ivers, Larry. *British Drums on the Southern Frontier: The Military
    Colonization of Georgia, 1733–1749.* Chapel Hill: University of North
    Carolina Press, 1974.
————. *Colonial Forts of South Carolina, 1670–1775.* Columbia: University
    of South Carolina Press, 1970.
Jackson, Harvey H. "The Carolina Connection: Jonathan Bryan, His
    Brothers, and the Founding of Georgia, 1733–1752." *Georgia Historical
    Quarterly* 68 (Summer 1984): 147–72.
————. "Consensus and Conflict: Factional Politics in Revolutionary
    Georgia, 1774–1777." *Georgia Historical Quarterly* 59 (Winter 1975):
    388–401.
————. "Georgia Whiggery: The Origins and Effects of a Many-Faceted
    Movement." In *Forty Years of Diversity: Essays on Colonial Georgia.*
    Edited by Harvey H. Jackson and Phinizy Spalding, 251–73. Athens:
    University of Georgia Press, 1984.
————. "Hugh Bryan and the Evangelical Movement in Colonial South
    Carolina," *William and Mary Quarterly,* 3d ser., 43 (Oct. 1986): 594–
    614.
————. *Lachlan McIntosh and the Politics of Revolutionary Georgia.*
    Athens: University of Georgia Press, 1979.
————. "The Rise of the Western Members: Revolutionary Politics and the

Georgia Backcountry." In *An Uncivil War: The Southern Backcountry during the American Revolution.* Edited by Ronald Hoffman, Thad W. Tate, and Peter J. Albert, 240–75. Charlottesville: University Press of Virginia, 1985.

James, William. *The Varieties of Religious Experience: A Study in Human Nature.* Enlarged ed. Appendices and Introduction by Joseph Ratner. New Hyde Park, N.Y.: University Books, 1963.

Jennings, Francis. *The Ambiguous Iroquois Empire: The Convenant Chain Confederation of Indian Tribes with English Colonies.* New York: Norton, 1984.

———. "The Indians' Revolution." *The American Revolution: Explorations in the History of American Radicalism.* Edited by Alfred Young, 319–48. De Kalb: Northern Illinois University Press, 1976.

———. *The Invasion of America: Indians, Colonialism, and the Cant of Conquest.* Chapel Hill: University of North Carolina Press, 1975.

Johnston, Edith Duncan. *The Houstouns of Georgia.* Athens: University of Georgia Press, 1950.

Jones, Charles Colcock, Jr. *The Dead Towns of Georgia.* Savannah: Morning News Steam Printing House, 1878.

———. *The History of Georgia.* 2 vols. Boston: Houghton Mifflin, 1883.

Jones, George Fenwick. "John Adam Treutlen's Origin and Rise to Prominence." In *Forty Years of Diversity: Essays on Colonial Georgia.* Edited by Harvey H. Jackson and Phinizy Spalding, 217–32. Athens: University of Georgia Press, 1984.

———. *The Salzburger Saga: Religious Exiles and Other Germans along the Savannah.* Athens: University of Georgia Press, 1984.

Jordan, Winthrop D. *White over Black: American Attitudes toward the Negro, 1550–1812.* Chapel Hill: University of North Carolina Press, 1968.

Kenny, William Howland, III. "Alexander Garden and George Whitefield: The Significance of Revivalism in South Carolina, 1738–1741." *South Carolina Historical Magazine* 71 (Jan. 1970): 1–16.

Klein, Rachel N. "Frontier Planters and the American Revolution: The South Carolina Backcountry, 1775–1782." In *An Uncivil War: The Southern Backcountry during the American Revolution.* Edited by Ronald Hoffman, Thad W. Tate, and Peter J. Albert, 37–69. Charlottesville: University Press of Virginia, 1985.

———. "Ordering the Backcountry: The South Carolina Regulation," *William and Mary Quarterly,* 3d ser., 38 (Oct. 1981): 661–80.

Klingberg, Frank. *An Appraisal of the Negro in Colonial South Carolina: A Study in Americanization.* Washington, D.C.: Associated Publishers, 1941.

Knollenberg, Bernard. *Origins of the American Revolution, 1759–1766.* New York: Macmillan, 1960.

Knox, Ronald. *Enthusiasm: A Chapter in the History of Religion.* New York: Oxford University Press, 1961.

Kulikoff, Allan. *Tobacco and Slaves: The Development of Southern Cultures in the Chesapeake, 1680–1800.* Chapel Hill: University of North Carolina Press, 1986.

Lamplugh, George R. *Politics on the Periphery: Factions and Parties in Georgia, 1783–1806.* Newark: University of Delaware Press, 1986.

Lanning, John Tate. "American Participation in the War of Jenkins' Ear." *Georgia Historical Quarterly* 11 (Sept. 1927): 191–204.

―――. *The Diplomatic History of Georgia: A Study in the Epoch of Jenkins' Ear.* Chapel Hill: University of North Carolina Press, 1936.

Lee, Umphrey. *The Historical Background of Early Methodist Enthusiasm.* New York: Columbia University Press, 1931.

Littlefield, Daniel C. *Rice and Slaves: Ethnicity and the Slave Trade in Colonial South Carolina.* Baton Rouge: Louisiana State University Press, 1981.

Lonn, Ella. *The Colonial Agents of the Southern Colonies.* Chapel Hill: University of North Carolina Press, 1945.

McCall, Hugh. *The History of Georgia, Containing Brief Sketches of the Most Remarkable Events up to the Present Day (1784).* 2 vols. Savannah: Seymour and Williams, 1811, 1816.

McCrady, Edward. *The History of South Carolina under the Proprietary Government, 1670–1719.* New York: Macmillan, 1901.

McCusker, John J. *Money and Exchange in Europe and America, 1600–1775: A Handbook.* Chapel Hill: University of North Carolina Press, 1978.

McCusker, John J., and Russell R. Menard. *The Economy of British America, 1607–1789.* Chapel Hill: University of North Carolina Press, 1985.

McLoughlin, William G. *Revivals, Awakenings, and Reform: An Essay on Religion and Social Change in America, 1607–1977.* Chicago: University of Chicago Press, 1978.

Main, Jackson Turner. *The Social Structure of Revolutionary America.* Princeton: Princeton University Press, 1965.

―――. *The Upper House in Revolutionary America, 1763–1788.* Madison: University of Wisconsin Press, 1967.

Merriwether, Robert L. *The Expansion of South Carolina, 1729–1765.* Kingsport, Tenn.: Southern Publishers, 1940.

Migliazzo, Arlin Charles. "Ethnic Diversity on the Southern Frontier: A Social History of Purrysburg, South Carolina, 1732–1792." Ph.D. diss., Washington State University, 1982.

Miller, John C. *Origins of the American Revolution.* Boston: Little, Brown, 1943.
_____. *Sam Adams, Pioneer in Propaganda.* Boston: Little, Brown, 1936.
Milling, Chapman J. *Red Carolinians.* Chapel Hill: University of North Carolina Press, 1940.
Morgan, David T. "The Great Awakening in South Carolina, 1740–1775." *South Atlantic Quarterly* 70 (Autumn 1971): 595–606.
Morgan, David T., Jr. "The Consequences of George Whitefield's Ministry in the Carolinas and Georgia, 1739–1740." *Georgia Historical Quarterly* 55 (Spring 1971): 62–81.
Morgan, Edmund S. *American Slavery, American Freedom: The Ordeal of Colonial Virginia.* New York: Norton, 1975.
Morgan, Edmund S., and Helen Morgan. *The Stamp Act Crisis: Prologue to Revolution.* Rev. ed. New York: Collier Books, 1962.
Mowat, Charles Loch. *East Florida as a British Province, 1763–1784.* Gainesville: University Presses of Florida, 1964.
_____. "The Enigma of William Drayton." *Florida Historical Quarterly* 12 (1943): 3–33.
Nash, Gary B. *Red, White, and Black: The Peoples of Early America.* Englewood Cliffs, N.J.: Prentice-Hall, 1974.
_____. *The Urban Crucible: Social Change, Political Consciousness, and the Origins of the American Revolution.* Cambridge: Harvard University Press, 1979.
O'Brien, Susan. "A Transatlantic Community of Saints: The Great Awakening as the First Evangelical Network, 1735–1755." *American Historical Review* 91 (Oct. 1986): 811–32.
O'Donnell, James H. *Southern Indians in the American Revolution.* Knoxville: University of Tennessee Press, 1973.
_____. "The Southern Indians in the War for American Independence, 1775–1783." In *Four Centuries of Southern Indians.* Edited by Charles M. Hudson. Athens: University of Georgia Press, 1975.
Panagopoulous, Epaminadous P. *New Smyrna: An Eighteenth-Century Greek Odyssey.* Gainesville: University Presses of Florida, 1976.
Pares, Richard. *Colonial Blockade and Neutral Rights, 1739–1763.* Oxford: Clarendon Press, 1939.
_____. *War and Trade in the West Indies, 1739–1763.* Oxford: Clarendon Press, 1936.
Quarles, Benjamin. *The Negro in the American Revolution.* New York: Norton, 1961.
Raboteau, Albert J. *Slave Religion: The "Invisible Institution" in the Antebellum South.* New York: Oxford University Press, 1978.
Redding, J. H. *The Life and Times of Jonathan Bryan, 1708–1788.* Savannah: Morning News Print, 1901.

Ritchie, Carson I. A. *Frontier Parish.* Rutherford, N.J.: Fairleigh Dickinson University Press, 1976.

Robinson, W. Stitt. *The Southern Colonial Frontier.* Albuquerque: University of New Mexico Press, 1979.

Rose, Willie Lee. *Slavery and Freedom.* Edited by William W. Freehling. New York: Oxford University Press, 1982.

Sanders, Lawrence Rowland. "Eighteenth Century Beaufort: A Study of South Carolina's Southern Parishes to 1800." Ph.D. diss., University of South Carolina, 1978.

Saye, Albert B. *A Constitutional History of Georgia, 1739–1945.* Athens: University of Georgia Press, 1948.

———. *New Viewpoints in Georgia History.* Athens: University of Georgia Press, 1943.

———. "Was Georgia a Debtor Colony?" *Georgia Historical Quarterly* 24 (Dec. 1940): 323–41.

Schlesinger, Arthur M. *The Colonial Merchants and the American Revolution.* 1917. Reprint. New York: Atheneum, 1968.

Screven, Frank B. "The Georgia Bryans and Screvens, 1685–1861." *Georgia Historical Quarterly* 40 (Dec. 1956): 326–48.

Searcy, Martha Condray. *The Georgia-Florida Contest in the American Revolution, 1776–1778.* Tuscaloosa: University of Alabama Press, 1985.

Semmel, Bernard. *The Methodist Revolution.* New York: Columbia University Press, 1973.

Sherman, Richard P. *Robert Johnson: Proprietary and Royal Governor of South Carolina.* Columbia: University of South Carolina Press, 1966.

Shy, John. *A People Numerous and Armed: Reflections on the Military Struggle for American Independence.* London: Oxford University Press, 1975.

———. *Toward Lexington: The Role of the British Army in the Coming of the American Revolution.* Princeton: Princeton University Press, 1965.

Siebert, William Henry. *Loyalists in East Florida, 1774 to 1785.* 2 vols. De Land: Florida State Historical Society, 1929.

Simmons, R. C. *The American Colonies: From Settlement to Independence.* New York: Norton, 1976.

Simms, Rev. James M. *The First Colored Baptist Church in North America.* Philadelphia: Lippincott, 1888.

Smith, Henry A. M. "Purrysburg." *South Carolina Historical Magazine* 10 (Oct. 1909): 187–219.

———. "Beaufort—The Original Plan and the Earliest Settlers." *South Carolina Historical Magazine* 9 (July 1908): 141–60.

Smith, Julia Floyd. *Slavery and Rice Culture in Low Country Georgia, 1750–1860.* Knoxville: University of Tennessee Press, 1985.

Smith, W. Calvin. "The Habershams: The Merchant Experience in Georgia."

In *Forty Years of Diversity: Essays on Colonial Georgia*. Edited by Harvey H. Jackson and Phinizy Spalding, 198–216. Athens: University of Georgia Press, 1984.

Spalding, Phinizy. *Oglethorpe in America*. Chicago: University of Chicago Press, 1977.

Strickland, Reba. *Religion and the State in Georgia in the Eighteenth Century*. New York: Columbia University Press, 1939.

Sturtevant, William C. "Creek into Seminole." In *North American Indians in Historical Perspective*. Edited by Eleanor B. Leacock and Nancy O. Lurie. New York: Random House, 1971.

Swanton, John R. *Early History of the Creek Indians and Their Neighbors*. Smithsonian Institution Bureau of American Ethnology Bulletin 73. Washington, D.C.: Government Printing Office, 1922.

––––––. "Social Organization and Social Usages of the Indians of the Creek Confederacy" and "Religious Beliefs and Medical Practices of the Creek Indians." In *Forty-Second Annual Report of the Bureau of American Ethnology, 1924–1925*, 25–472. Washington, D.C.: Government Printing Office, 1928.

Szatmary, Daniel P. *Shays' Rebellion: The Making of an Agrarian Insurrection*. Amherst: University of Massachusetts Press, 1980.

Taylor, Paul S. *Georgia Plan: 1732–1752*. Berkeley: University of California Press, 1972.

Temperley, Harold William Vazeille. "The Causes of the War of Jenkins' Ear, 1739." *Transactions of the Royal Historical Society*, 3d ser., 3 (1909): 197–236.

Tepaske, John Jay. *The Governorship of Spanish Florida, 1700–1763*. Durham: Duke University Press, 1964.

Todd, John R., and Hutson, Francis. *Prince William's Parish and Plantations*. Richmond: Garnett and Massie, 1935.

Tracy, Joseph. *The Great Awakening*. Boston: Lewis Tappan, 1845. Reprint. New York: Arno Press and the New York Times, 1969.

Turner, Frederick Jackson. *The Frontier in American Society*. New York: Holt, 1920.

Usner, Daniel H. "The Frontier Exchange Economy of the Lower Mississippi Valley in the Eighteenth Century." *William and Mary Quarterly*, 3d ser., 44 (Apr. 1987): 165–92.

Ver Steeg, Clarence L. *Origins of a Southern Mosaic*. Athens: Universitiy of Georgia Press, 1975.

Wallace, David Duncan. *The History of South Carolina*. 3 vols. New York: American Historical Association, 1934.

––––––. *The Life of Henry Laurens, with a Sketch of the Life of Lieutenant-Colonel John Laurens*. New York: Putnam's, 1915.

Walsh, Richard. *Charleston's Sons of Liberty: A Study of the Artisans, 1763–1789*. Columbia: University of South Carolina Press, 1959.

Wearmouth, Robert. *Methodism and the Common People of the Eighteenth Century*. London: Epworth Press, 1945.

Weir, Robert. *Colonial South Carolina: A History*. New York: KTO Press, 1983.

Wertenbaker, Thomas J. *The Golden Age of Colonial Culture*. Ithaca: Cornell University Press, 1949.

Willis, William S. "Divide and Rule: White, Red, and Black in the Southeast." *Journal of Negro History* 48 (July 1963): 157–76.

Wood, Betty. *Slavery in Colonial Georgia, 1730–1775*. Athens: University of Georgia Press, 1984.

Wood, Gordon. *The Creation of the American Republic, 1776–1787*. Chapel Hill: University of North Carolina Press, 1969.

Wood, Peter H. *Black Majority: Negroes in Colonial South Carolina from 1670 through the Stono Rebellion*. New York: Norton, 1974.

———. "La Salle: Discovery of a Lost Explorer." *American Historical Review* 89 (Apr. 1984): 294–323.

Wood, Peter H., Gregory A. Waselkov, and M. Thomas Hatley, eds. *Powhatan's Mantle: Indians in the Colonial Southeast*. Lincoln: University of Nebraska Press, 1989.

Wright. Esmond. *Fabric of Freedom, 1763–1800*. Rev. ed. New York: Hill and Wang, 1978.

Wright, J. Leitch, Jr. *Creeks and Seminoles: Destruction and Regeneration of the Muscogulge People*. Lincoln: University of Nebraska Press, 1987.

———. *Florida in the American Revolution*. Gainesville: University Presses of Florida, 1964.

INDEX